AN AGE OF LICENSE
BY LUCY KNISLEY

2011

...Was a year of travel! Through coincidence, work, and luck, I was offered opportunities to take trips.

I took as many as possible.

Recovering from heartbreak, I was determined to spend my travels having adventures and being a free agent.

Some trips are more than distance traveled in miles.

FOOD
Growth
Love
ART
SEX

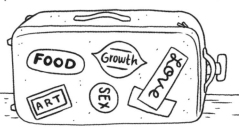

Sometimes travel can show us how our life *is*...

Or give us a glimpse of how it **can be**...

Being untethered, I could float away,
lifted to a great height
where everything is new,
and I could look back on my life
with new perspective,
and go, "Oh!"

PASSPORT

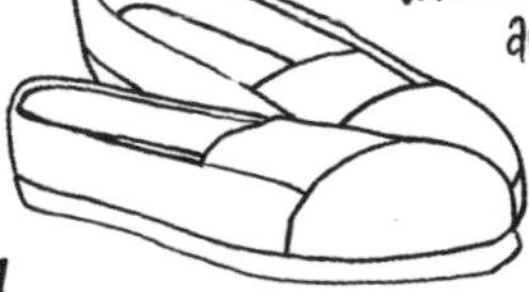

About a year ago...

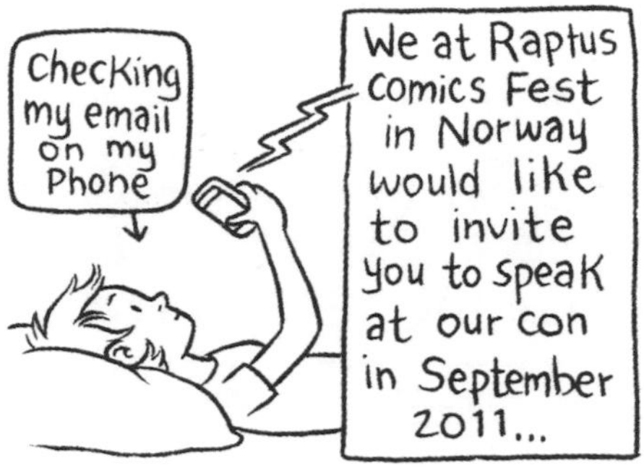
Checking my email on my Phone
We at Raptus comics Fest in Norway would like to invite you to speak at our con in September 2011...

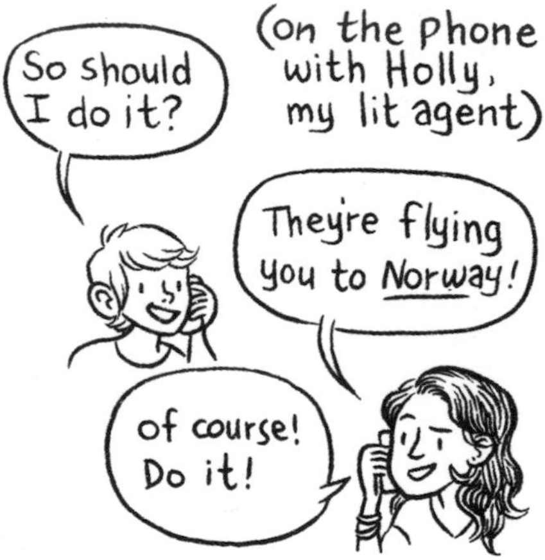
So should I do it?
(on the Phone with Holly, my lit agent)
They're flying you to Norway!
of course! Do it!

About six months ago...

(MOM)

...So Hilary and Jen* and I are going to stay in the house in France for the _whole_ _month!_

*Two of my mom's friends

...Is there extra room?

Dear Lucy, We'd be happy to fly you out of another city assuming the cost is the same...

...Looks like it's the same cost from Paris, so we can do that. See you in September!
—Arild
Raptus Comics Fest

About five months ago...

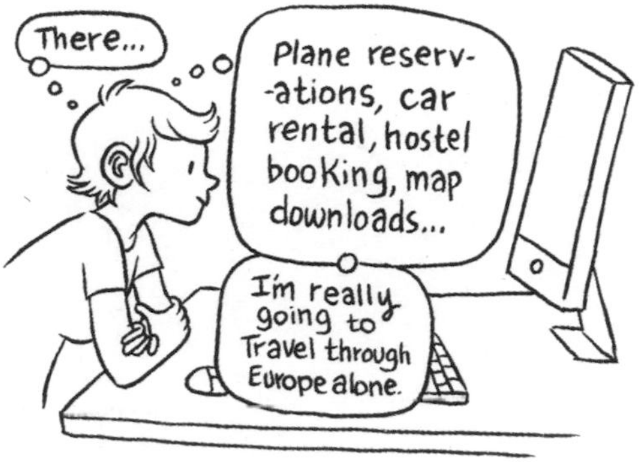
There...
Plane reserv-
-ations, car
rental, hostel
booking, map
downloads...
I'm really
going to
Travel through
Europe alone.

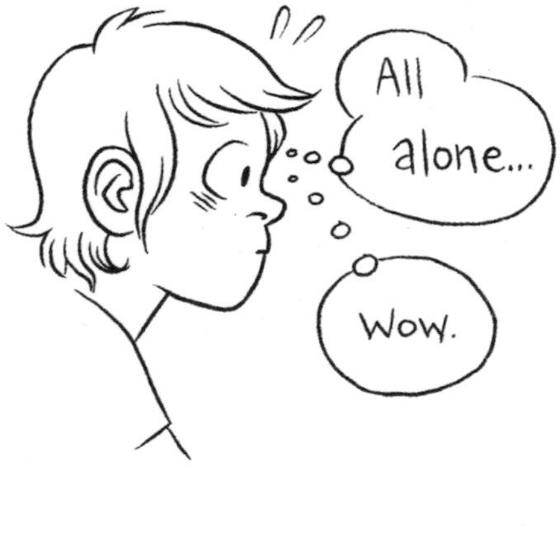
All
alone...
Wow.

Sept. 1, 2011 – 2AM

One week until I leave for this Europe trip, and I thought I'd check my itinerary quickly before bed. ...3 HOURS and a lot of nervousness later...

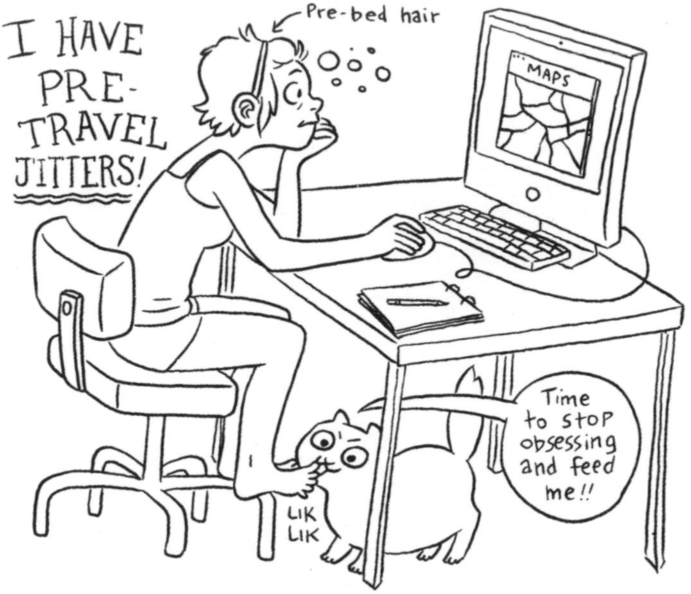

I HAVE PRE-TRAVEL JITTERS!
Pre-bed hair
MAPS
Time to stop obsessing and feed me!!
LIK LIK

Lying in bed not sleeping, I think about all the reasons I'm doing this...

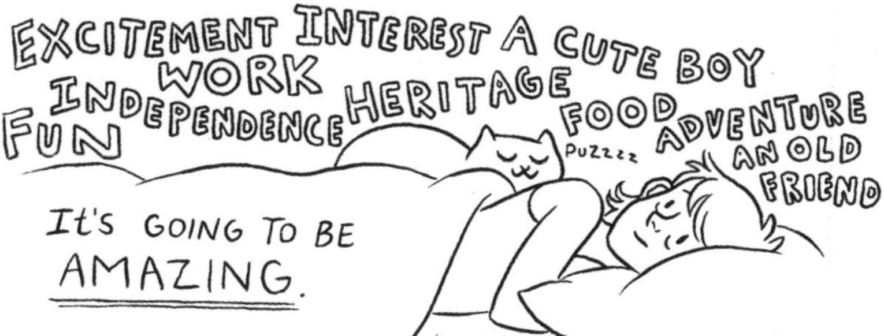

EXCITEMENT INTEREST A CUTE BOY
WORK
INDEPENDENCE HERITAGE
FUN
FOOD
ADVENTURE
AN OLD FRIEND
PUZZZZ
It's GOING TO BE AMAZING.

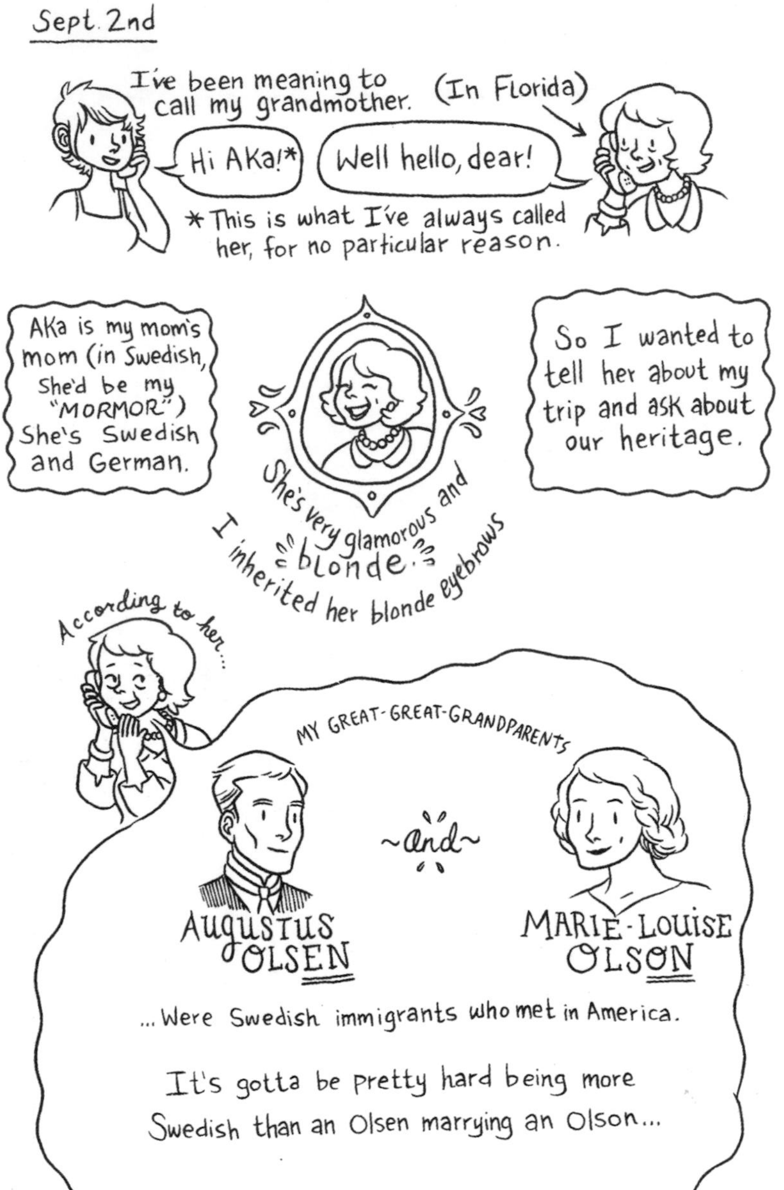

Sept. 2nd
I've been meaning to call my grandmother.
(In Florida)
Hi AKa!*
Well hello, dear!
* This is what I've always called her, for no particular reason.
AKa is my mom's mom (in Swedish, She'd be my "MORMOR") She's Swedish and German.
She's very glamorous and blonde.
I inherited her blonde eyebrows
So I wanted to tell her about my trip and ask about our heritage.
According to her...
MY GREAT-GREAT-GRANDPARENTS
AUGUSTUS OLSEN
~and~
MARIE-LOUISE OLSON
...Were Swedish immigrants who met in America.
It's gotta be pretty hard being more Swedish than an Olsen marrying an Olson...

At home.

I met with my friend MK to get her recommendations for Berlin and Stockholm.

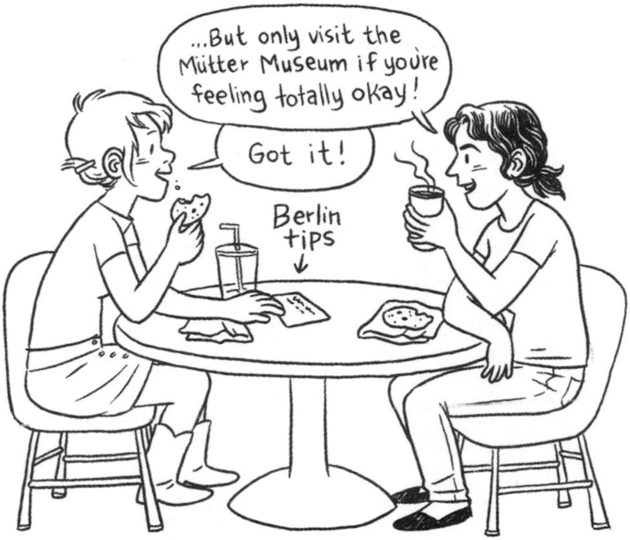
...But only visit the Mütter Museum if you're feeling totally okay!
Got it!
Berlin tips

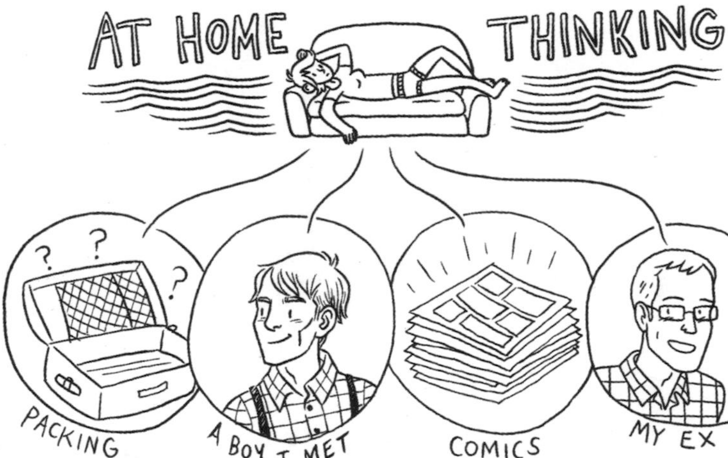
AT HOME THINKING
PACKING
A BOY I MET
COMICS
MY EX

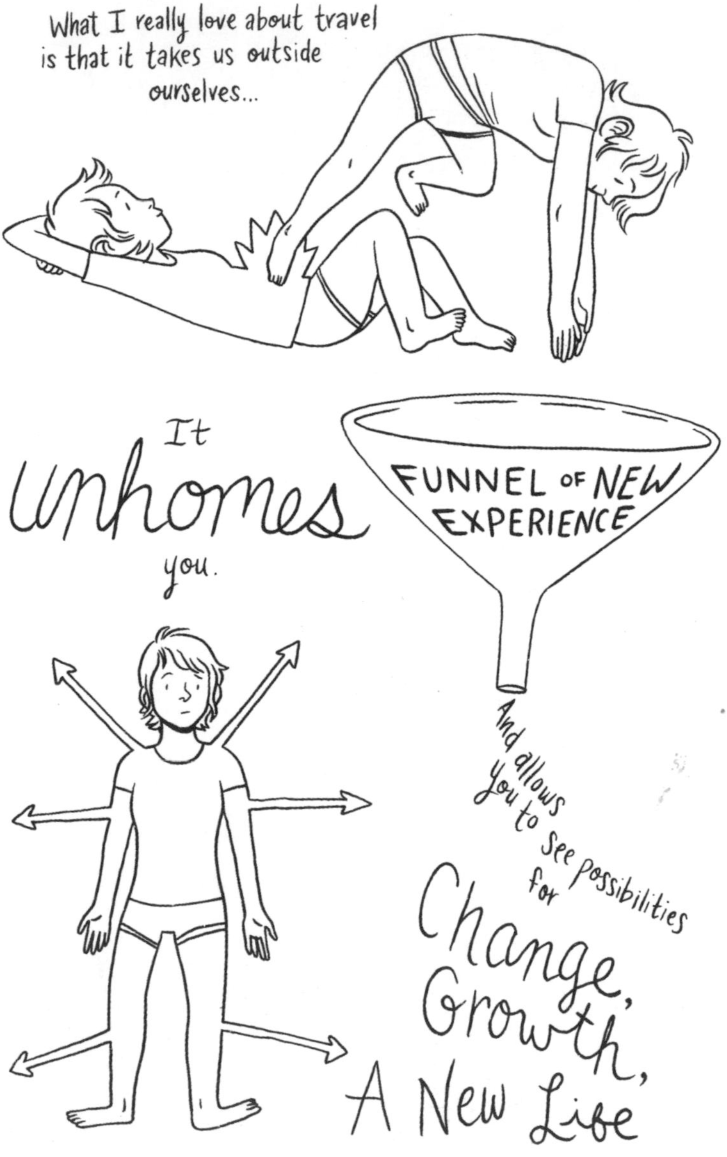
What I really love about travel is that it takes us outside ourselves...
It unhomes you.
FUNNEL OF NEW EXPERIENCE
And allows you to see possibilities for
Change, Growth, A New Life

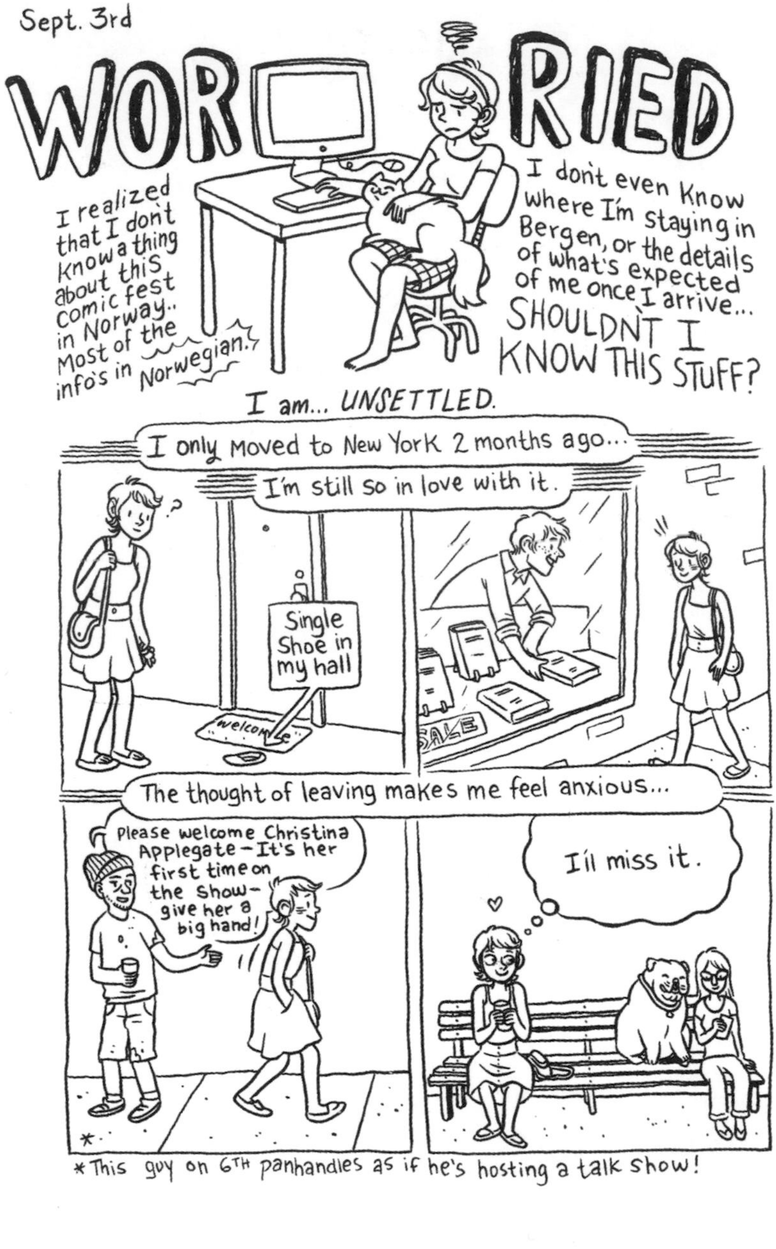
Sept. 3rd
WORRIED
I realized that I don't know a thing about this comic fest in Norway.. Most of the info's in Norwegian!
I don't even know where I'm staying in Bergen, or the details of what's expected of me once I arrive...
SHOULDN'T I KNOW THIS STUFF?
I am... UNSETTLED.
I only moved to New York 2 months ago...
I'm still so in love with it.
Single Shoe in my hall
welcome
SALE
The thought of leaving makes me feel anxious...
Please welcome Christina Applegate - It's her first time on the show - give her a big hand!
I'll miss it.
*This guy on 6TH panhandles as if he's hosting a talk show!

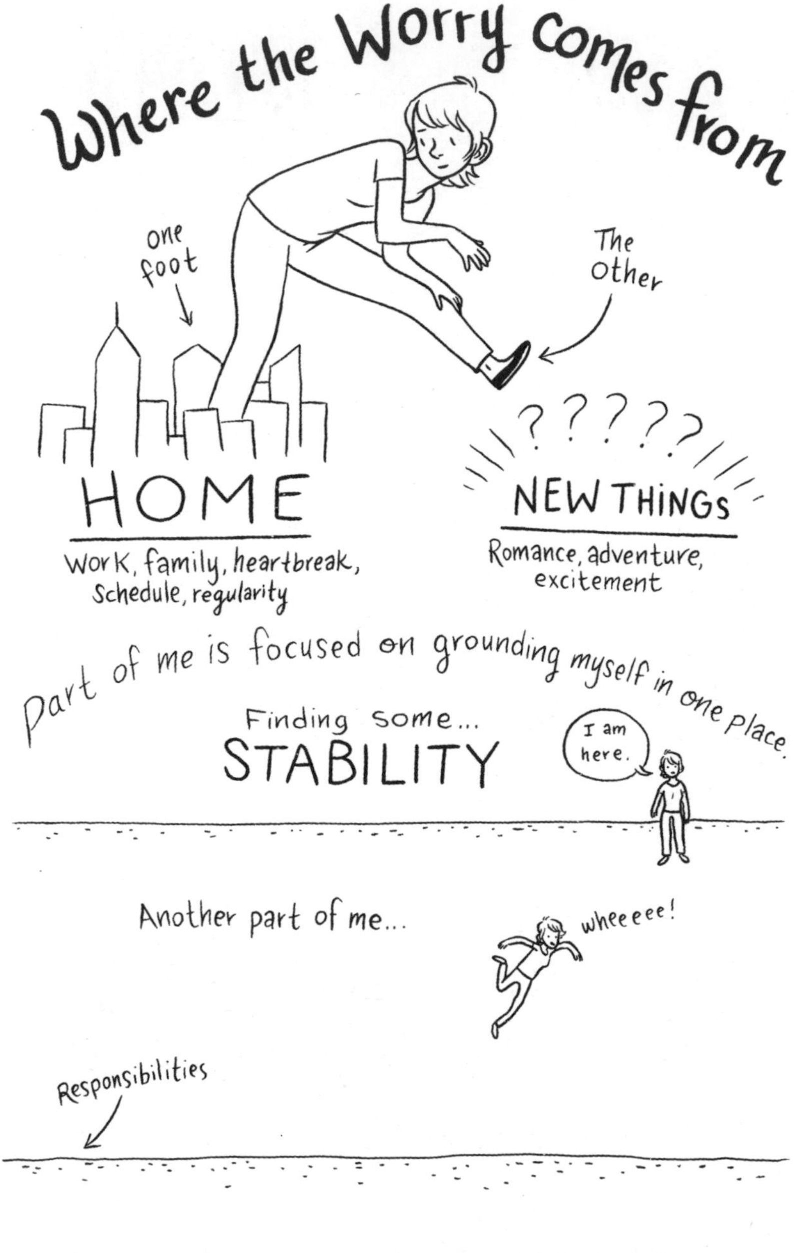
Where the Worry comes from
one foot
The other
HOME
Work, family, heartbreak, Schedule, regularity
?????
NEW THINGS
Romance, adventure, excitement
Part of me is focused on grounding myself in one place.
Finding some...
STABILITY
I am here.
Another part of me...
wheeeee!
Responsibilities

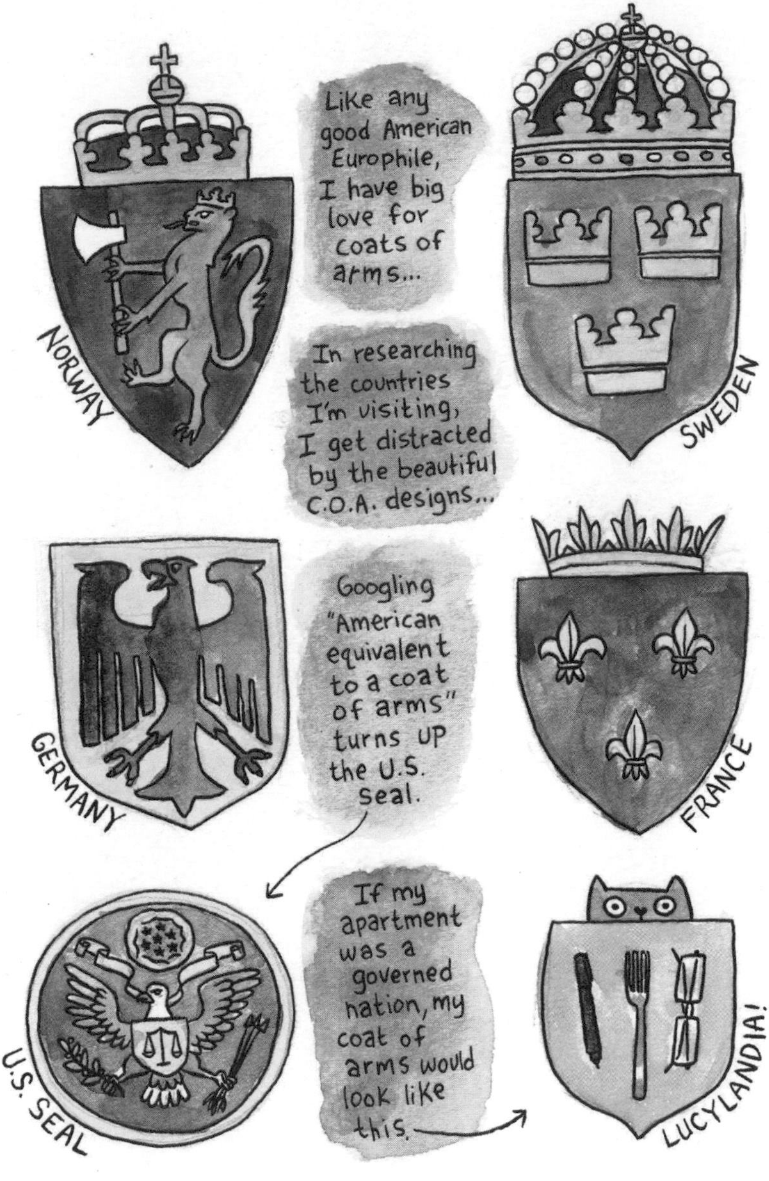
Like any good American Europhile, I have big love for coats of arms...
In researching the countries I'm visiting, I get distracted by the beautiful C.O.A. designs...
Googling "American equivalent to a coat of arms" turns up the U.S. seal.
If my apartment was a governed nation, my coat of arms would look like this.
NORWAY
SWEDEN
GERMANY
FRANCE
U.S. SEAL
LUCYLANDIA!

I AM ROMANTICALLY CONFLICTED

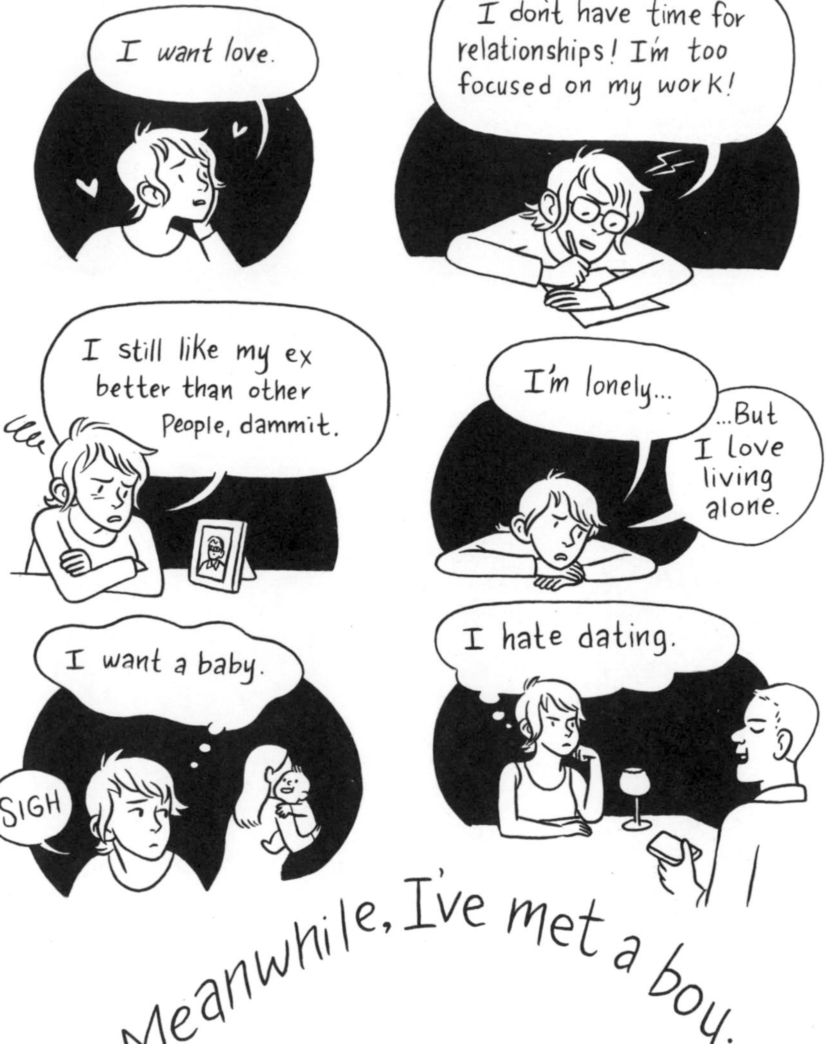
I want love.
I don't have time for relationships! I'm too focused on my work!
I still like my ex better than other people, dammit.
I'm lonely...
...But I love living alone.
I want a baby.
SIGH
I hate dating.
Meanwhile, I've met a boy.

A · FEW · WEEKS · AGO

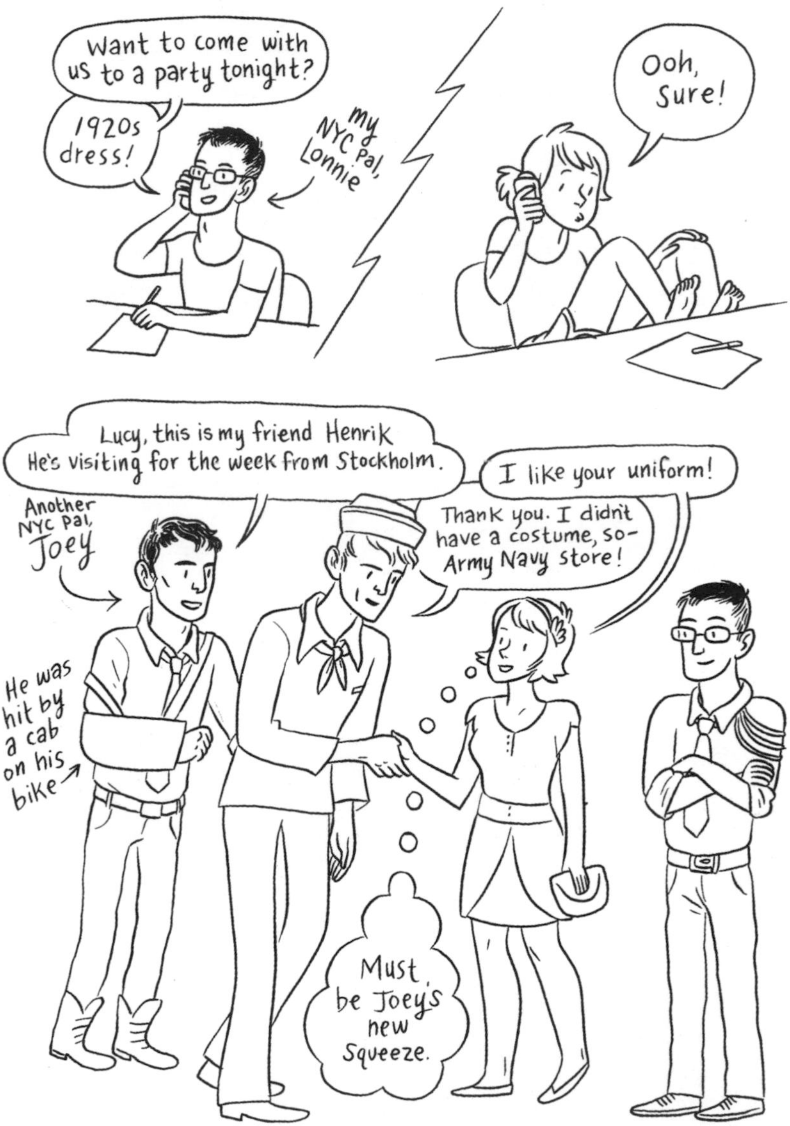
Want to come with us to a party tonight?
1920s dress!
my NYC Pal, Lonnie
Ooh, Sure!
Lucy, this is my friend Henrik He's visiting for the week from Stockholm.
Another NYC Pal, Joey
He was hit by a cab on his bike
I like your uniform!
Thank you. I didn't have a costume, so- Army Navy store!
Must be Joey's new Squeeze.

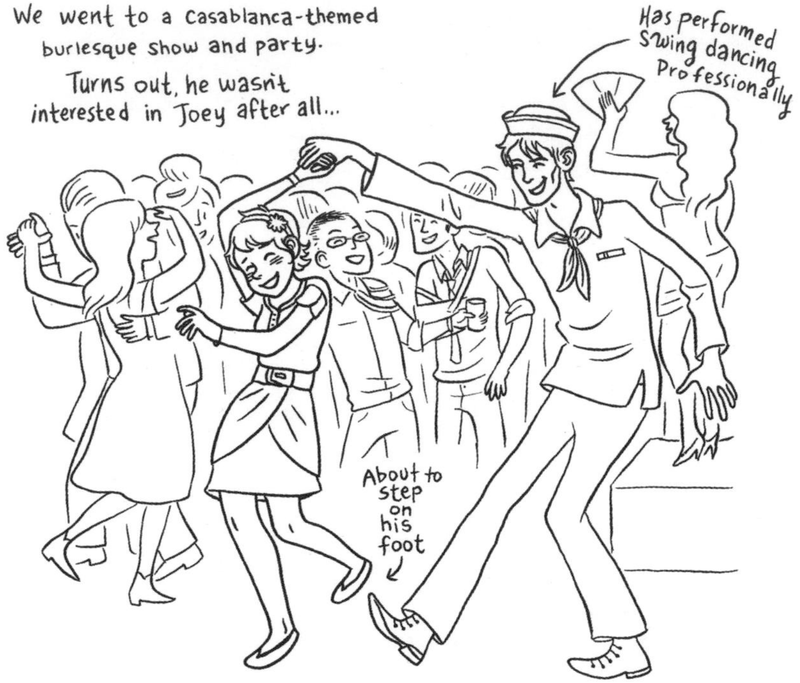
We went to a casablanca-themed burlesque show and party.
Turns out, he wasn't interested in Joey after all...
Has performed swing dancing professionally
About to step on his foot

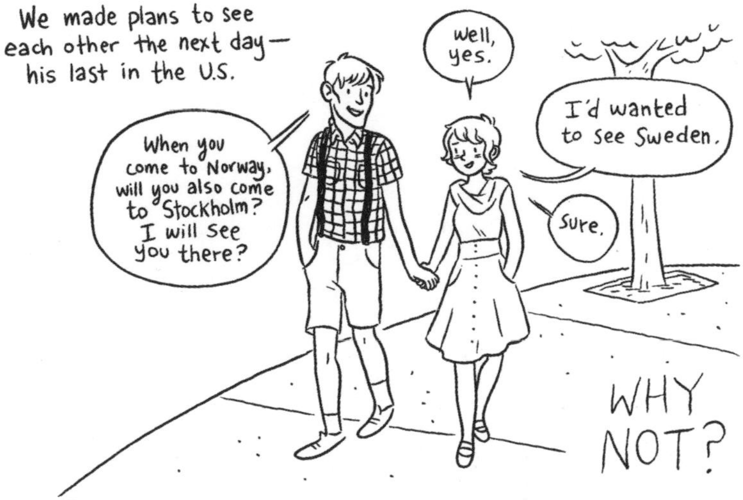
We made plans to see each other the next day— his last in the U.S.
When you come to Norway, will you also come to Stockholm? I will see you there?
Well, yes.
I'd wanted to see Sweden.
Sure.
WHY NOT?

~The Basic Plan~

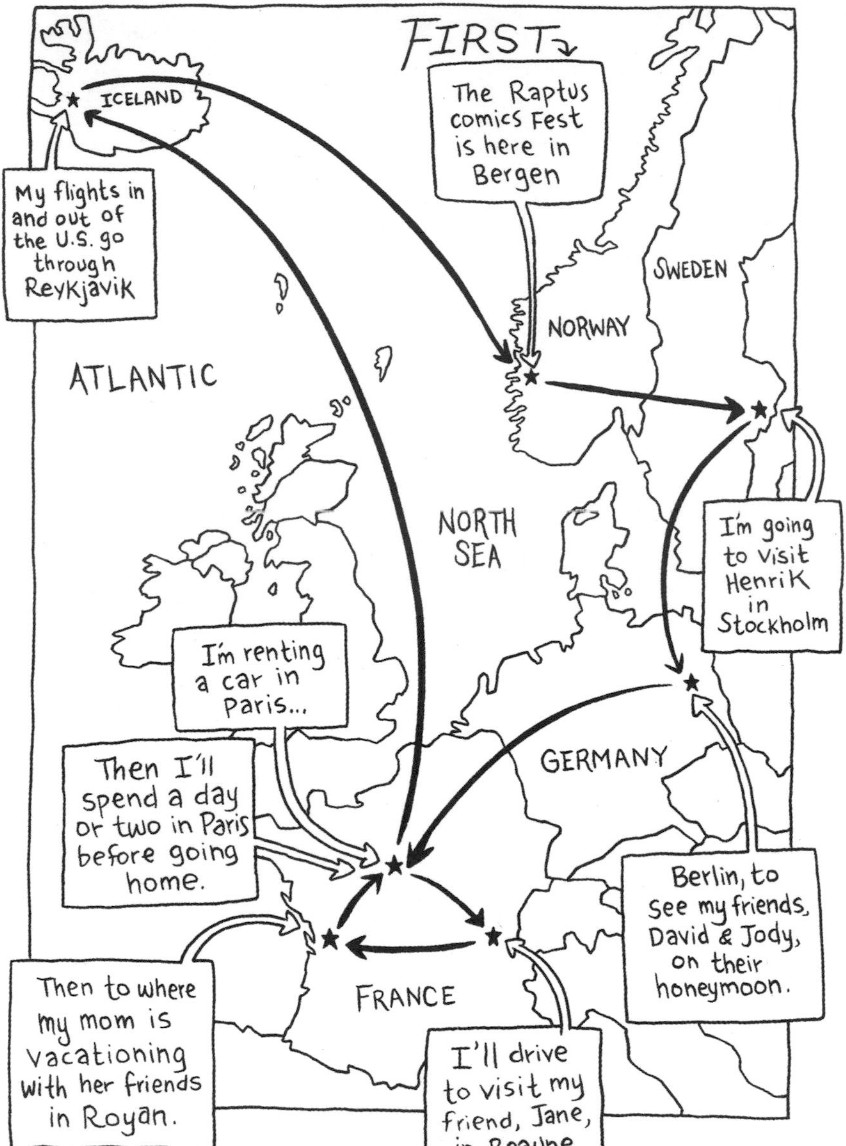
FIRST
The Raptus comics Fest is here in Bergen
My flights in and out of the U.S. go through Reykjavik
ICELAND
ATLANTIC
NORWAY
SWEDEN
NORTH SEA
I'm going to visit Henrik in Stockholm
I'm renting a car in Paris...
Then I'll spend a day or two in Paris before going home.
GERMANY
Berlin, to see my friends, David & Jody, on their honeymoon.
FRANCE
Then to where my mom is vacationing with her friends in Royan.
I'll drive to visit my friend, Jane, in Beaune

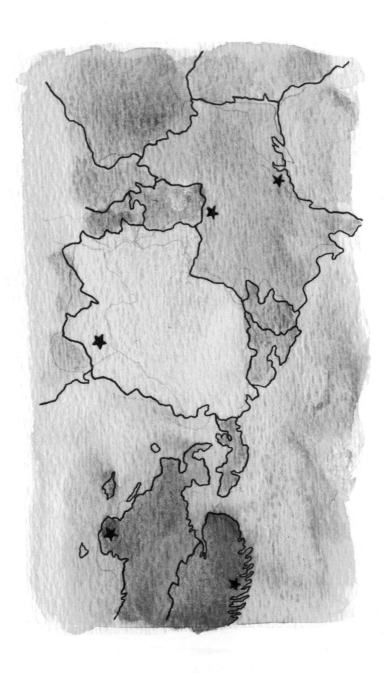

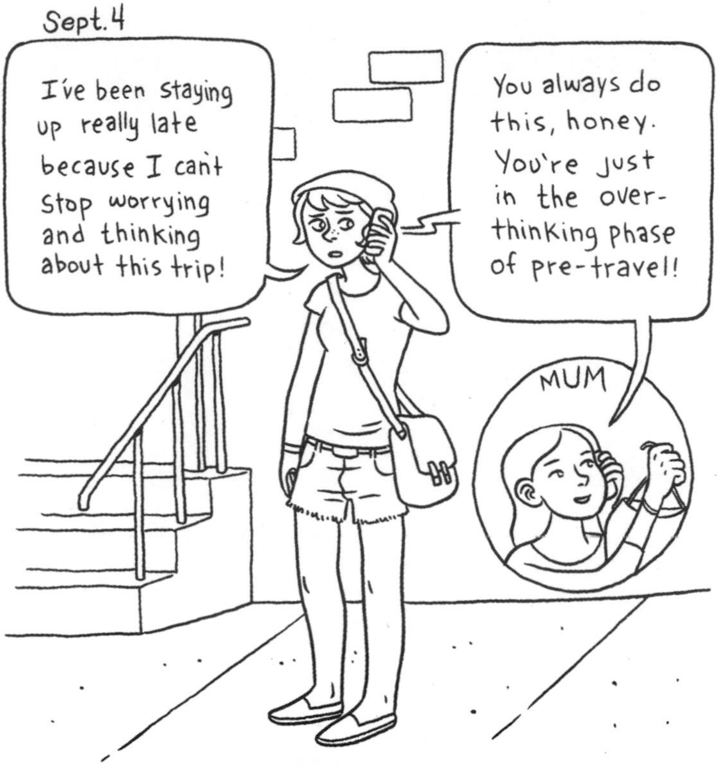
Sept. 4
I've been staying up really late because I can't stop worrying and thinking about this trip!
You always do this, honey. You're just in the over-thinking phase of pre-travel!
MUM

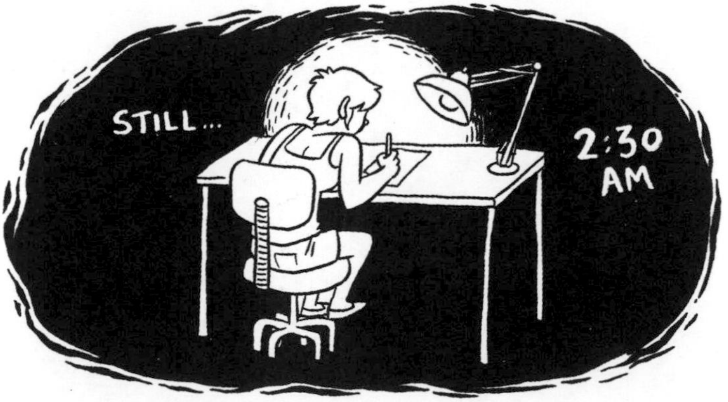
STILL...
2:30 AM

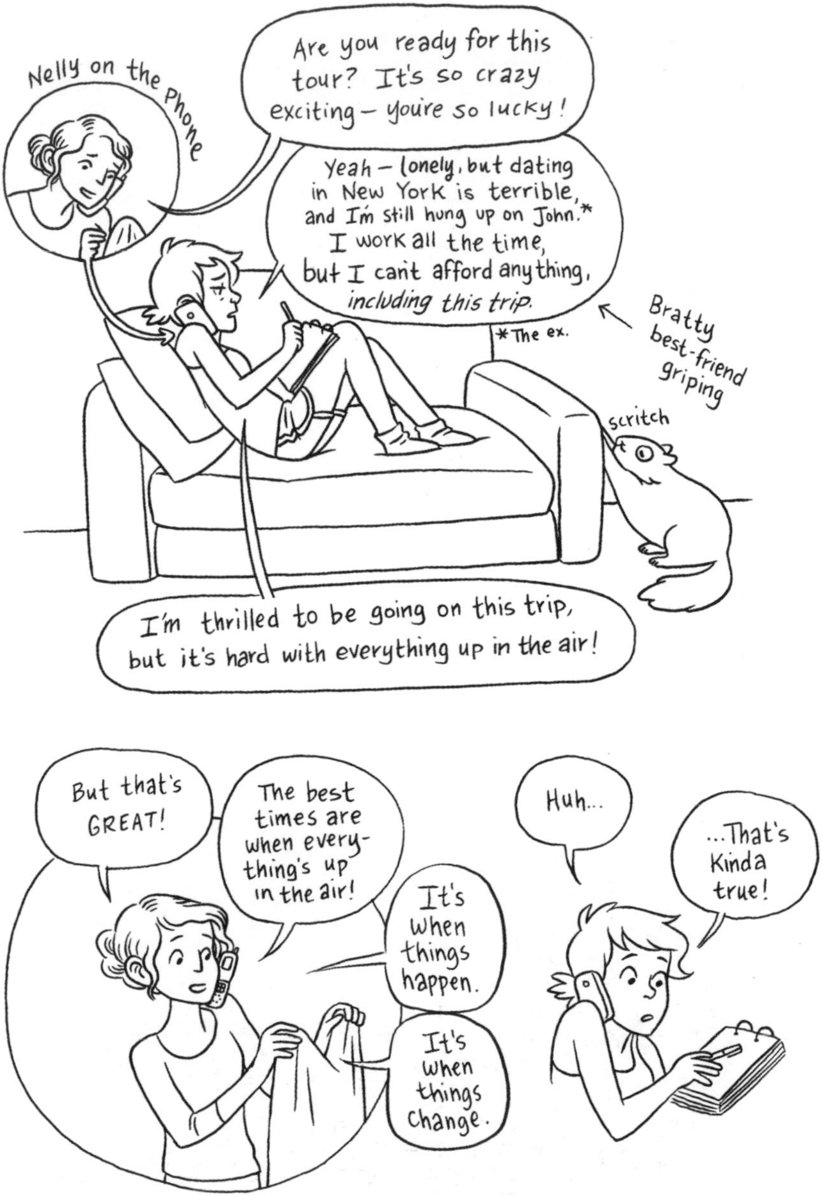
Nelly on the Phone
Are you ready for this tour? It's so crazy exciting – you're so lucky!
Yeah – lonely, but dating in New York is terrible, and I'm still hung up on John.* I work all the time, but I can't afford anything, *including this trip.*
*The ex.
Bratty best-friend griping
scritch
I'm thrilled to be going on this trip, but it's hard with everything up in the air!
But that's GREAT!
The best times are when every-thing's up in the air!
It's when things happen.
It's when things change.
Huh...
...That's kinda true!

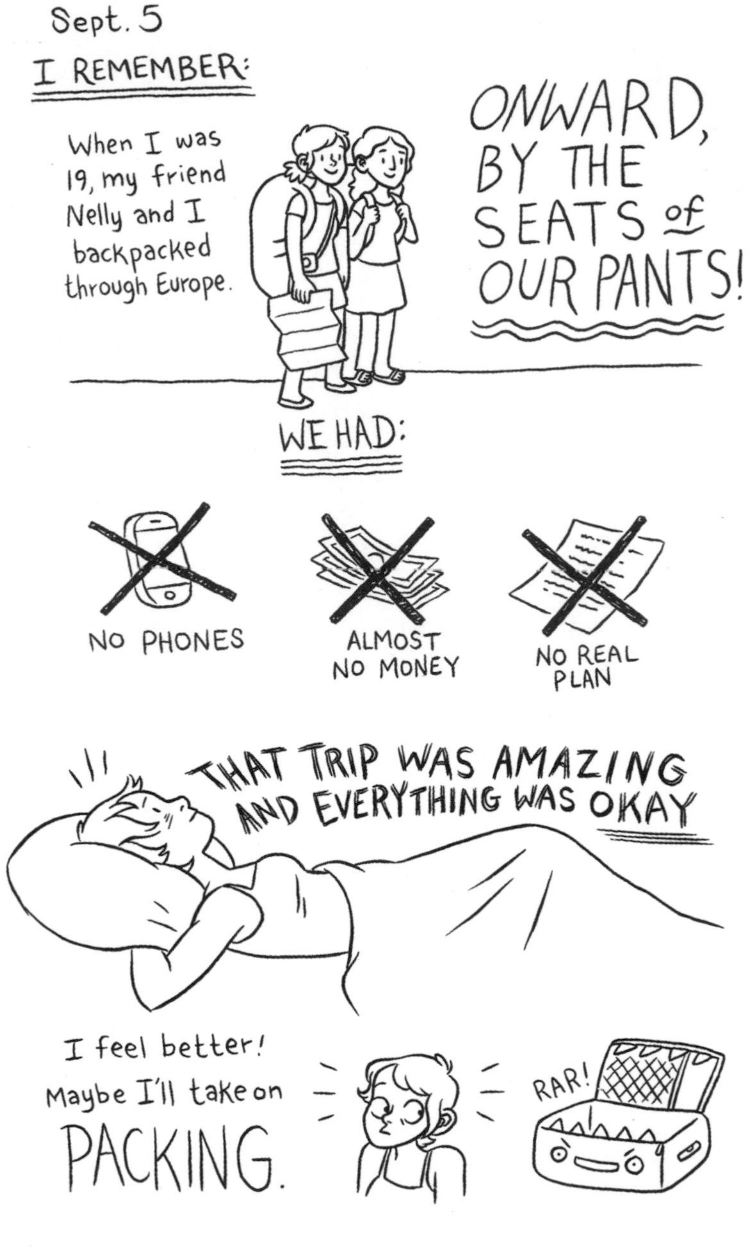
Sept. 5
I REMEMBER:
When I was 19, my friend Nelly and I backpacked through Europe.
ONWARD, BY THE SEATS of OUR PANTS!
WE HAD:
NO PHONES
ALMOST NO MONEY
NO REAL PLAN
THAT TRIP WAS AMAZING AND EVERYTHING WAS OKAY
I feel better! Maybe I'll take on PACKING.
RAR!

Packing impossibilities.

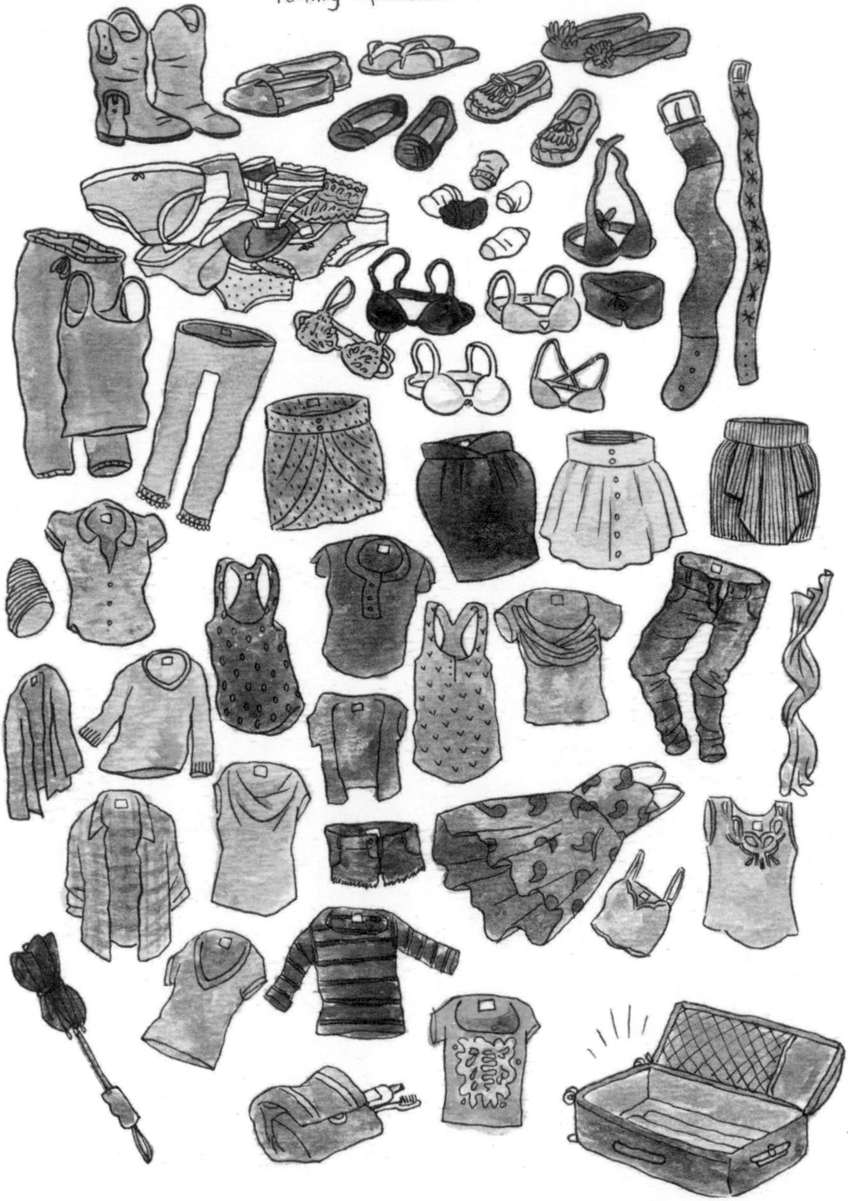

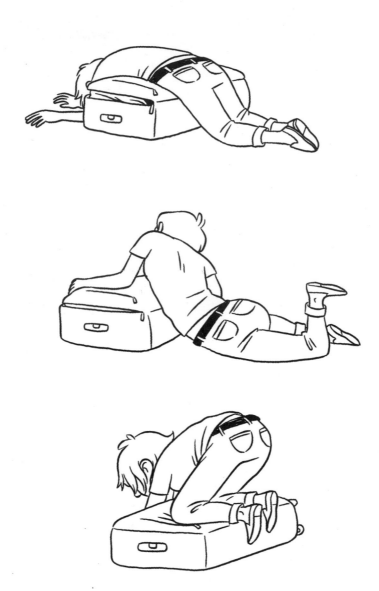

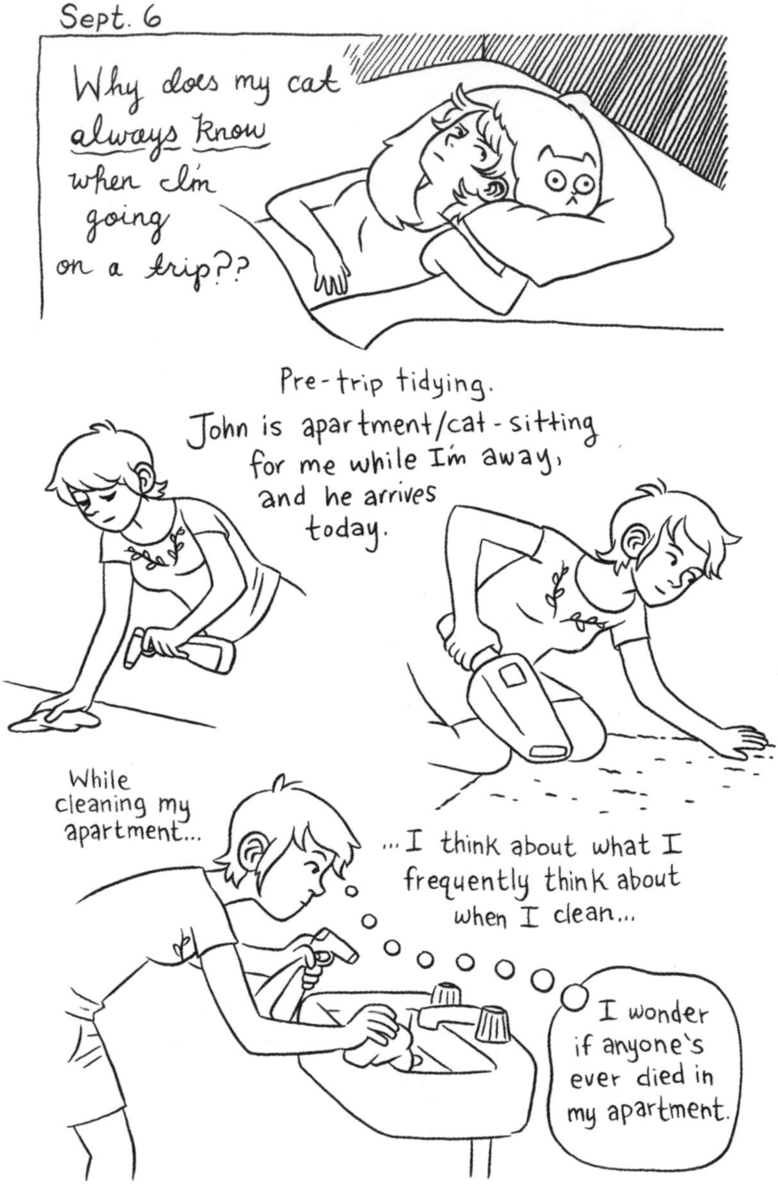
Sept. 6
Why does my cat always know when I'm going on a trip??
Pre-trip tidying.
John is apartment/cat-sitting for me while I'm away, and he arrives today.
While cleaning my apartment...
...I think about what I frequently think about when I clean...
I wonder if anyone's ever died in my apartment.

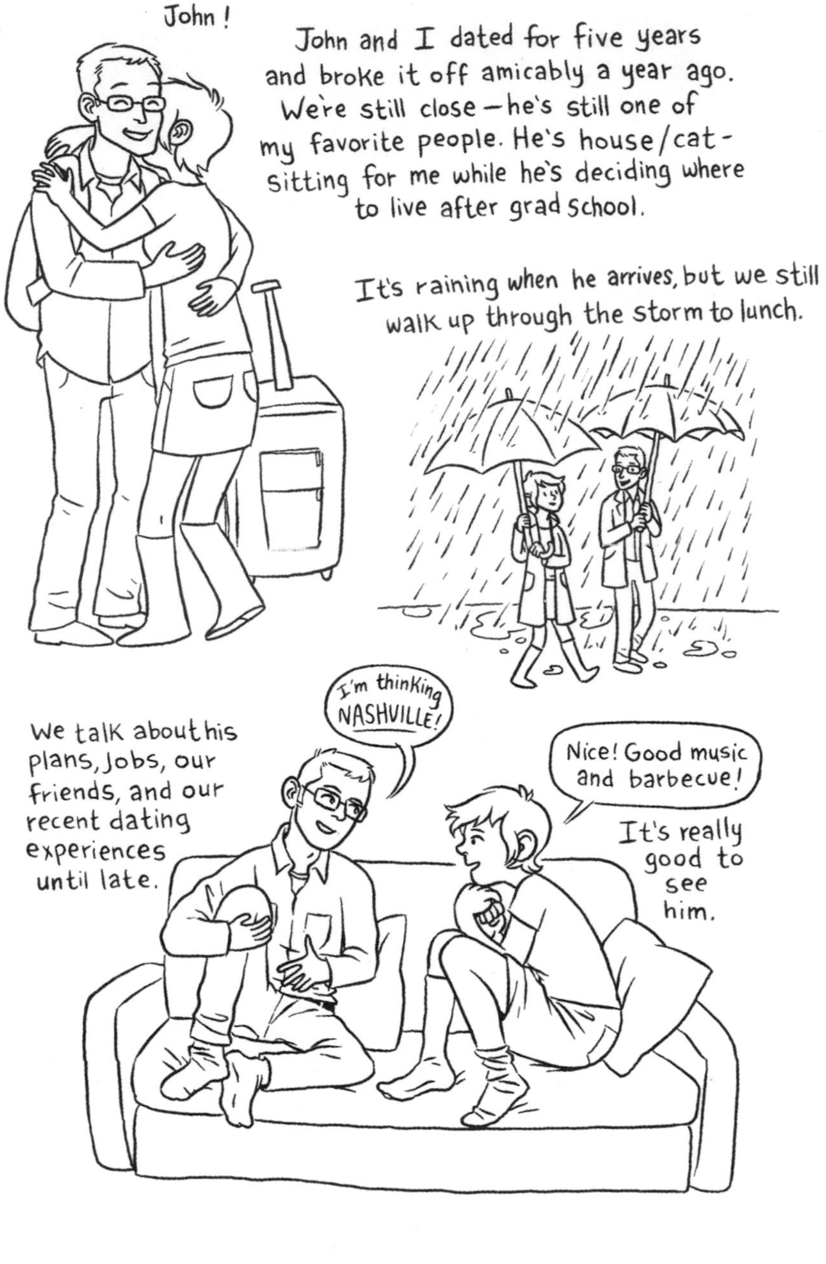
John!
John and I dated for five years and broke it off amicably a year ago. We're still close—he's still one of my favorite people. He's house/cat-sitting for me while he's deciding where to live after grad school.
It's raining when he arrives, but we still walk up through the storm to lunch.
We talk about his plans, jobs, our friends, and our recent dating experiences until late.
I'm thinking NASHVILLE!
Nice! Good music and barbecue!
It's really good to see him.

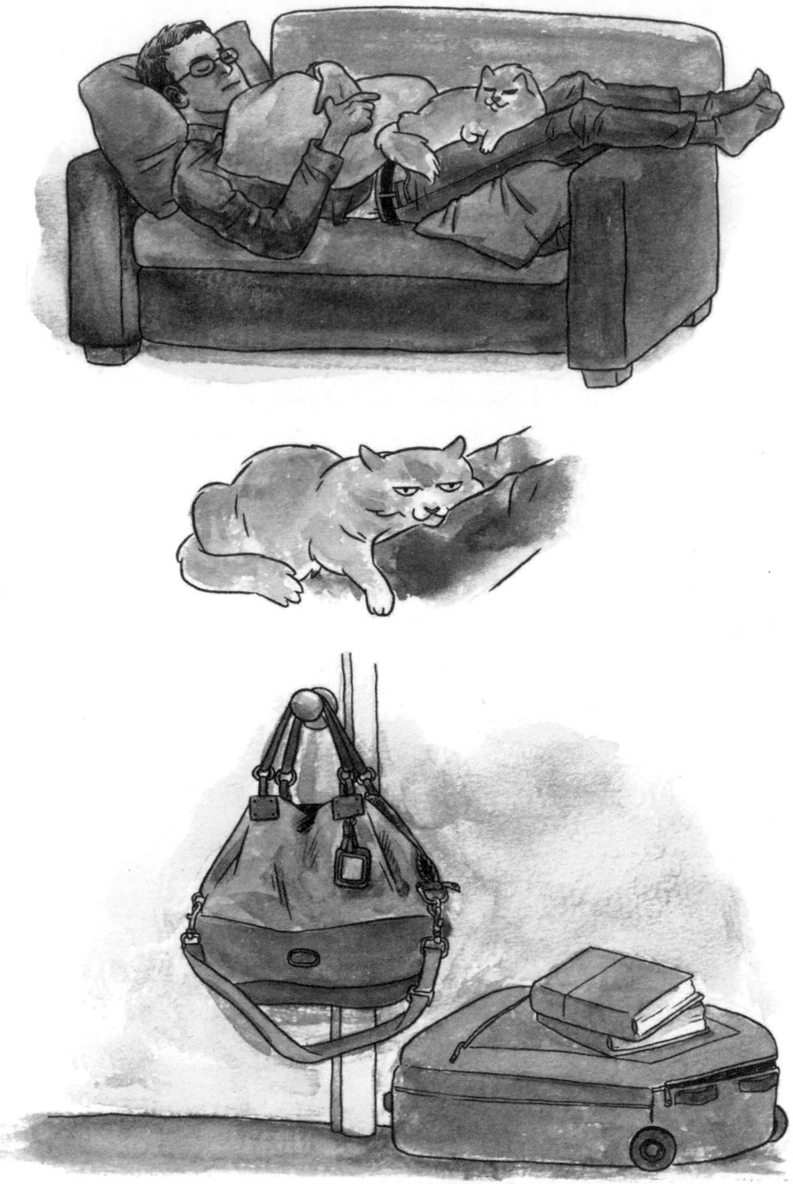

John is great. Independent, smart, funny...
...but he doesn't want kids, and I do.

Not right <u>now</u>, but someday.

And that "someday" loomed too darkly
to sustain, so we parted ways.

But "someday" is still so abstract and far off
that sometimes the lines get blurred.

Being in a sort of state of limbo can make it
hard to find someone new, to look ahead instead of
behind me, or to commit to any kind of future plan...

...But it's nice anyway.

LOVE

IS COMPLICATED

I'm not sure I'm very good at it.

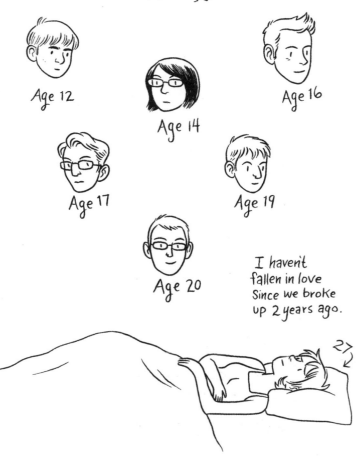

Age 12

Age 14

Age 16

Age 17

Age 19

Age 20

I haven't
fallen in love
since we broke
up 2 years ago.

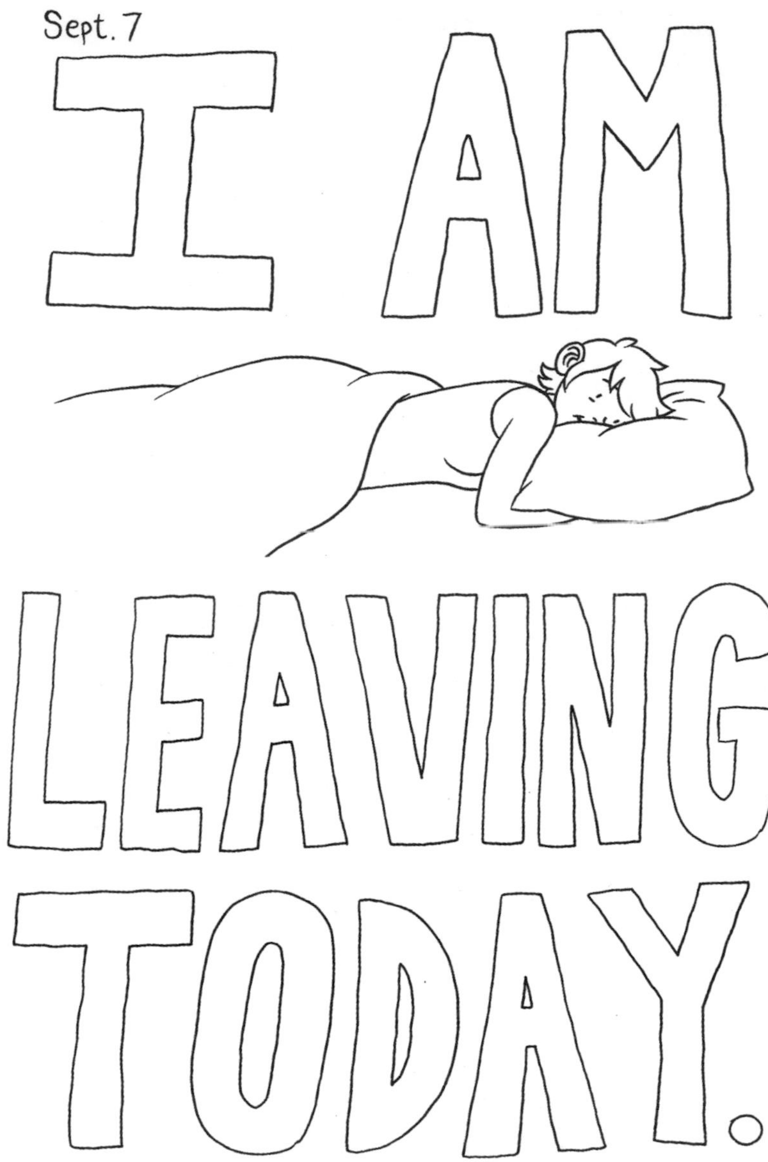
Sept. 7
I AM
LEAVING
TODAY.

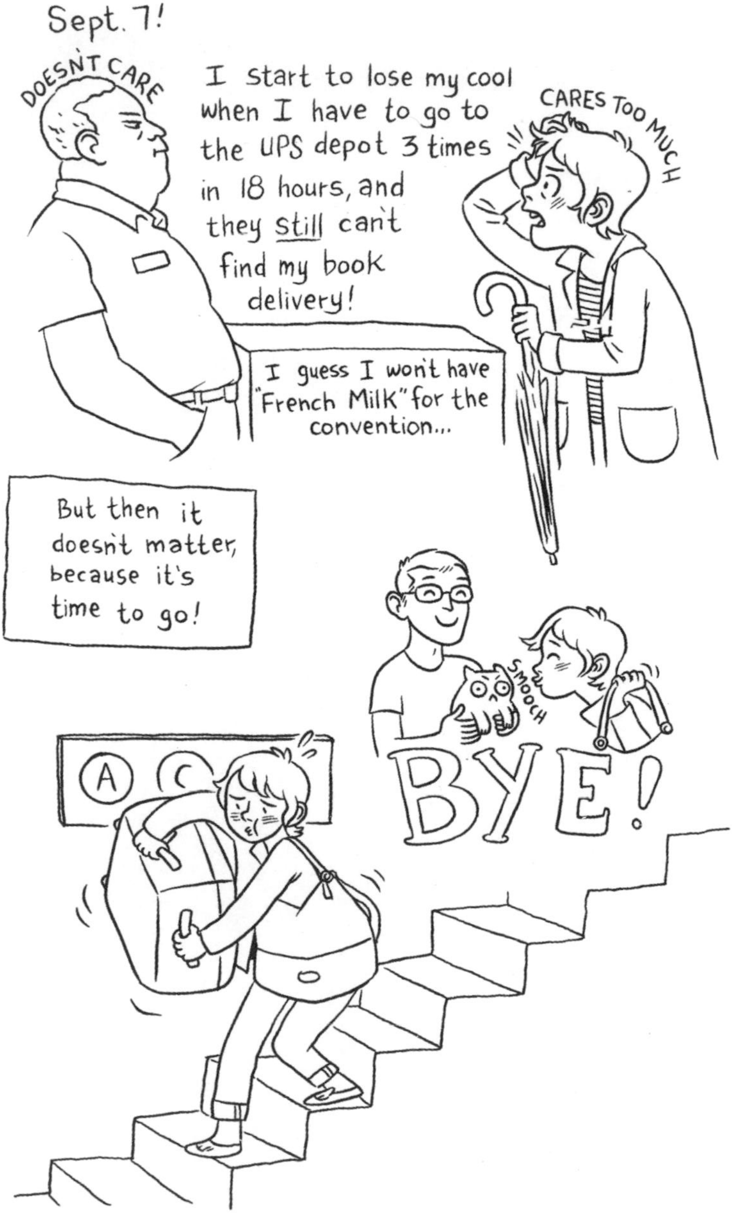
Sept. 7!
DOESN'T CARE
I start to lose my cool when I have to go to the UPS depot 3 times in 18 hours, and they still can't find my book delivery!
CARES TOO MUCH
I guess I won't have "French Milk" for the convention...
But then it doesn't matter, because it's time to go!
SMOOCH
BYE!
A

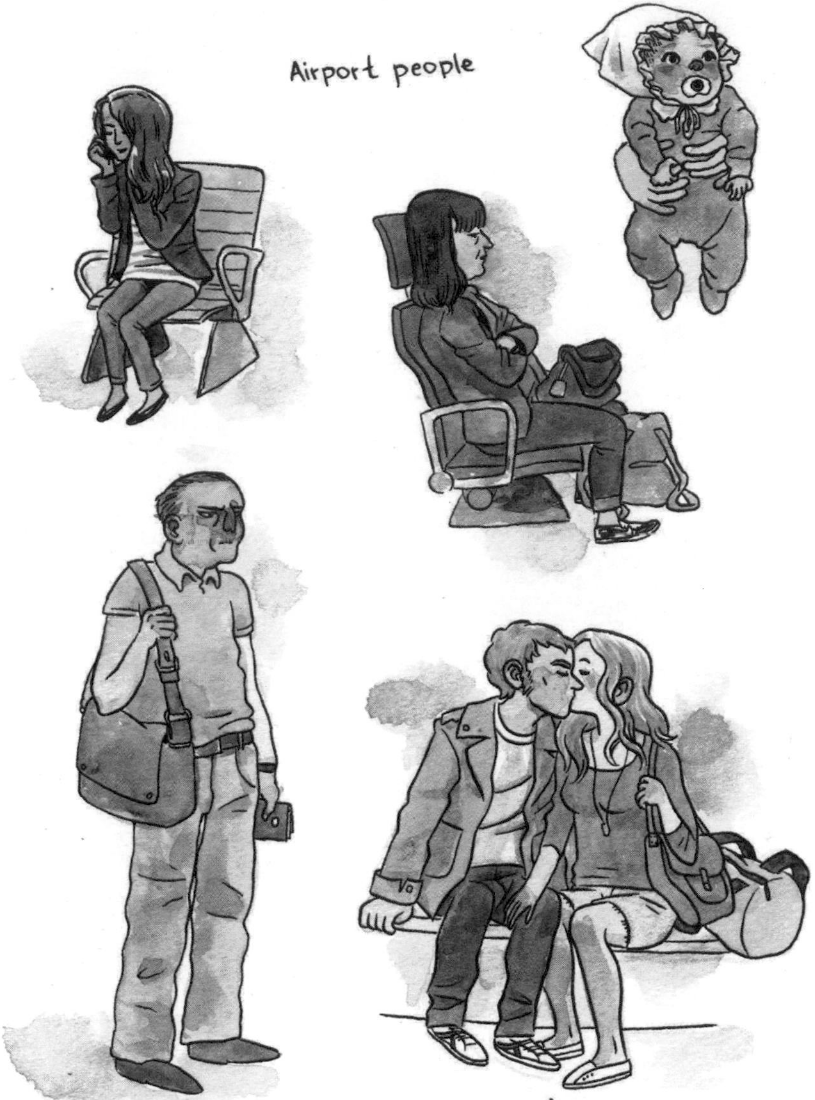
Airport people
They were French!

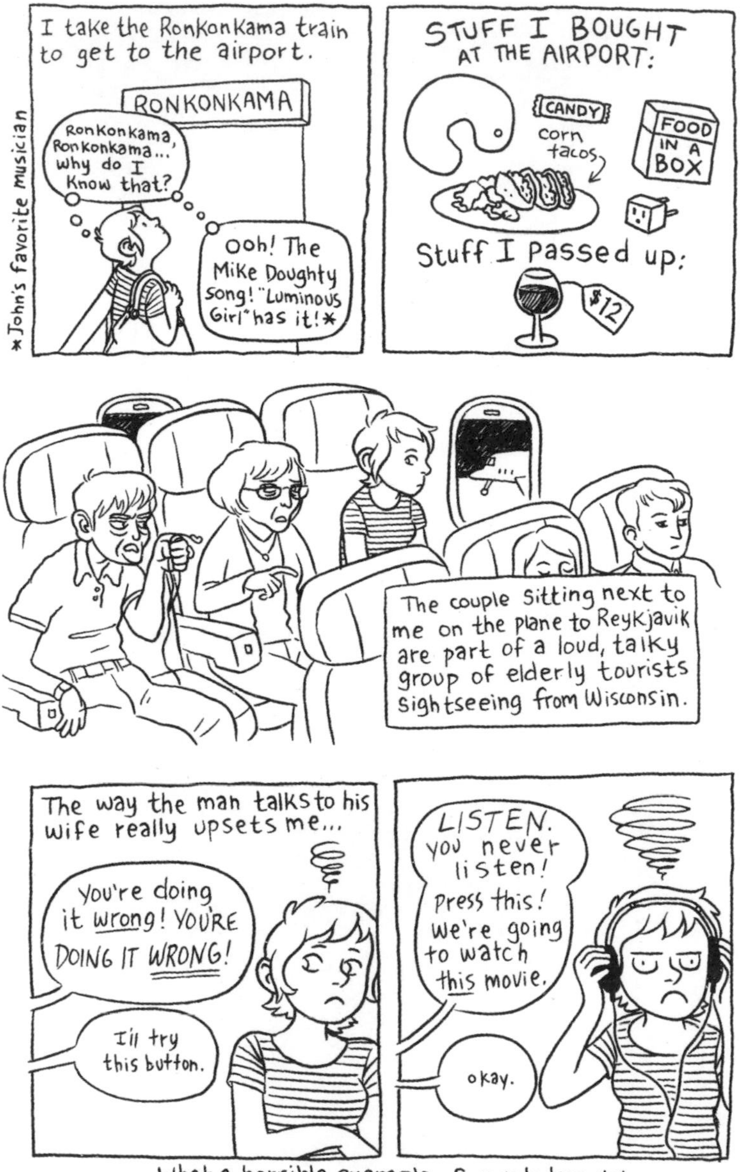
I take the RonKonKama train to get to the airport.
RONKONKAMA
RonKonKama, RonKonKama..., why do I Know that?
Ooh! The Mike Doughty song! "Luminous Girl" has it!*
*John's favorite musician
STUFF I BOUGHT AT THE AIRPORT:
CANDY
corn tacos
FOOD IN A BOX
Stuff I passed up:
$12
The couple sitting next to me on the plane to Reykjavik are part of a loud, talky group of elderly tourists sightseeing from Wisconsin.
The way the man talks to his wife really upsets me...
You're doing it wrong! YOU'RE DOING IT WRONG!
I'll try this button.
LISTEN. You never listen! Press this! We're going to watch this movie.
okay.

What a horrible example of coupledom. Ugh.
Is this the happy ending of romance?

TO BERGEN, NORWAY

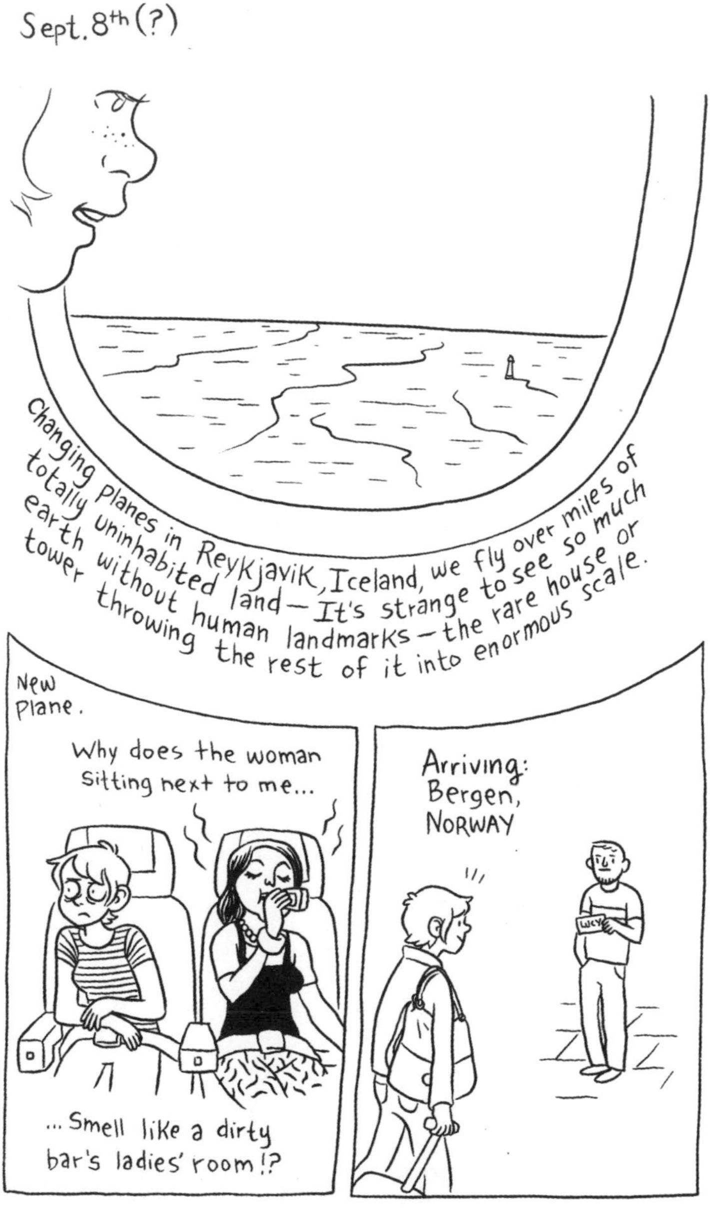
Sept. 8th (?)
Changing planes in Reykjavik, Iceland, we fly over miles of totally uninhabited land — It's strange to see so much earth without human landmarks — the rare house or tower throwing the rest of it into enormous scale.
New plane.
Why does the woman sitting next to me...
... Smell like a dirty bar's ladies' room!?
Arriving: Bergen, NORWAY
LUCY

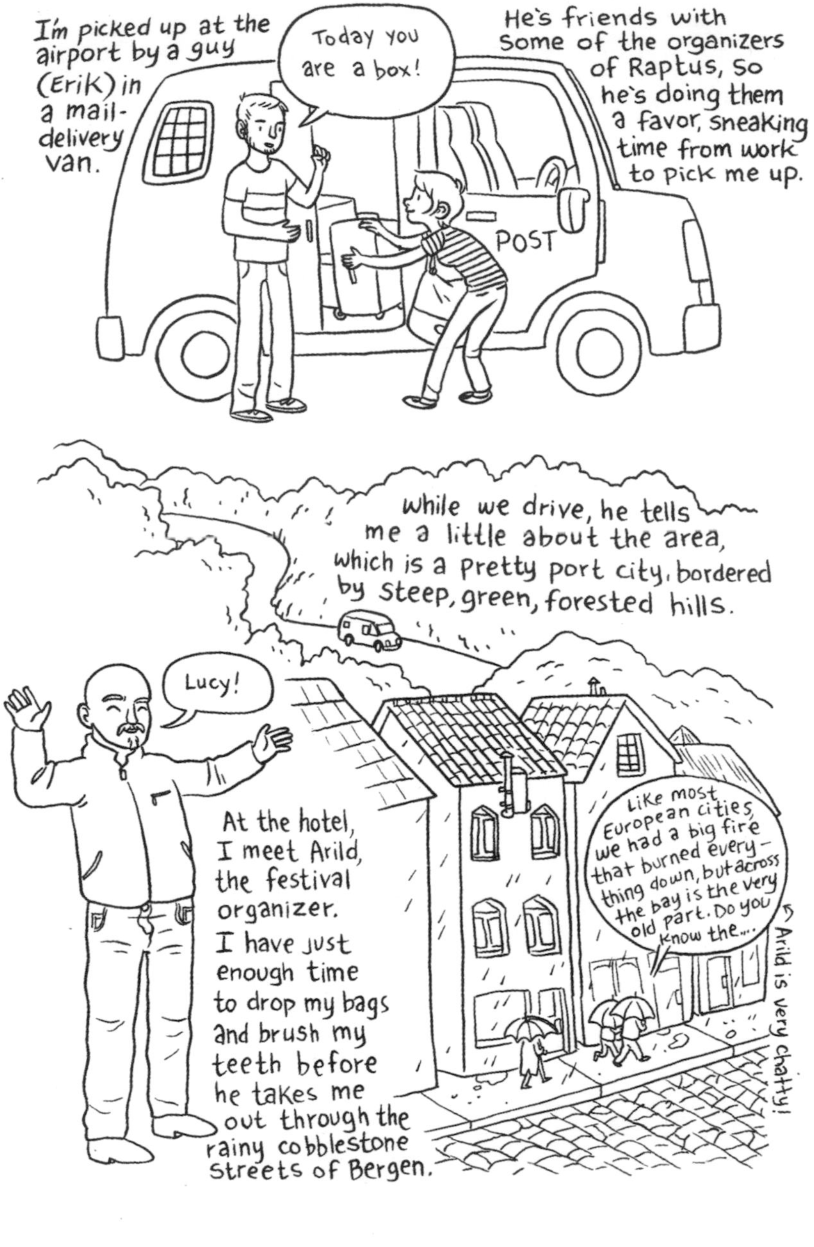
I'm picked up at the airport by a guy (Erik) in a mail-delivery van.
Today you are a box!
He's friends with some of the organizers of Raptus, so he's doing them a favor, sneaking time from work to pick me up.
POST
While we drive, he tells me a little about the area, which is a pretty port city, bordered by steep, green, forested hills.
Lucy!
At the hotel, I meet Arild, the festival organizer. I have just enough time to drop my bags and brush my teeth before he takes me out through the rainy cobblestone streets of Bergen.
Like most European cities, we had a big fire that burned everything down, but across the bay is the very old part. Do you know the....
Arild is very chatty!

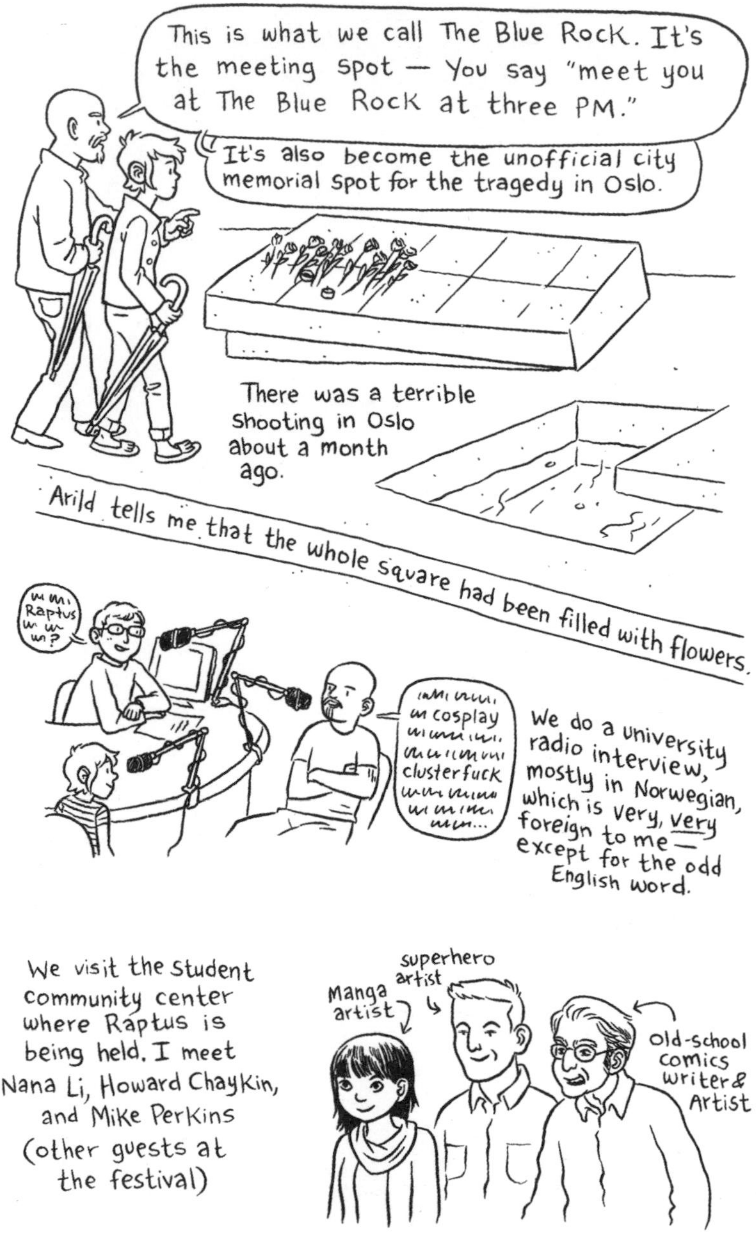
This is what we call The Blue Rock. It's the meeting spot — You say "meet you at The Blue Rock at three PM."
It's also become the unofficial city memorial spot for the tragedy in Oslo.
There was a terrible shooting in Oslo about a month ago.
Arild tells me that the whole square had been filled with flowers.
Raptus
cosplay
clusterfuck
We do a university radio interview, mostly in Norwegian, which is very, very foreign to me— except for the odd English word.
We visit the Student community center where Raptus is being held. I meet Nana Li, Howard Chaykin, and Mike Perkins (other guests at the festival)
Manga artist
superhero artist
Old-school comics writer & Artist

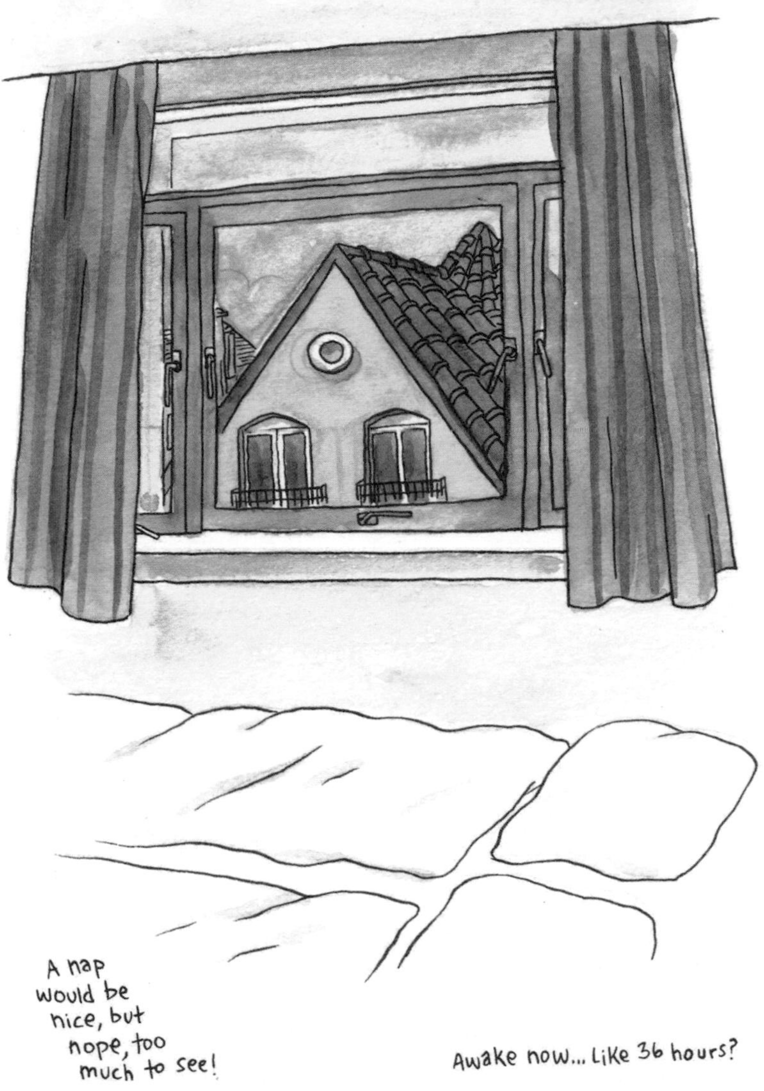
A nap would be nice, but nope, too much to see!
Awake now... Like 36 hours?

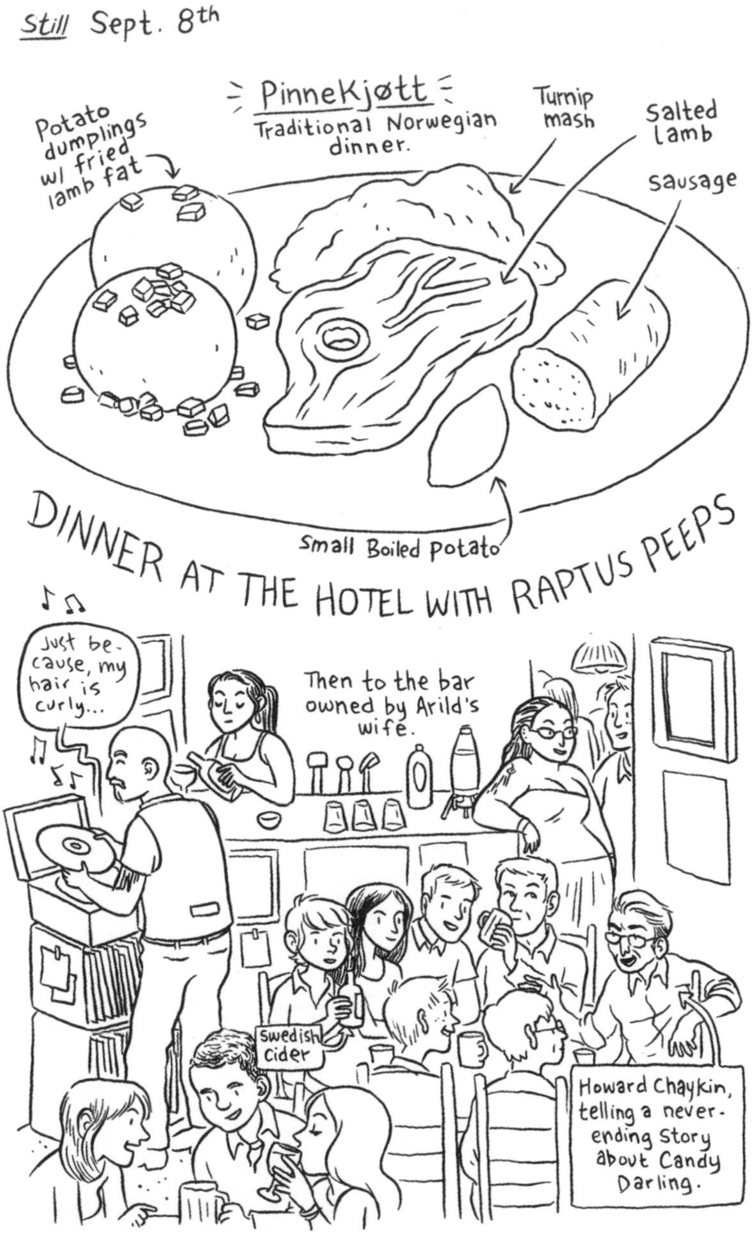
Still Sept. 8th
PinneKjøtt
Traditional Norwegian dinner.
Potato dumplings w/ fried lamb fat
Turnip mash
Salted lamb
sausage
Small Boiled Potato
DINNER AT THE HOTEL WITH RAPTUS PEEPS
Just be-cause, my hair is curly...
Then to the bar owned by Arild's wife.
Swedish Cider
Howard Chaykin, telling a never-ending story about Candy Darling.

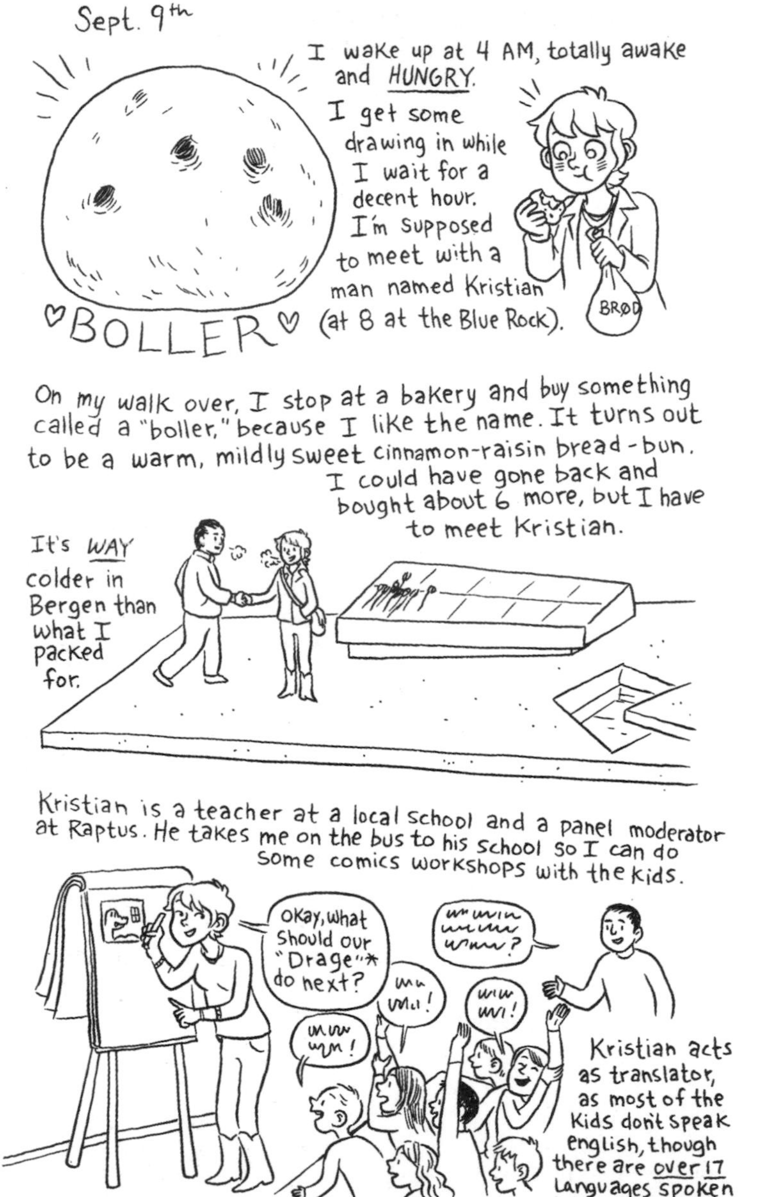
Sept. 9th
I wake up at 4 AM, totally awake and HUNGRY.
I get some drawing in while I wait for a decent hour. I'm supposed to meet with a man named Kristian (at 8 at the Blue Rock).
♡BOLLER♡
BRØD
On my walk over, I stop at a bakery and buy something called a "boller," because I like the name. It turns out to be a warm, mildly sweet cinnamon-raisin bread-bun.
I could have gone back and bought about 6 more, but I have to meet Kristian.
It's WAY colder in Bergen than what I packed for.
Kristian is a teacher at a local school and a panel moderator at Raptus. He takes me on the bus to his school so I can do some comics workshops with the kids.
Okay, what should our "Drage"* do next?
Kristian acts as translator, as most of the kids don't speak english, though there are over 17 languages spoken among the students!
*Norwegian for DRAGON!

I do two short workshops with grades 4&5 and a longer one with grade 6, which includes me drawing portraits of all 25 students.

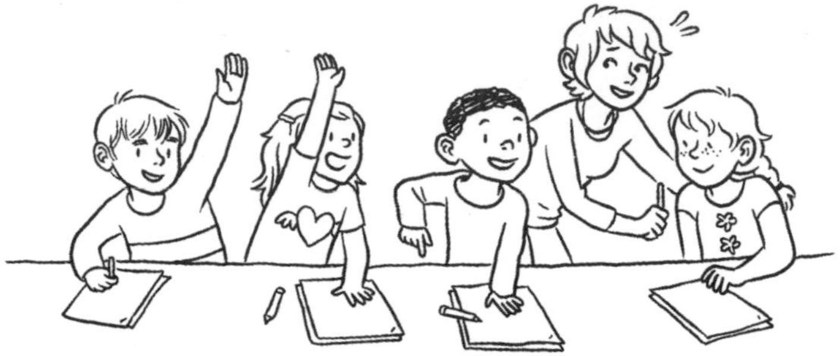

It's only 3 classes, but it still totally wipes me out!

SOME HIGHLIGHTS

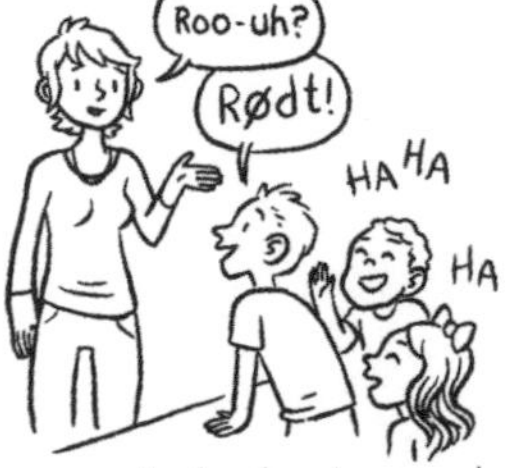
Roo-uh?
Rødt!
HA HA
HA

The Kids trying to teach me how to say "RED" in Norwegian.

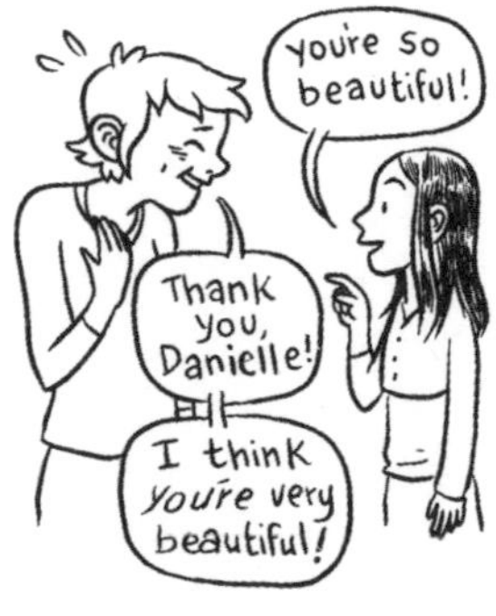
You're so beautiful!
Thank you, Danielle!
I think *you're* very beautiful!

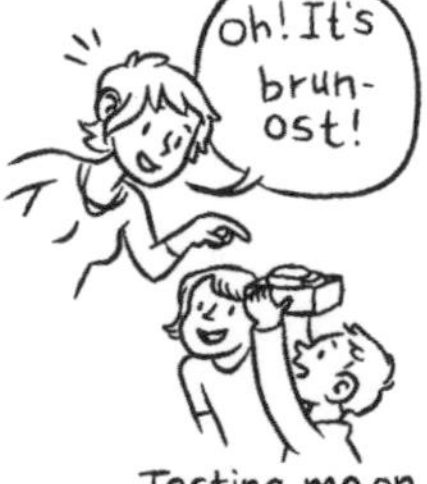
Oh! It's brun-ost!

Testing me on my ability to recognize cheeses.

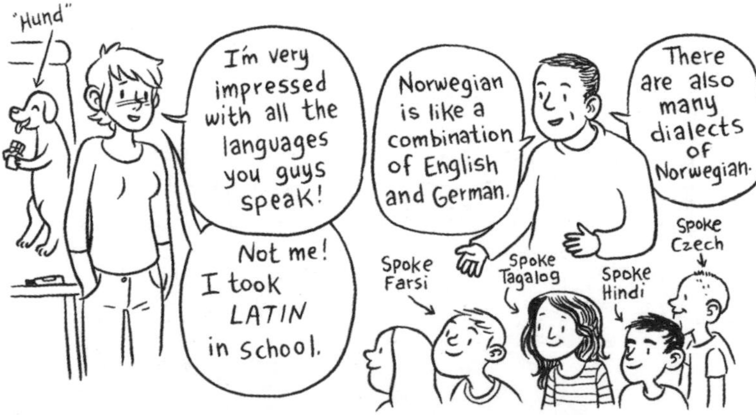
"Hund"
I'm very impressed with all the languages you guys speak!
Not me! I took LATIN in school.
Norwegian is like a combination of English and German.
There are also many dialects of Norwegian.
Spoke Farsi
Spoke Tagalog
Spoke Hindi
Spoke Czech

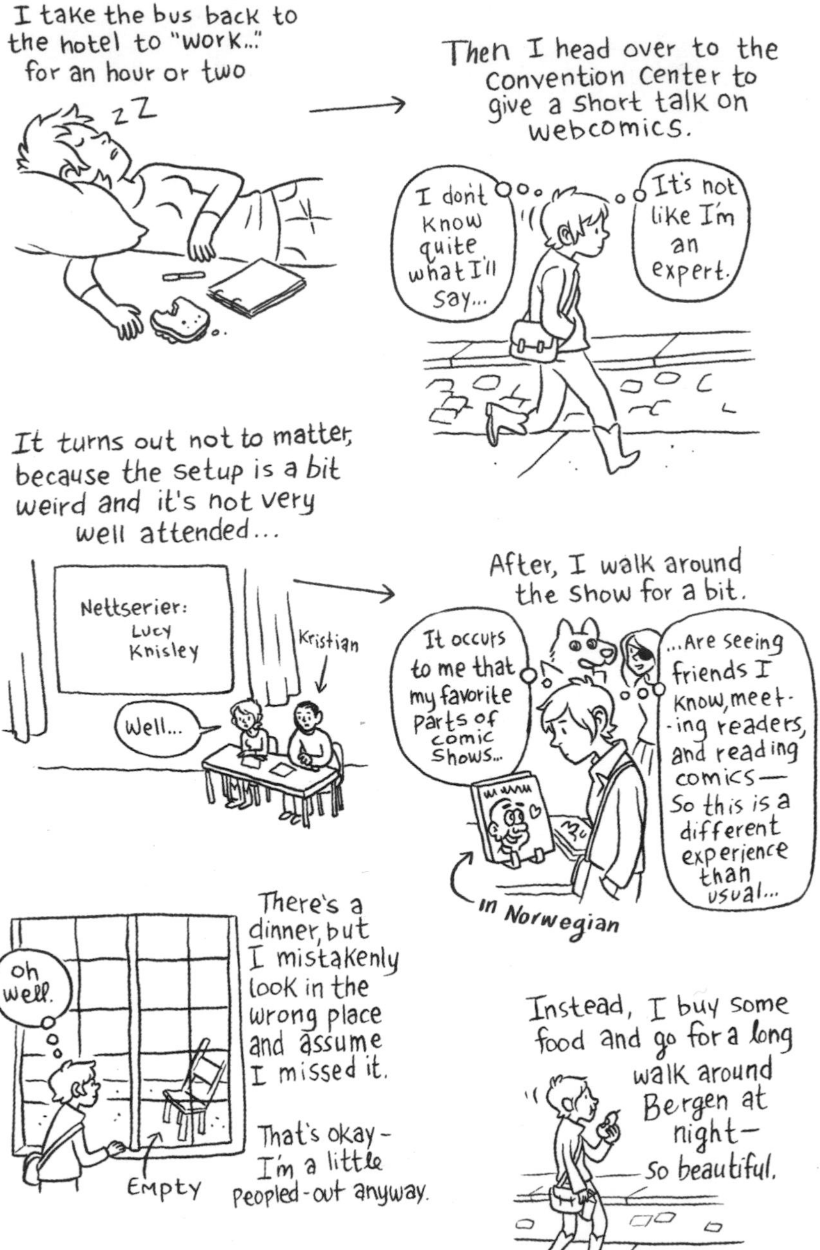
I take the bus back to the hotel to "work..." for an hour or two
zZ
Then I head over to the convention center to give a short talk on webcomics.
I don't know quite what I'll say...
It's not like I'm an expert.
It turns out not to matter, because the setup is a bit weird and it's not very well attended...
Nettserier: Lucy Knisley
Kristian
Well...
After, I walk around the show for a bit.
It occurs to me that my favorite parts of comic shows...
...Are seeing friends I know, meet-ing readers, and reading comics— So this is a different experience than usual...
in Norwegian
There's a dinner, but I mistakenly look in the wrong place and assume I missed it.
oh well.
Empty
That's okay - I'm a little peopled-out anyway.
Instead, I buy some food and go for a long walk around Bergen at night— So beautiful.

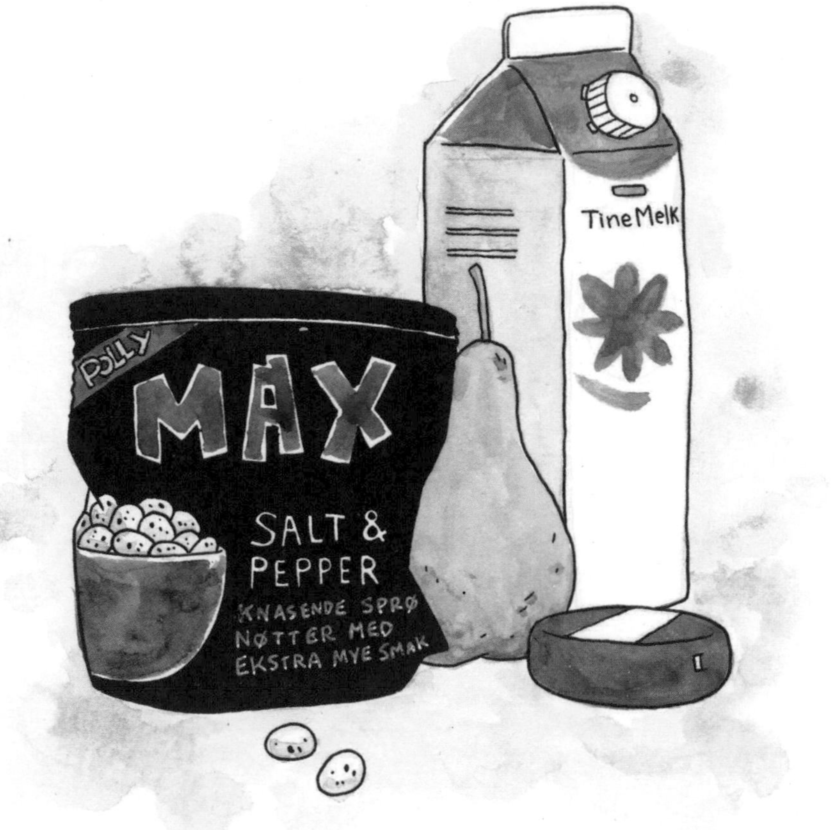
POLLY
MAX
SALT &
PEPPER
KNASENDE SPRØ
NØTTER MED
EKSTRA MYE SMAK
Tine Melk

These were peanuts
coated with a salty
corn puff kinda stuff.
TOTALLY ADDICTIVE!

Earlier, I'd asked around about special Norwegian foods I should try during my visit. I was told about a traditional type of cured fish called "Lutefisk."

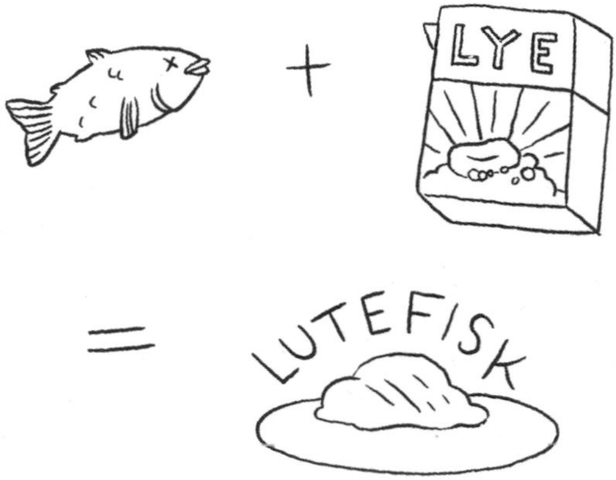
LYE
LUTEFISK

It's a very pungent, gelatinous dish that most Norwegians I asked about it seemed to revile. I'd give it a try, but I haven't seen it yet.

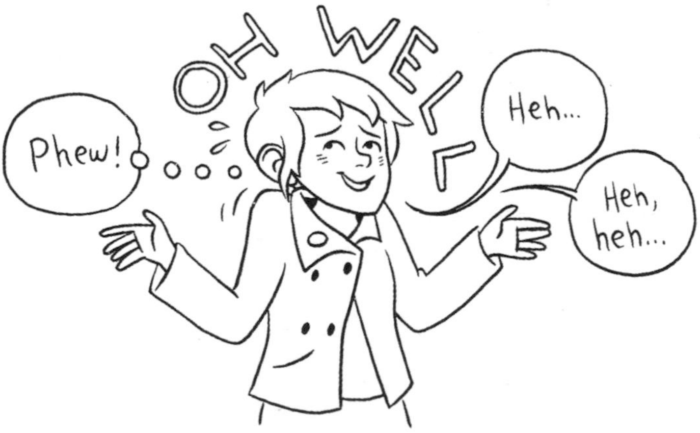
OH WELL
Phew!
Heh...
Heh, heh...

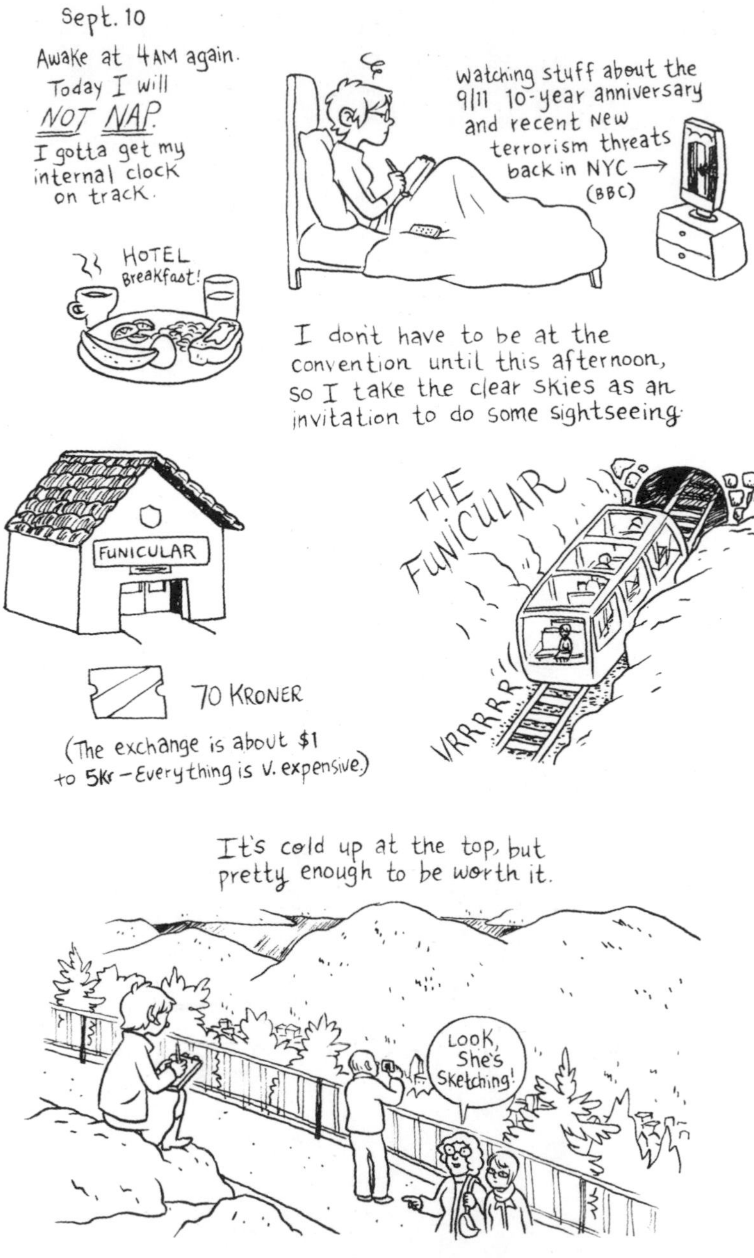
Sept. 10
Awake at 4AM again. Today I will NOT NAP. I gotta get my internal clock on track.
HOTEL Breakfast!
Watching stuff about the 9/11 10-year anniversary and recent new terrorism threats back in NYC → (BBC)
I don't have to be at the convention until this afternoon, so I take the clear skies as an invitation to do some sightseeing.
FUNICULAR
70 KRONER
(The exchange is about $1 to 5Kr - Everything is v. expensive.)
THE FUNICULAR
VRRRRR
It's cold up at the top, but pretty enough to be worth it.
Look, She's Sketching!

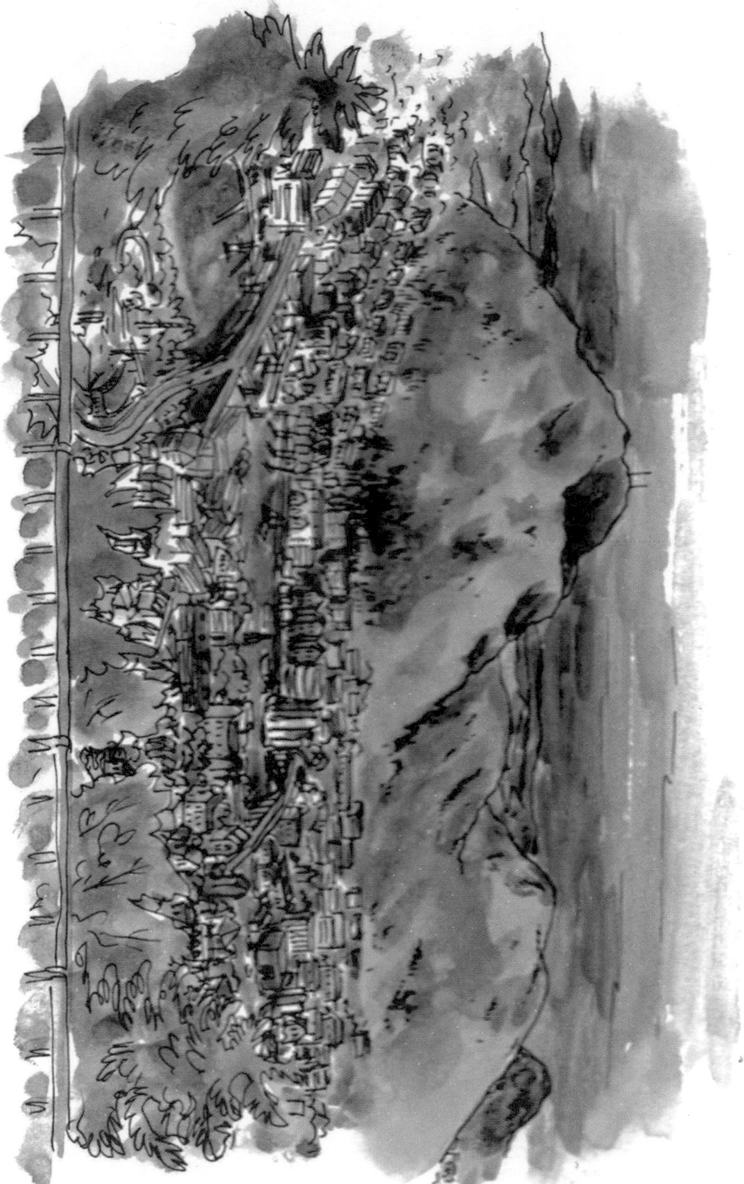

FUNNY MUSIC I'VE HEARD IN BERGEN

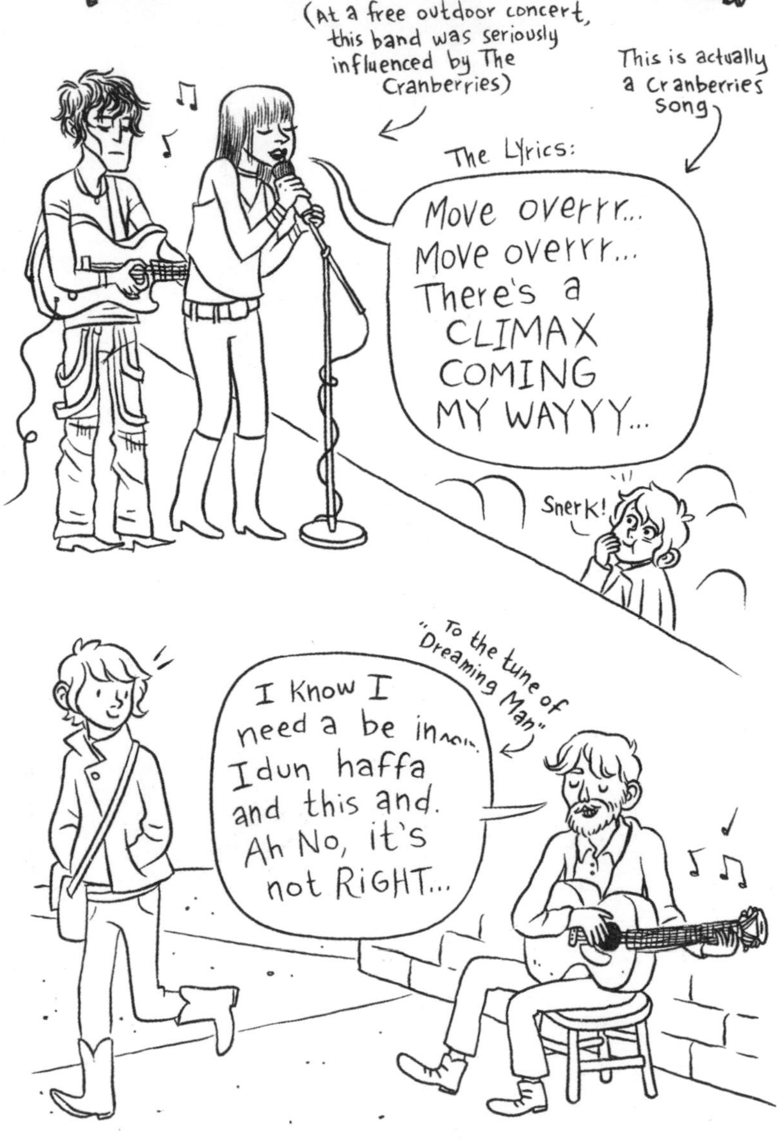

(At a free outdoor concert, this band was seriously influenced by The Cranberries)
This is actually a Cranberries song
The Lyrics:
Move overrr... Move overrr... There's a CLIMAX COMING MY WAYYY...
Snerk!
"To the tune of "Dreaming Man"
I Know I need a be in
Idun haffa and this and. Ah No, it's not RIGHT...

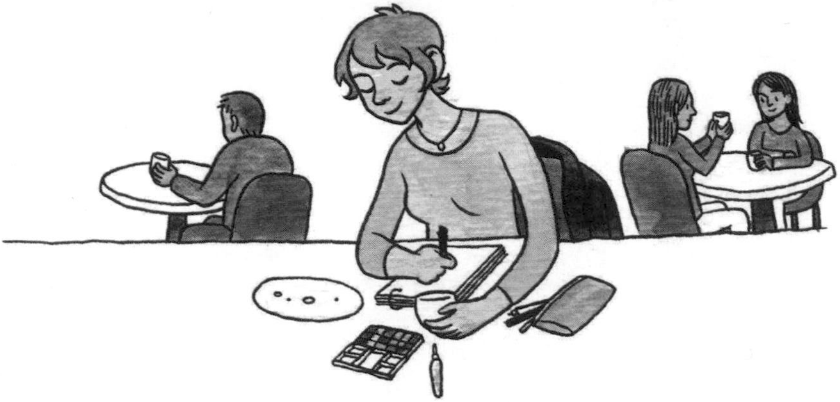

Drawing in cafe's is one of my favorite activities.
Sometimes it seems so romantic,
sneaking glances at other patrons
so I can draw them and speculate
about their secret lives.

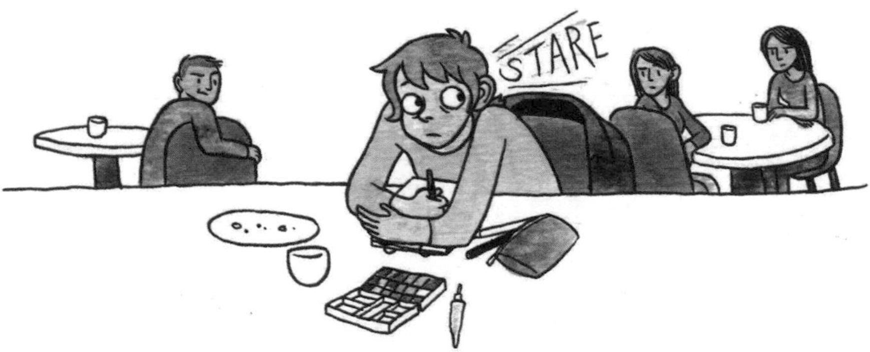
STARE

But the reality is actually probably a bit creepy.

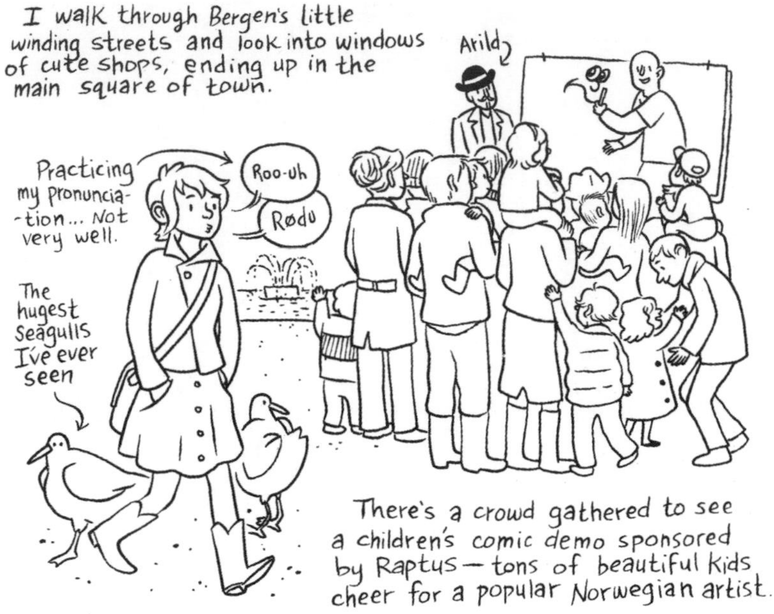
I walk through Bergen's little winding streets and look into windows of cute shops, ending up in the main square of town.
Arild
Practicing my pronunciation... Not very well.
Roo-uh
Rødu
The hugest seagulls I've ever seen
There's a crowd gathered to see a children's comic demo sponsored by Raptus — tons of beautiful kids cheer for a popular Norwegian artist.

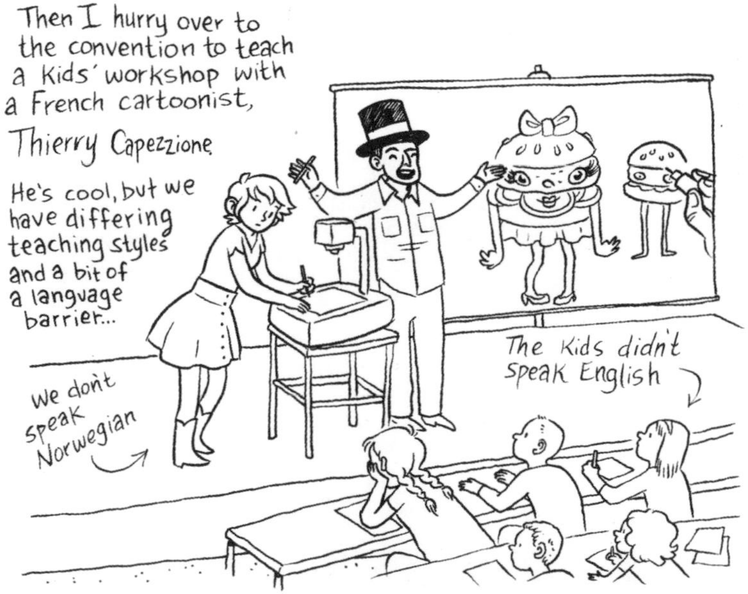
Then I hurry over to the convention to teach a kids' workshop with a French cartoonist, Thierry Capezzione
He's cool, but we have differing teaching styles and a bit of a language barrier...
The kids didn't speak English
we don't speak Norwegian

Kristian takes me out to "the best beer bar in Bergen" afterwards.

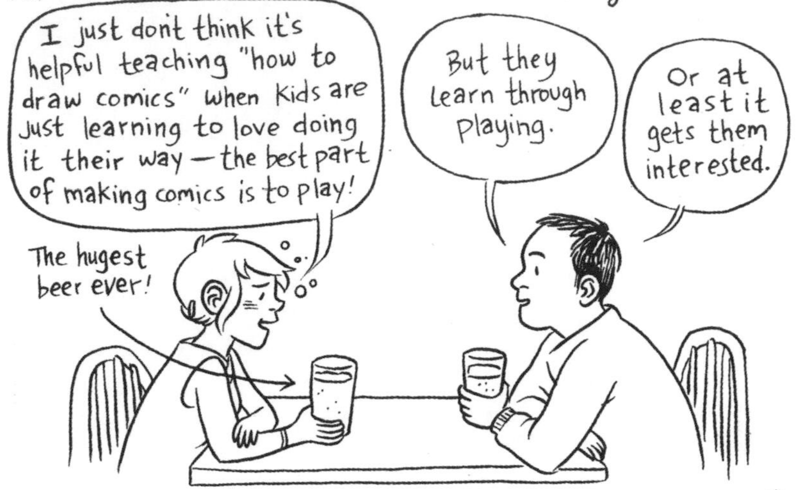
I just don't think it's helpful teaching "how to draw comics" when kids are just learning to love doing it their way — the best part of making comics is to play!
But they learn through playing.
Or at least it gets them interested.
The hugest beer ever!

(Kristian agrees to translate my travelogue into Norwegian!)

RAPTUS BANKETT (Banquet)

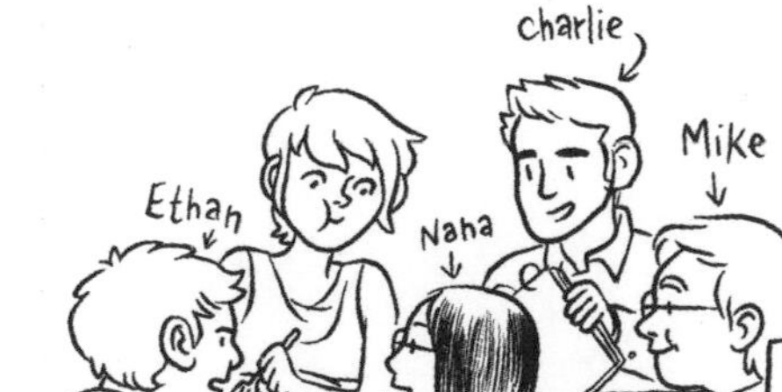
Charlie
Mike
Ethan
Naha

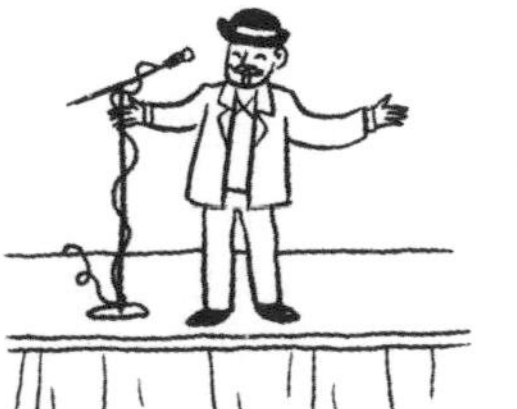

We drink, talk about materials in comics, and eat a vast array of cool buffet food.

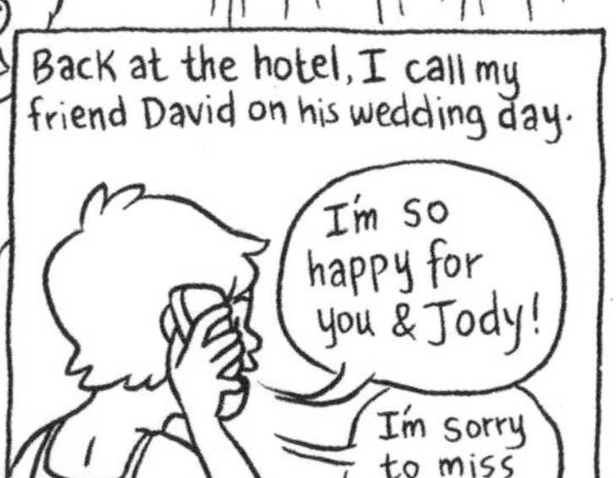
Back at the hotel, I call my friend David on his wedding day.
I'm so happy for you & Jody!
I'm sorry to miss it...

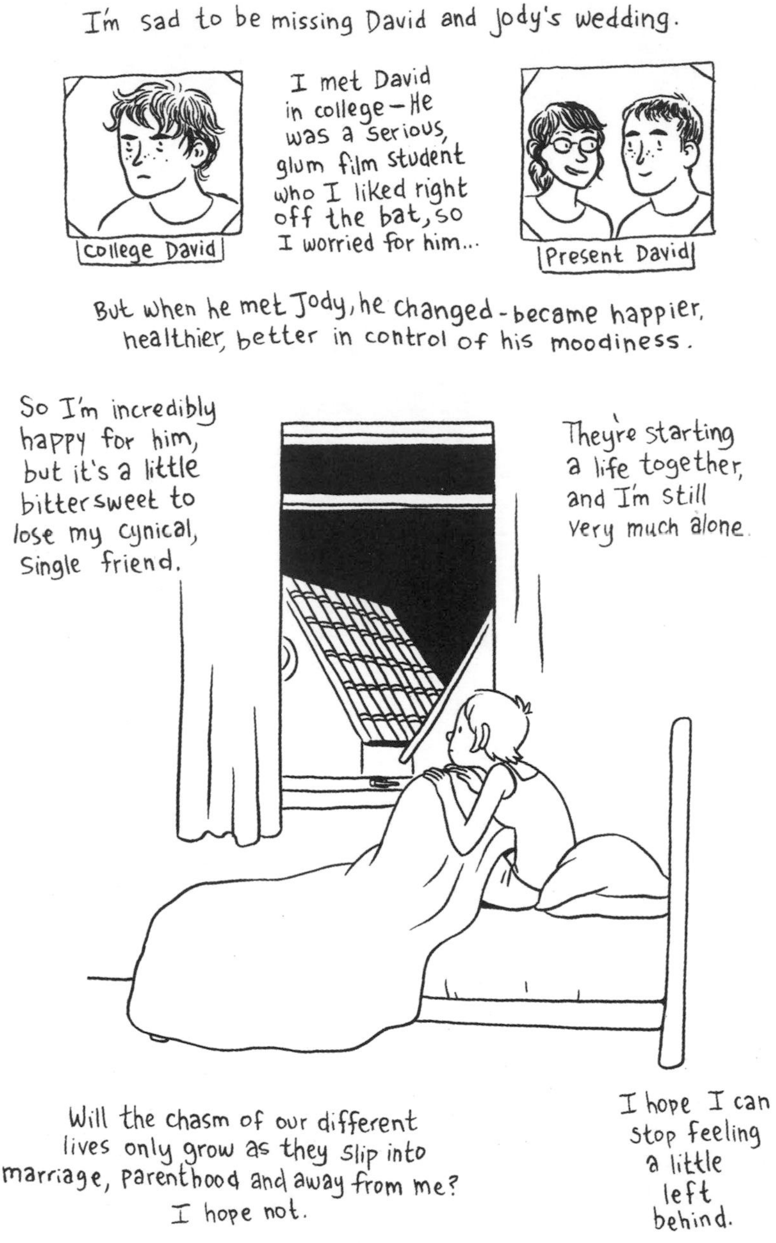
I'm sad to be missing David and Jody's wedding.
I met David in college—He was a serious, glum film student who I liked right off the bat, so I worried for him...
College David
Present David
But when he met Jody, he changed-became happier, healthier, better in control of his moodiness.
So I'm incredibly happy for him, but it's a little bittersweet to lose my cynical, single friend.
They're starting a life together, and I'm still very much alone.
Will the chasm of our different lives only grow as they slip into marriage, parenthood and away from me? I hope not.
I hope I can stop feeling a little left behind.

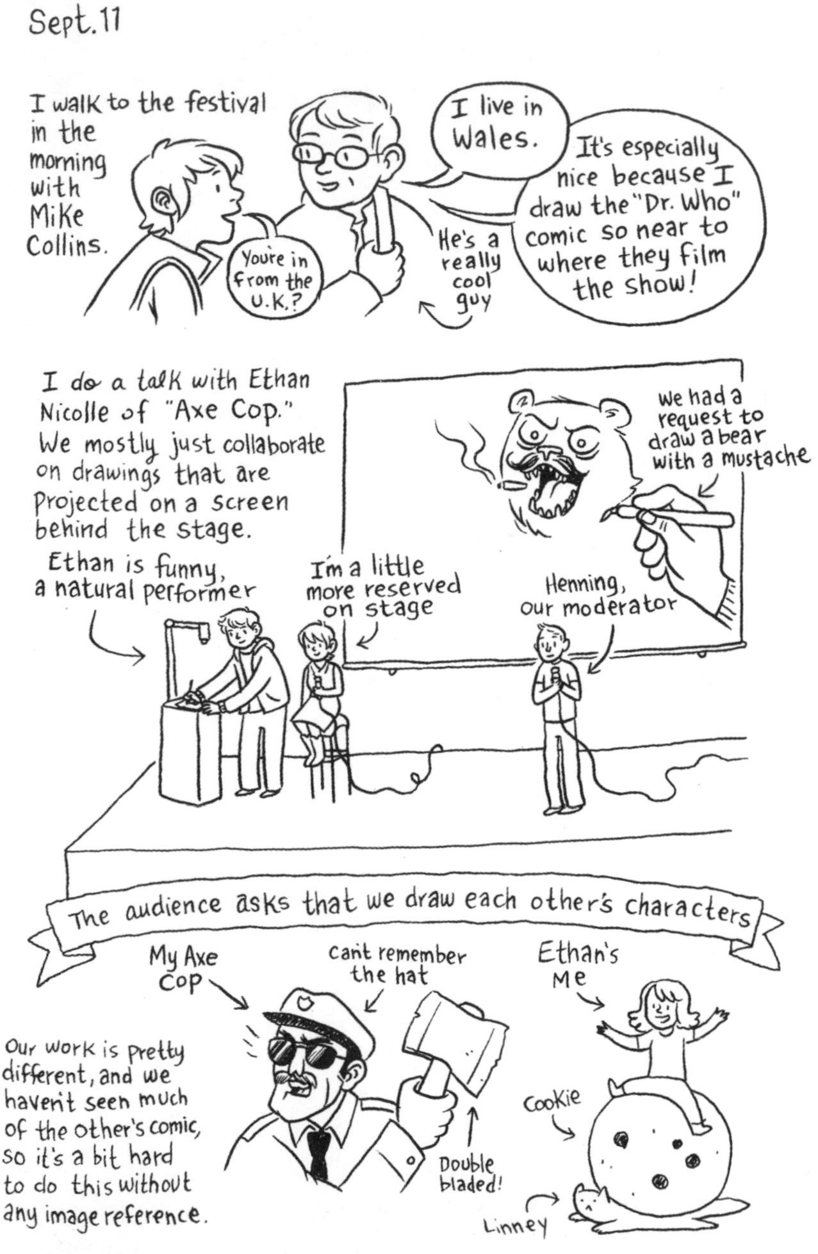
Sept. 11
I walk to the festival in the morning with Mike Collins.
You're in from the U.K.?
I live in Wales.
It's especially nice because I draw the "Dr. Who" comic so near to where they film the show!
He's a really cool guy
I do a talk with Ethan Nicolle of "Axe Cop." We mostly just collaborate on drawings that are projected on a screen behind the stage.
We had a request to draw a bear with a mustache
Ethan is funny, a natural performer
I'm a little more reserved on stage
Henning, our moderator
The audience asks that we draw each other's characters
My Axe Cop
Can't remember the hat
Ethan's Me
Our work is pretty different, and we haven't seen much of the other's comic, so it's a bit hard to do this without any image reference.
Double bladed!
Cookie
Linney

I do a signing and quickly sell out of the few books I brought.

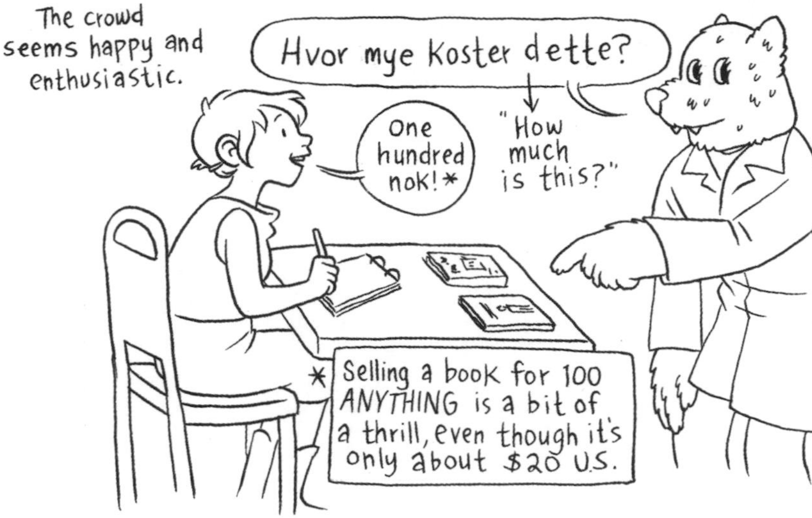
The crowd seems happy and enthusiastic.
Hvor mye Koster dette?
"How much is this?"
One hundred nok!*
* Selling a book for 100 ANYTHING is a bit of a thrill, even though it's only about $20 U.S.

Then I give my big talk on graphic travelogues. I've prepared a lot for this, so I'm more nervous than I should be, but it seems to go well.

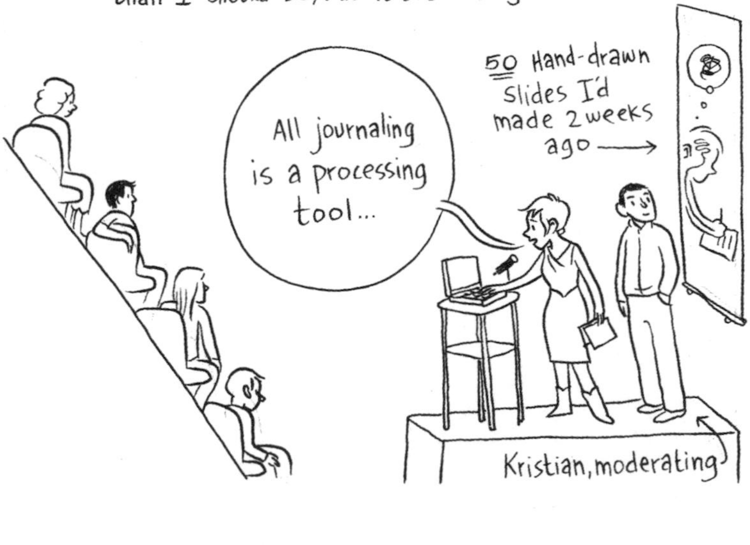
All journaling is a processing tool...
50 Hand-drawn slides I'd made 2 weeks ago
Kristian, moderating

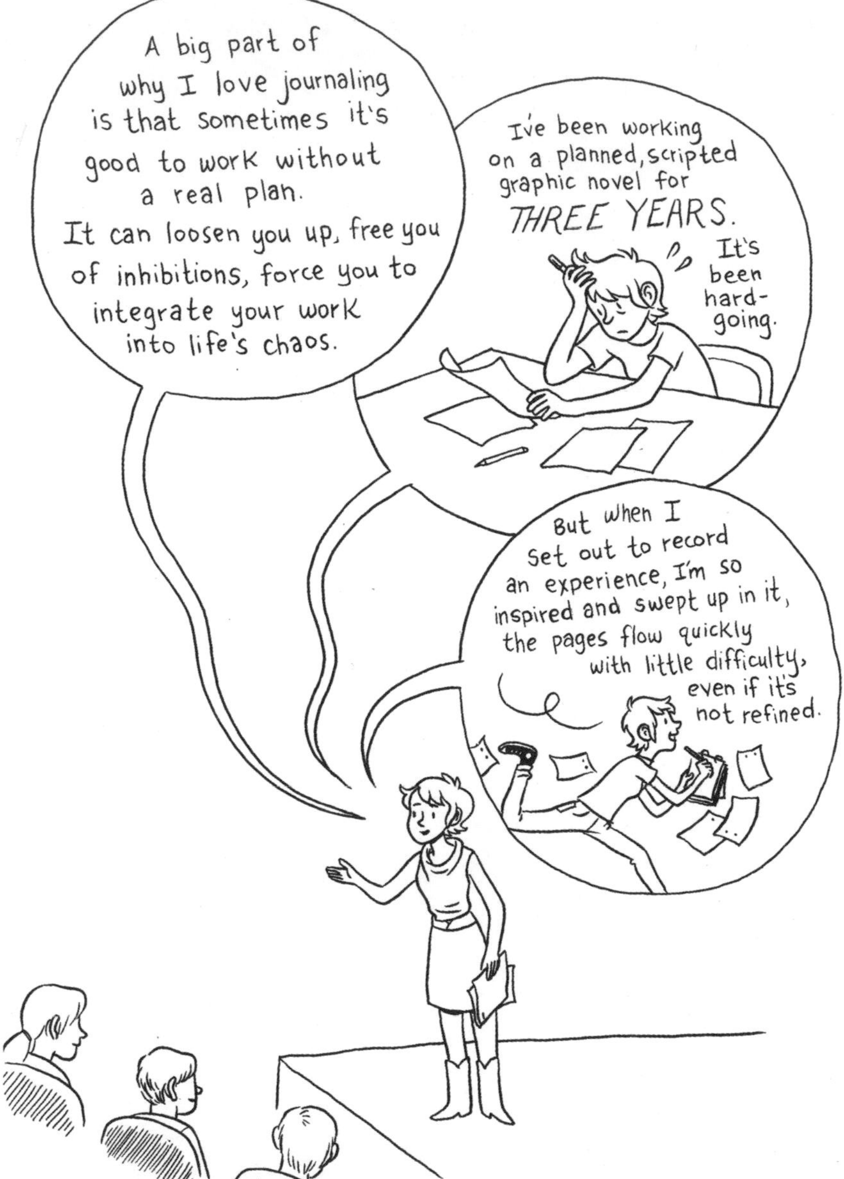
A big part of why I love journaling is that sometimes it's good to work without a real plan. It can loosen you up, free you of inhibitions, force you to integrate your work into life's chaos.
I've been working on a planned, scripted graphic novel for THREE YEARS.
It's been hard-going.
But when I set out to record an experience, I'm so inspired and swept up in it, the pages flow quickly with little difficulty, even if it's not refined.

A NOTE FROM THE FUTURE

(A page completed after my trip)

UNBEKNOWNST TO ME, while I wandered the show, meeting people and exploring the Norwegian comics scene, I was apparently **BEING STALKED.**

comics are a medium suited to immediacy...

<crass sexual innuendo>

LUCY KNISLEY ON TRAVEL COMICS

SCHEDULE

Heh Heh

I learned this info when I got home, and my friend Kristian sent me a copy of the zine two guys had made, about following me around the show and the various sexual and demeaning fantasies they had about me...

JUST A QUICK SUGGESTION:

Maybe don't make a zine about **STALKING SOMEONE.** Especially a sexually explicit one, in which you follow a professional artist around a show (at which she is an invited guest) without her knowledge, and then publish your zine & sell it at the show next year.

Heh Heh

IT'S CREEPY

And unprofessional and unkind.

Just TALK TO HER, LIKE AN ADULT.

& NOW TO BACK TO THE STORY...

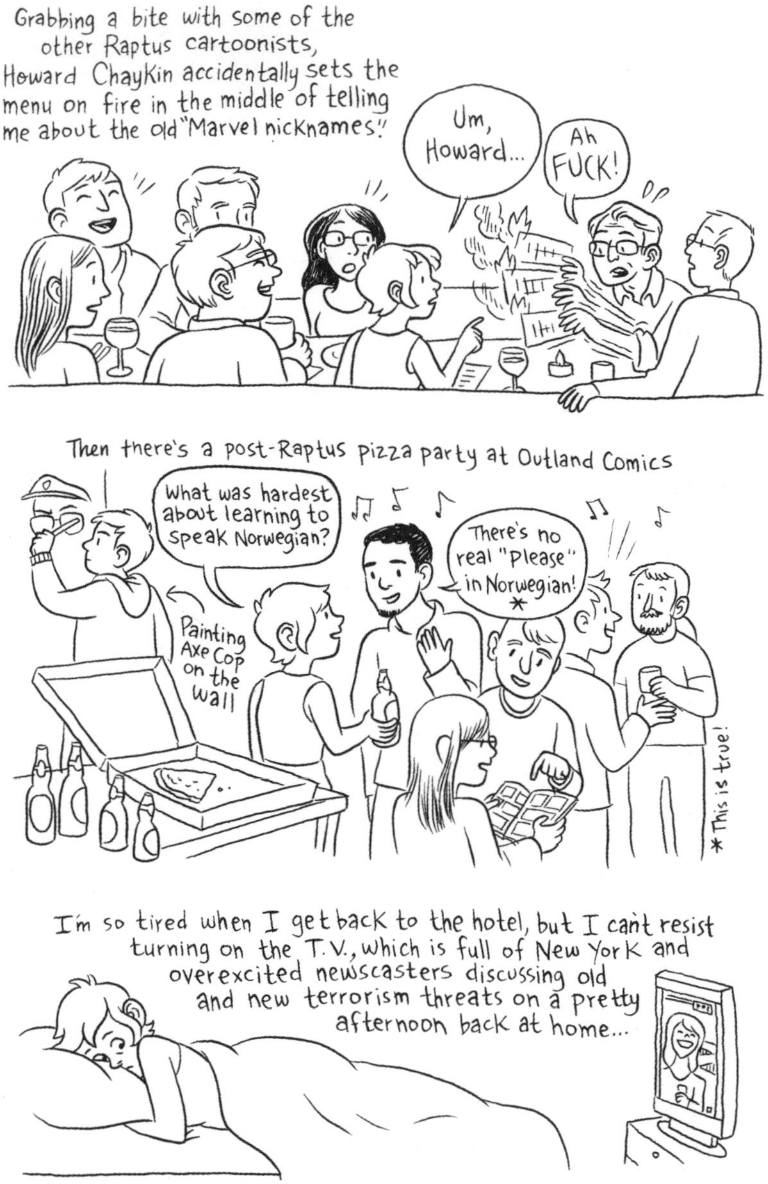
Grabbing a bite with some of the other Raptus cartoonists, Howard Chaykin accidentally sets the menu on fire in the middle of telling me about the old "Marvel nicknames."
Um, Howard...
Ah FUCK!
Then there's a post-Raptus pizza party at Outland Comics
What was hardest about learning to speak Norwegian?
Painting Axe Cop on the wall
There's no real "please" in Norwegian! *
* This is true!
I'm so tired when I get back to the hotel, but I can't resist turning on the T.V., which is full of New York and overexcited newscasters discussing old and new terrorism threats on a pretty afternoon back at home...

I hate the newscaster's enthusiasm
for showing the old footage.

Terrified flashbacks.

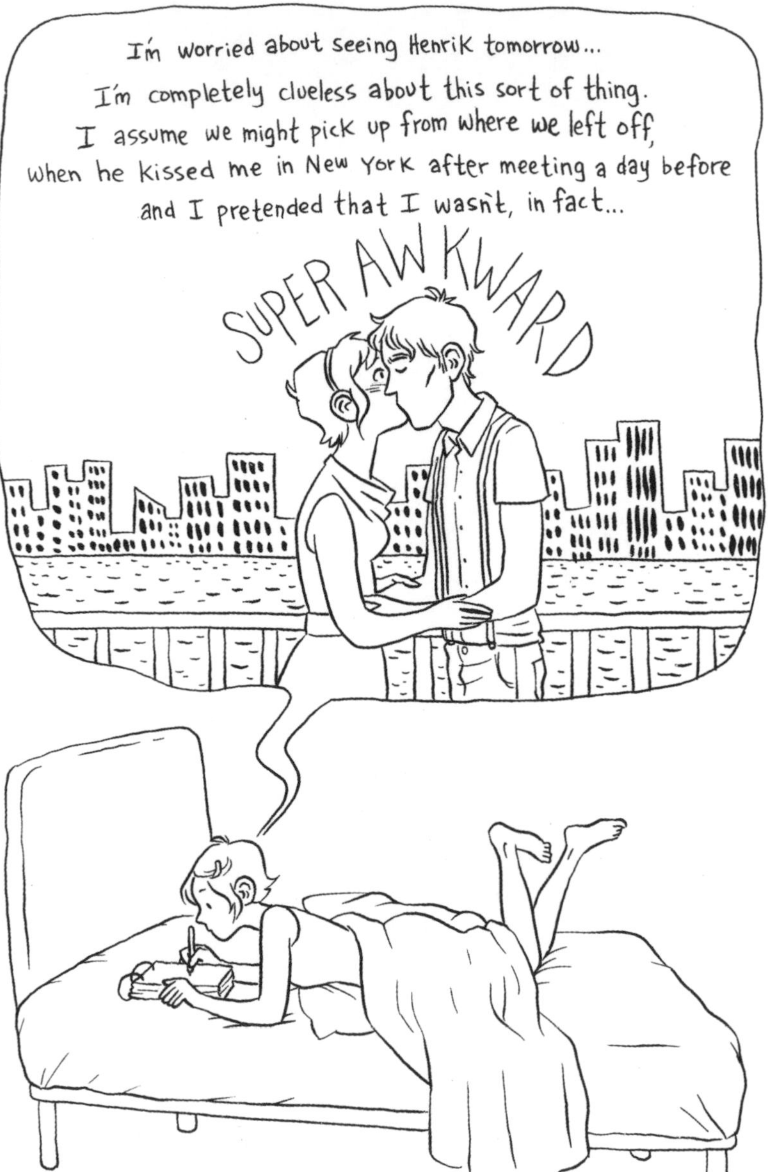
I'm worried about seeing Henrik tomorrow...
I'm completely clueless about this sort of thing.
I assume we might pick up from where we left off,
when he kissed me in New York after meeting a day before
and I pretended that I wasn't, in fact...
SUPER AWKWARD

TO STOCKHOLM, SWEDEN

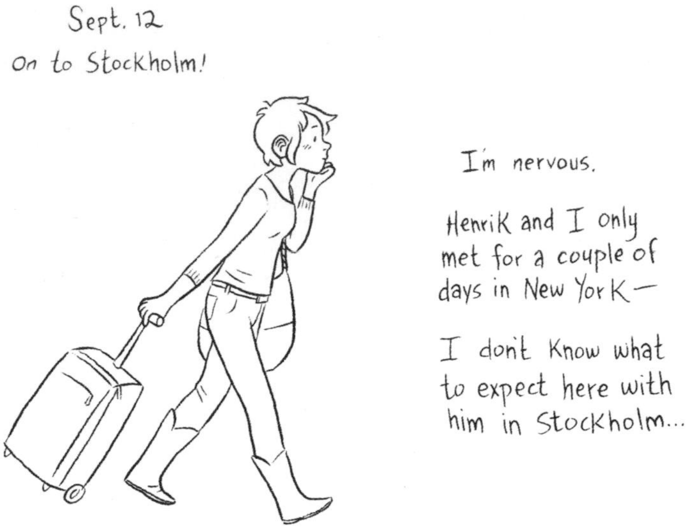
Sept. 12
On to Stockholm!
I'm nervous.
Henrik and I only met for a couple of days in New York—
I don't know what to expect here with him in Stockholm...

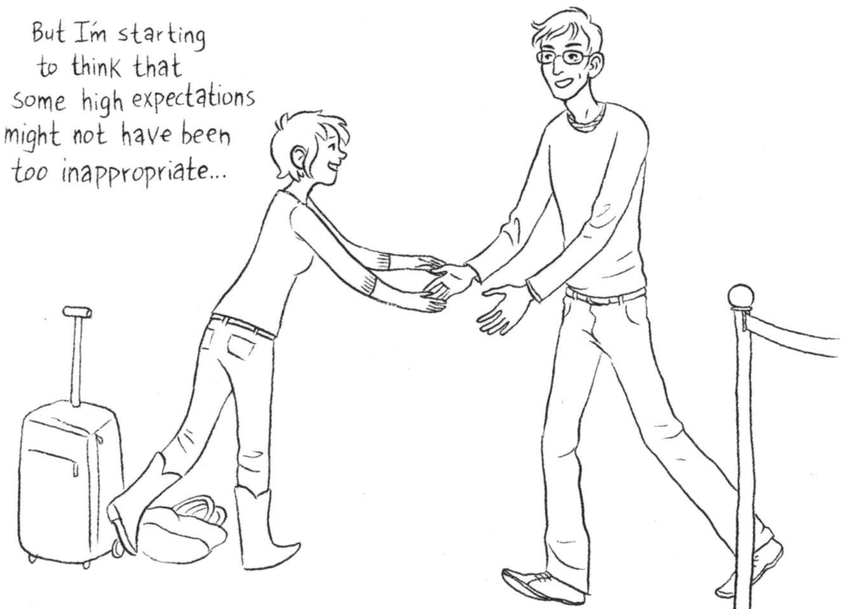
But I'm starting to think that some high expectations might not have been too inappropriate...

Henrik takes me to A nearby airfield

WHOOOSSSH!

Picking apples from the tree outside the Commune where he lives.

Frogs on the path

The Lake

I feel I should apologize for the lapse in diligent journaling that occurred during my brief stay in Stockholm...

What I saw of Stockholm was so beautiful — palaces and gorgeous little squares in Gamla Stan (Old Town) and boats in shining water, but...

To be honest, I was a little...
...distracted...

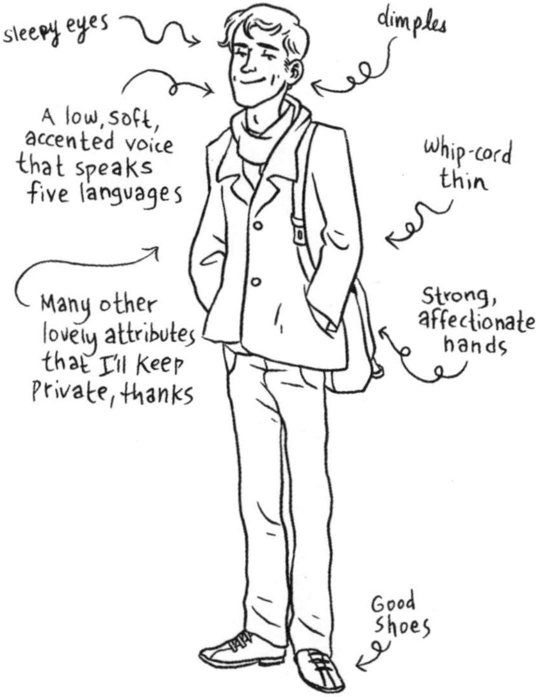
sleepy eyes
dimples
A low, soft, accented voice that speaks five languages
whip-cord thin
Many other lovely attributes that I'll keep private, thanks
Strong, affectionate hands
Good shoes

No, you know what?

I don't apologize.

From here, it's just snapshots.

It's funny to think that I came on this trip to give a talk on making travelogues, and now I'm suddenly finding it very difficult to actually work on mine...

Sometimes linearity can just vanish, deserting even the most diligently rational storytellers.

And things just become moments, impossible to ever really capture...

Sorry, I'm not sure I got the recipe Just right...

wild raspberry Jam

Vegan Swedish Pancakes

Traditional yellow pea Soup

Truthfully, I could barely eat at all!

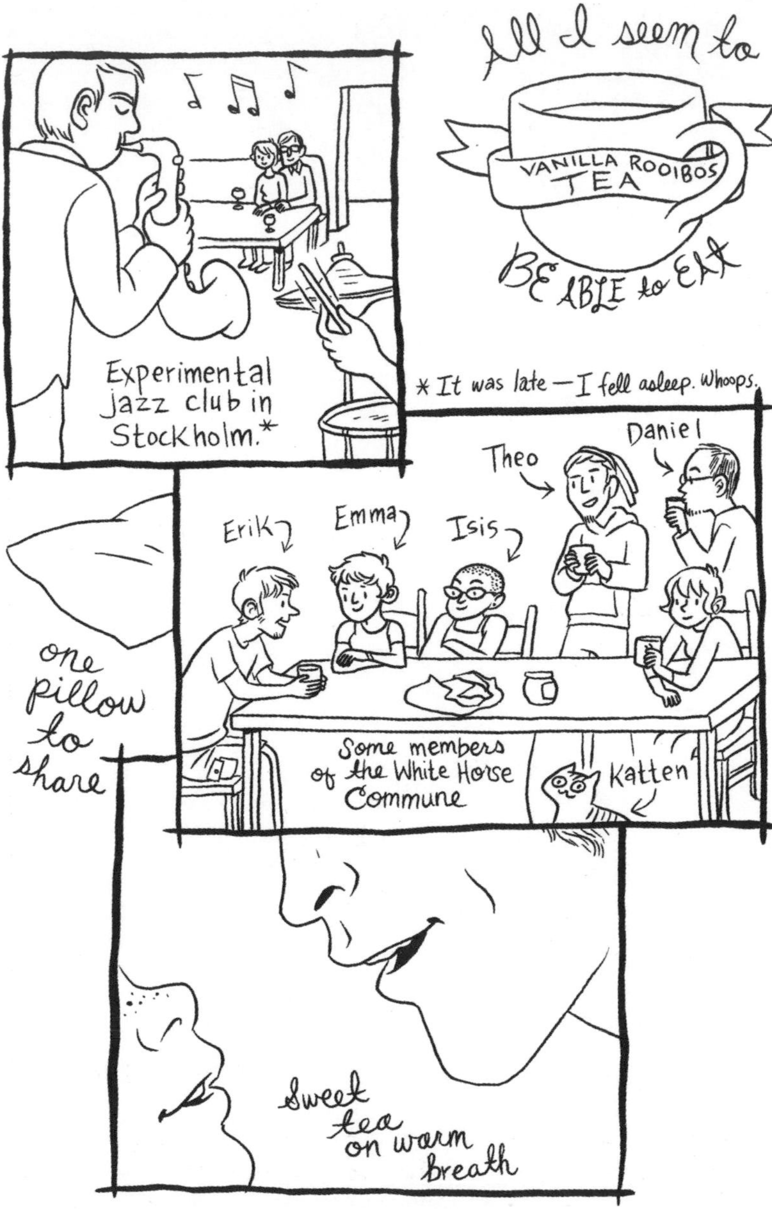
Experimental jazz club in Stockholm.*
All I seem to
VANILLA ROOIBOS TEA
BE ABLE to EAT
* It was late — I fell asleep. Whoops.
Theo
Daniel
Erik
Emma
Isis
Some members of the White Horse Commune
Katten
one pillow to share
Sweet tea on warm breath

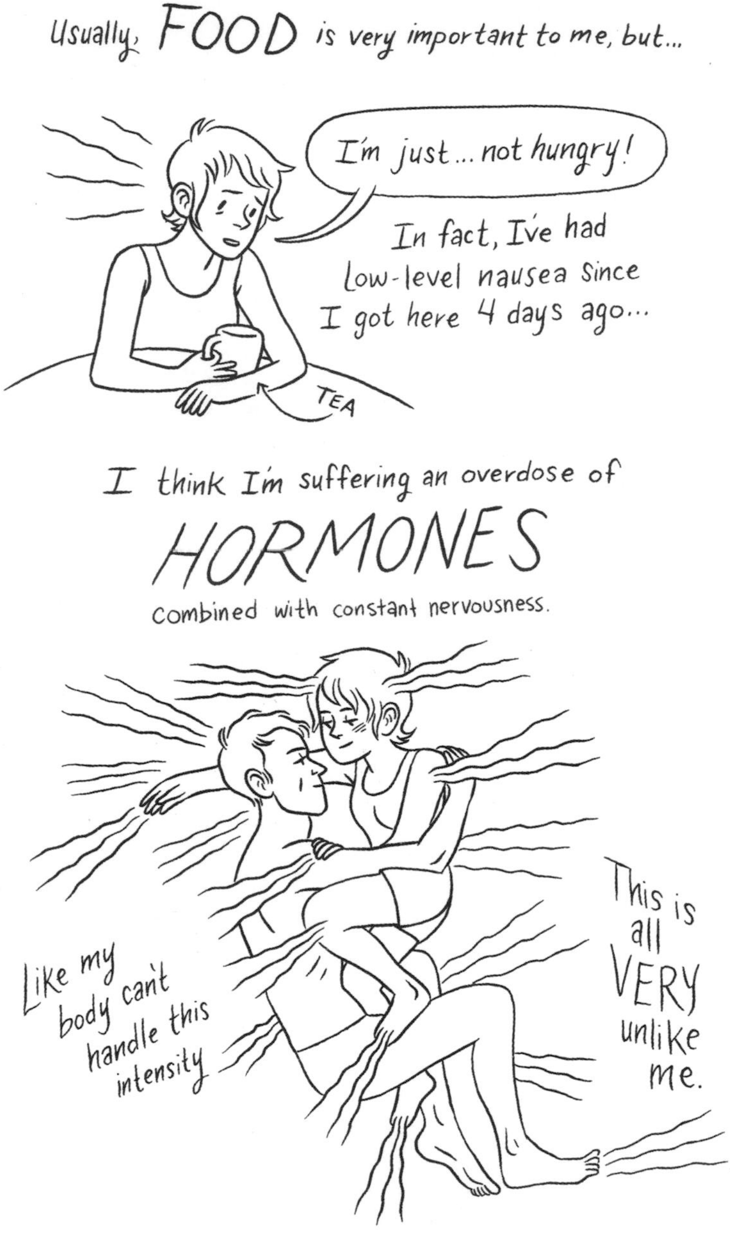
Usually, FOOD is very important to me, but...
I'm just... not hungry!
In fact, I've had low-level nausea since I got here 4 days ago...
TEA
I think I'm suffering an overdose of
HORMONES
combined with constant nervousness.
Like my body can't handle this intensity
This is all VERY unlike me.

The White Horse

Henrik lives in a commune
just outside of Stockholm.
It's actually a pretty famous
Swedish commune. There's a
movie about it.

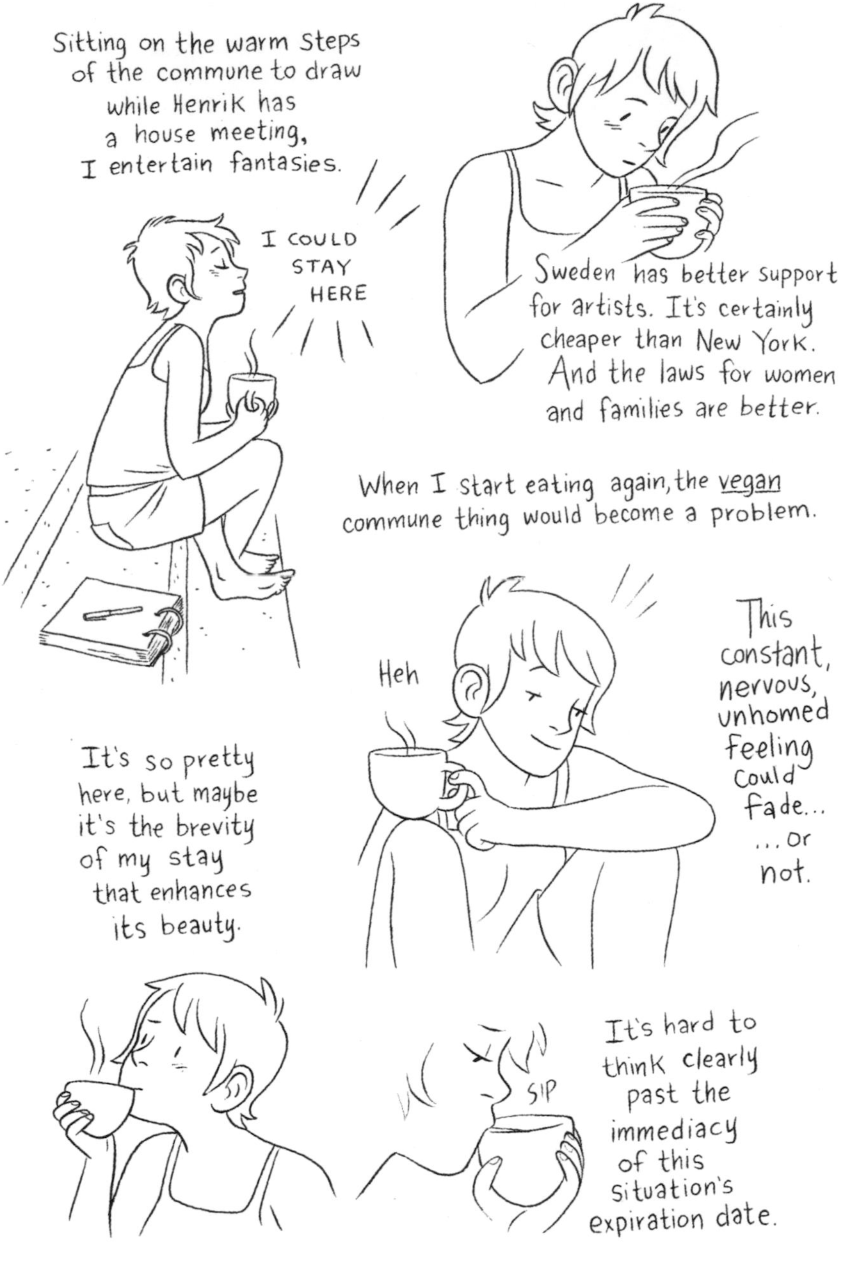
Sitting on the warm steps of the commune to draw while Henrik has a house meeting, I entertain fantasies.
I COULD STAY HERE
Sweden has better support for artists. It's certainly cheaper than New York. And the laws for women and families are better.
When I start eating again, the vegan commune thing would become a problem.
Heh
This constant, nervous, unhomed feeling could fade...
...or not.
It's so pretty here, but maybe it's the brevity of my stay that enhances its beauty.
SIP
It's hard to think clearly past the immediacy of this situation's expiration date.

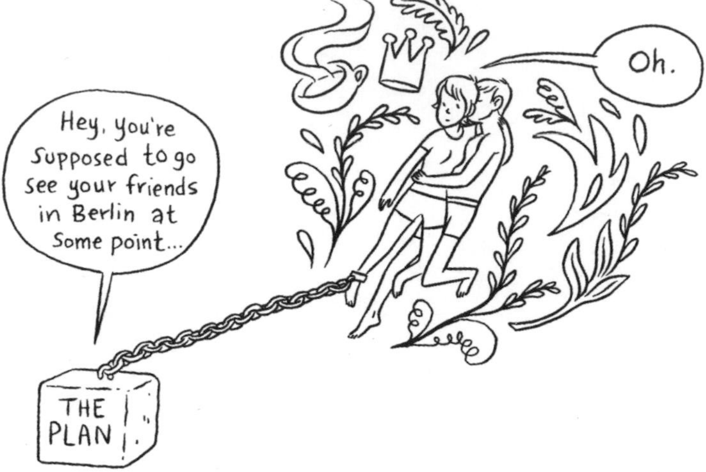
Hey, you're supposed to go see your friends in Berlin at some point...
Oh.
THE PLAN

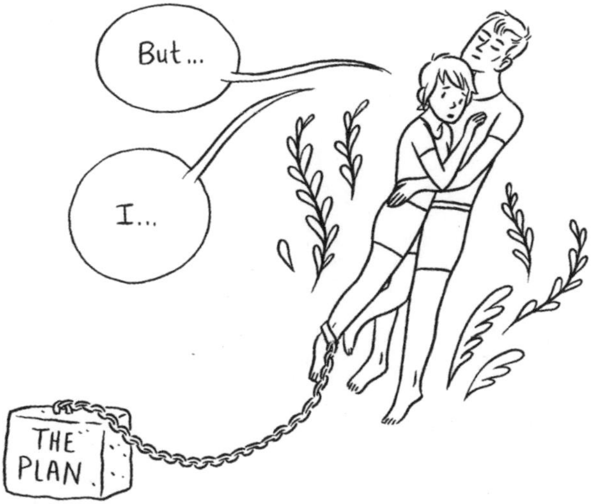
But...
I...
THE PLAN

Walking to the tram stop.

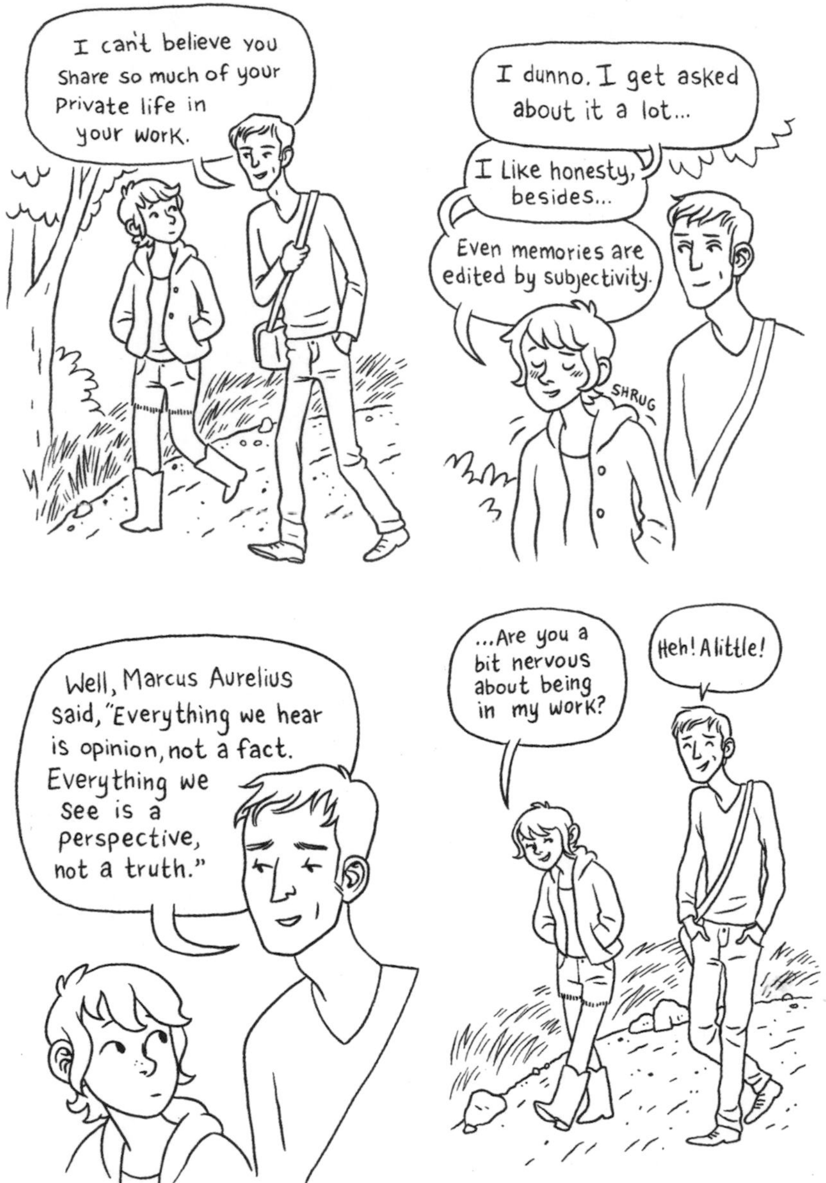
I can't believe you share so much of your private life in your work.
I dunno. I get asked about it a lot...
I like honesty, besides...
Even memories are edited by subjectivity.
SHRUG
Well, Marcus Aurelius said, "Everything we hear is opinion, not a fact. Everything we see is a perspective, not a truth."
...Are you a bit nervous about being in my work?
Heh! A little!

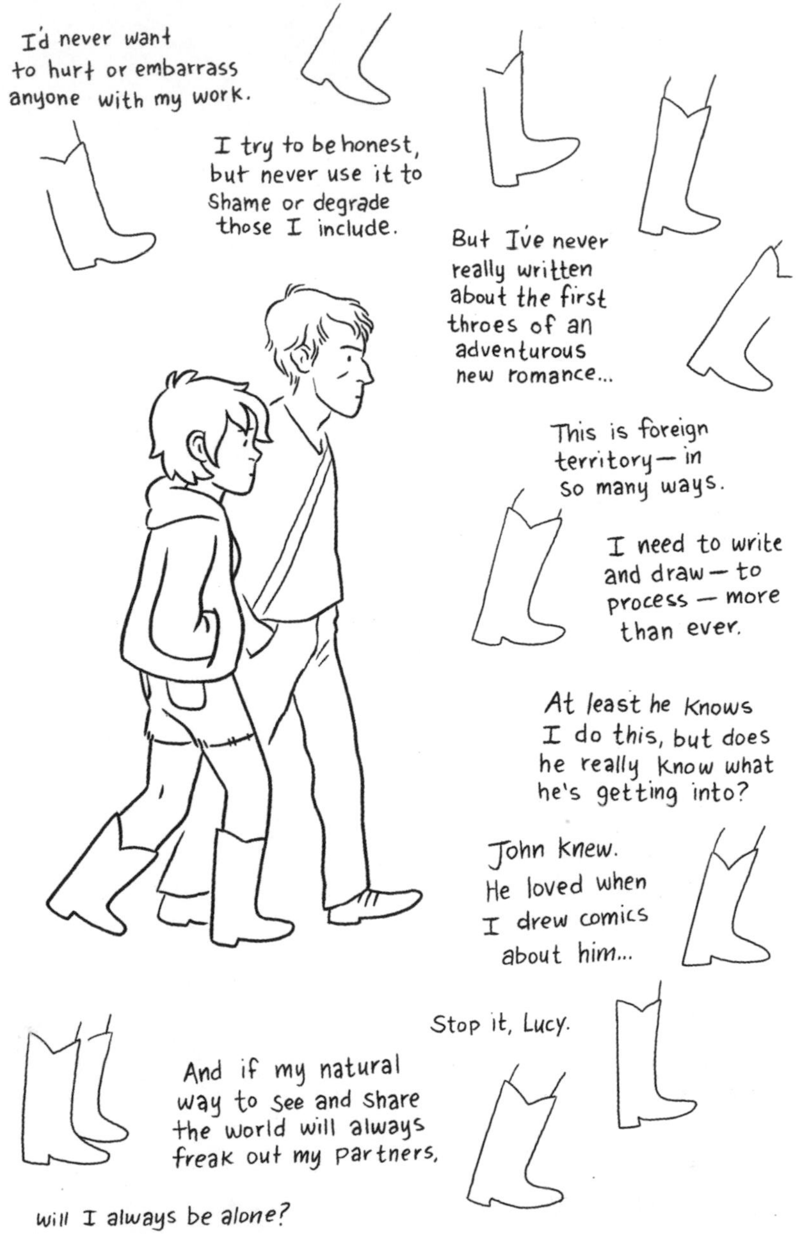
I'd never want to hurt or embarrass anyone with my work.
I try to be honest, but never use it to shame or degrade those I include.
But I've never really written about the first throes of an adventurous new romance...
This is foreign territory— in so many ways.
I need to write and draw — to process — more than ever.
At least he knows I do this, but does he really know what he's getting into?
John knew. He loved when I drew comics about him...
Stop it, Lucy.
And if my natural way to see and share the world will always freak out my partners,
will I always be alone?

Henrik takes me into the city, where we walk around, and I buy a Sugar bun on his recommendation.

Chunky Sugar

It's not very good, but it's the first non-vegan food I've had in days.

While rushing for the tram, my hair clip falls out and is lost.

Hurry!

We'll miss it!

Later, when we're safely on the tram, Henrik asks

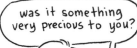

was it something very precious to you?

No, I say.

But I think about this for a long time and I'm not sure why.

Part of Stockholm's Gamla Stan

It feels like I'm living in a Joni Mitchell song.

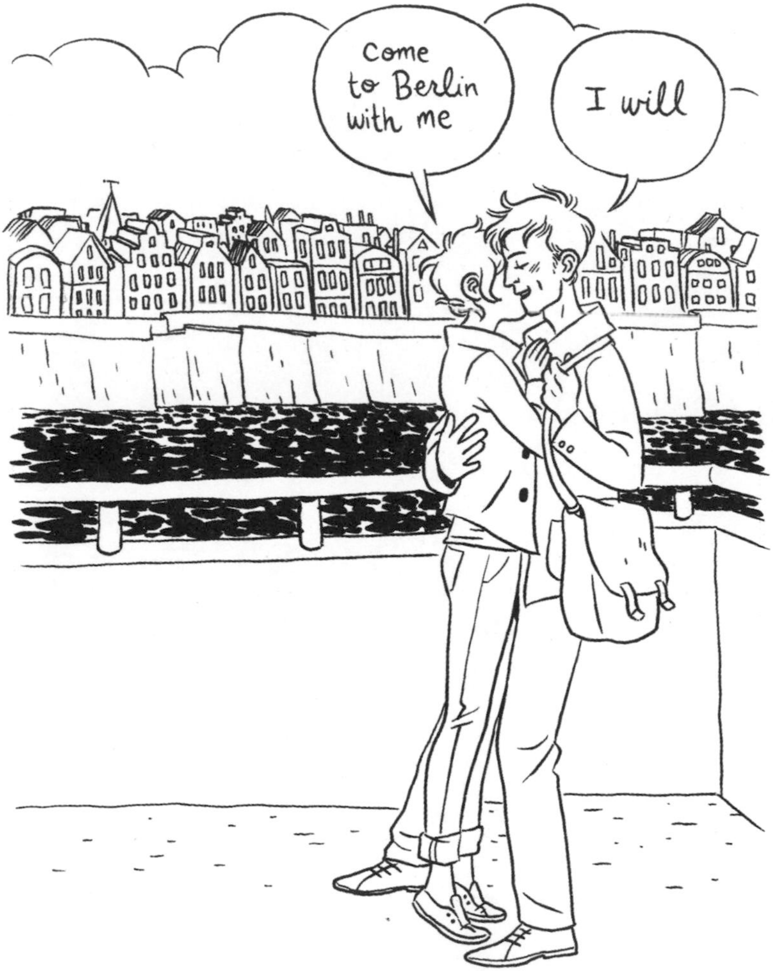
Come to Berlin with me
I will

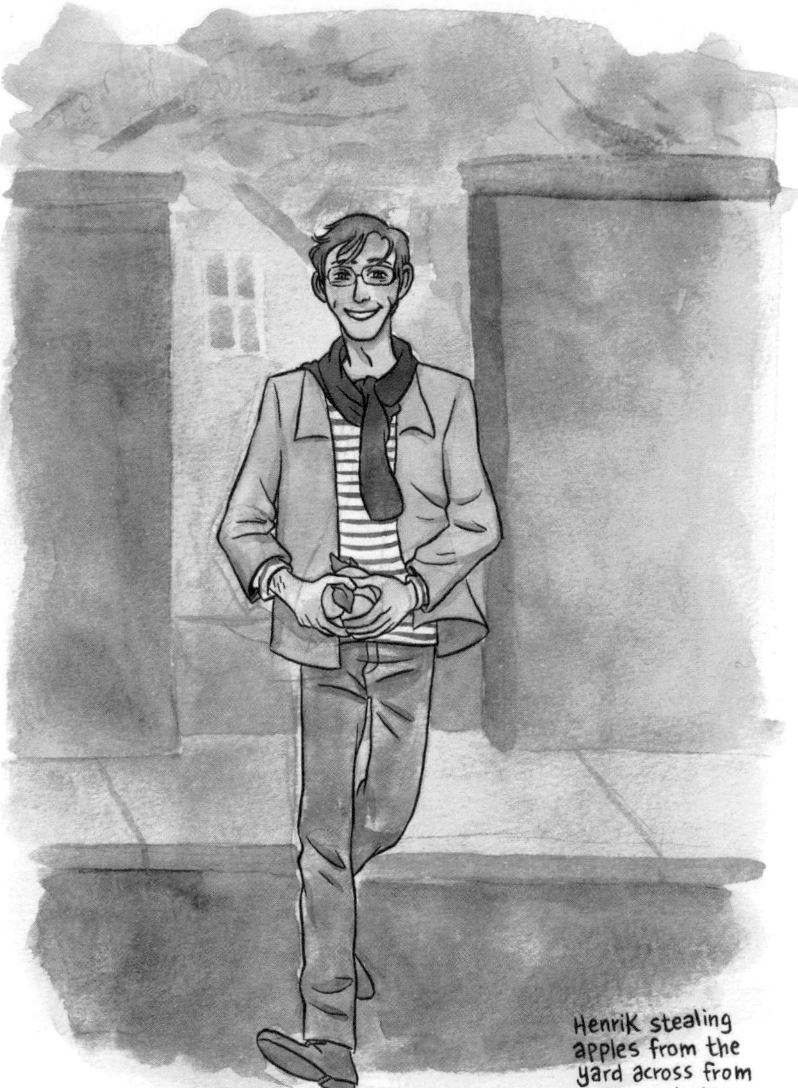
Henrik stealing apples from the yard across from the bus station on the way to the airport.

TO BERLIN, GERMANY

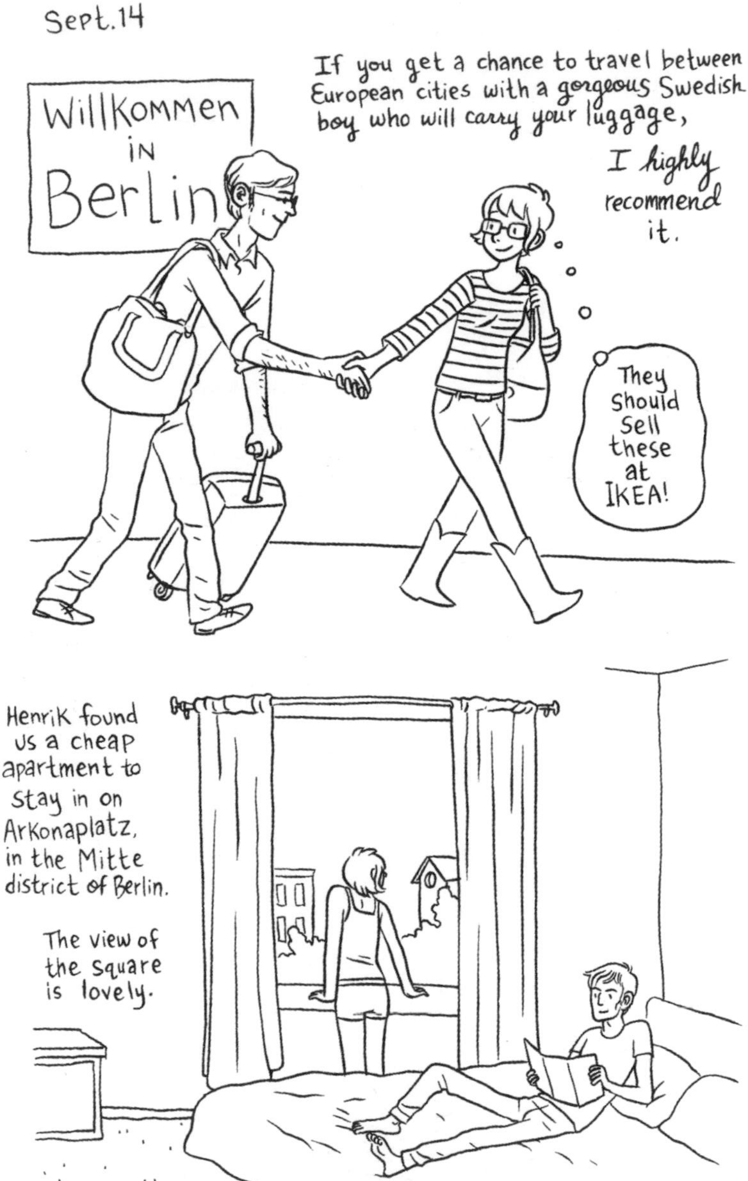
Sept. 14
Willkommen in Berlin
If you get a chance to travel between European cities with a gorgeous Swedish boy who will carry your luggage,
I *highly* recommend it.
They should sell these at IKEA!
Henrik found us a cheap apartment to stay in on Arkonaplatz, in the Mitte district of Berlin.
The view of the square is lovely.

DAVID & JODY

Sept. 15

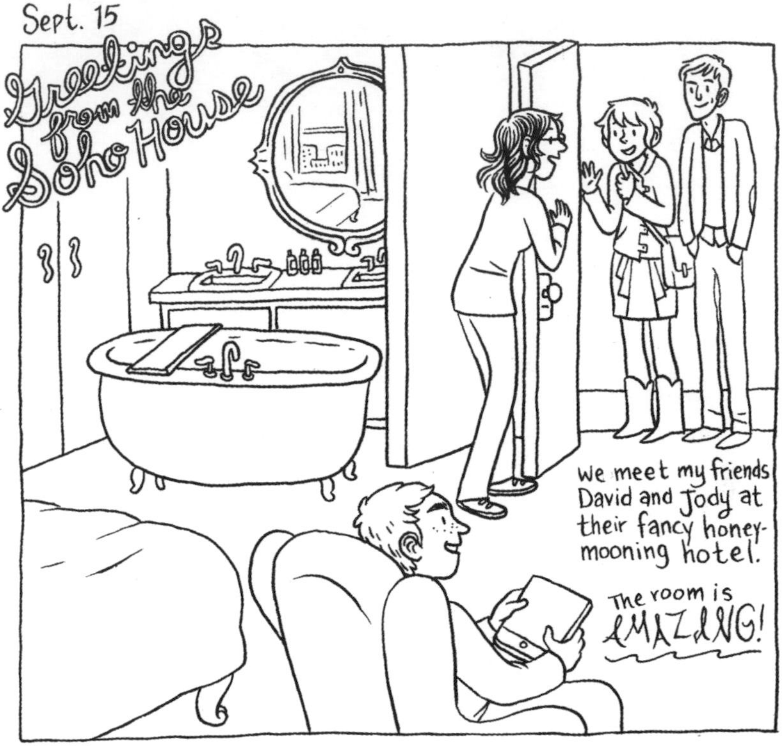

Greetings from the Soho House
We meet my friends David and Jody at their fancy honey-mooning hotel.
The room is AMAZING!

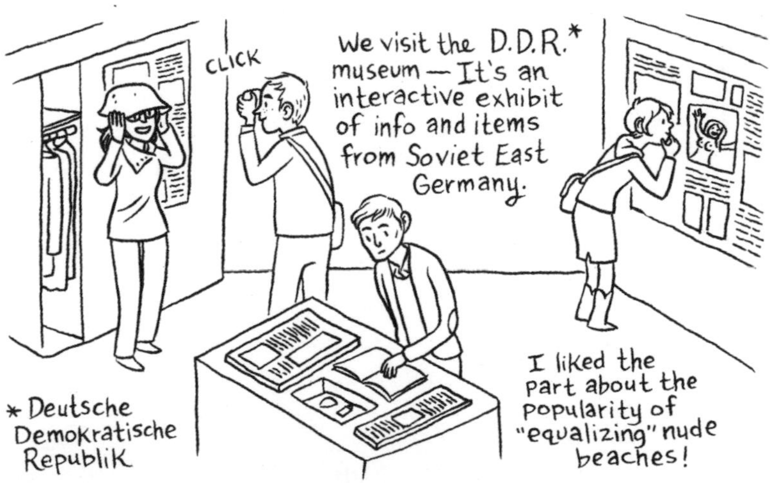

CLICK
We visit the D.D.R.* museum — It's an interactive exhibit of info and items from Soviet East Germany.
I liked the part about the popularity of "equalizing" nude beaches!

* Deutsche Demokratische Republik

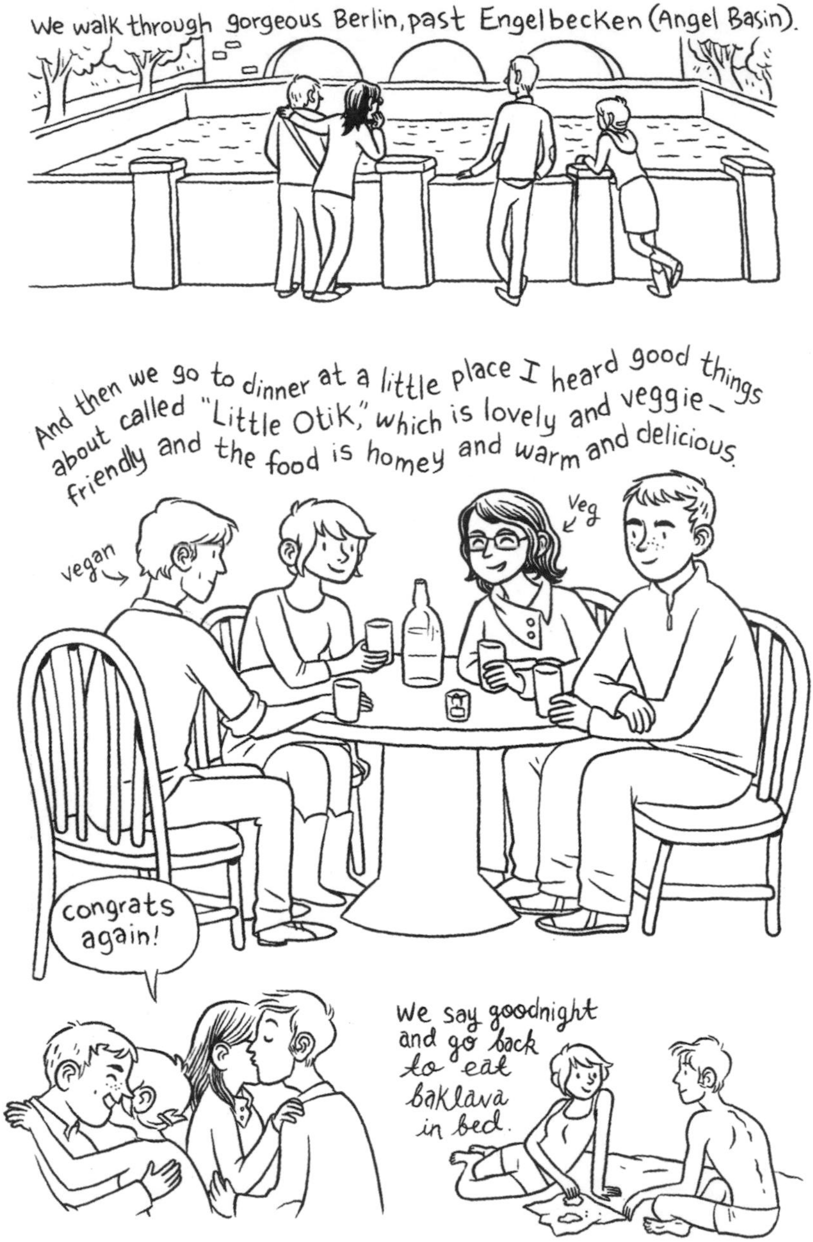
We walk through gorgeous Berlin, past Engelbecken (Angel Basin).
And then we go to dinner at a little place I heard good things about called "Little Otik," which is lovely and veggie-friendly and the food is homey and warm and delicious.
vegan
Veg
congrats again!
We say goodnight and go back to eat baklava in bed.

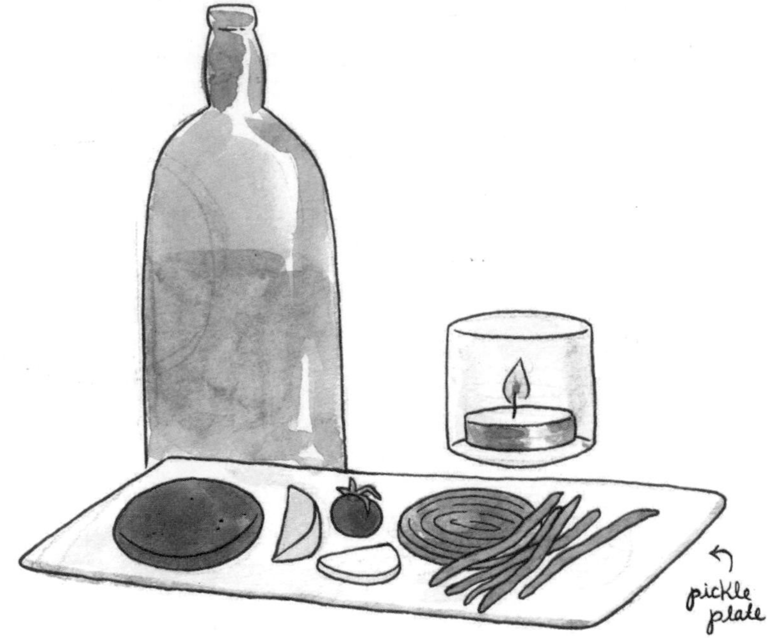
pickle plate

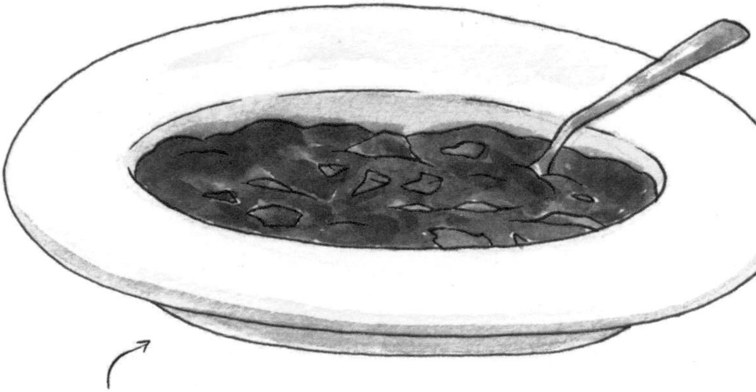

Papa Pomodoro @ Little Otik
(Garlic tomato soup with good bread cooked into it and purple basil on top)

Sept. 16

I'm supposed to leave for France today, but...I just can't yet.

Dear Jane,
I'm going to be a day late coming to Beaune to visit you — Sorry!

Changed my Flight

It's a good thing these inter-Europe airlines are so inexpensive!

We don't make it out of the apartment 'til 3.

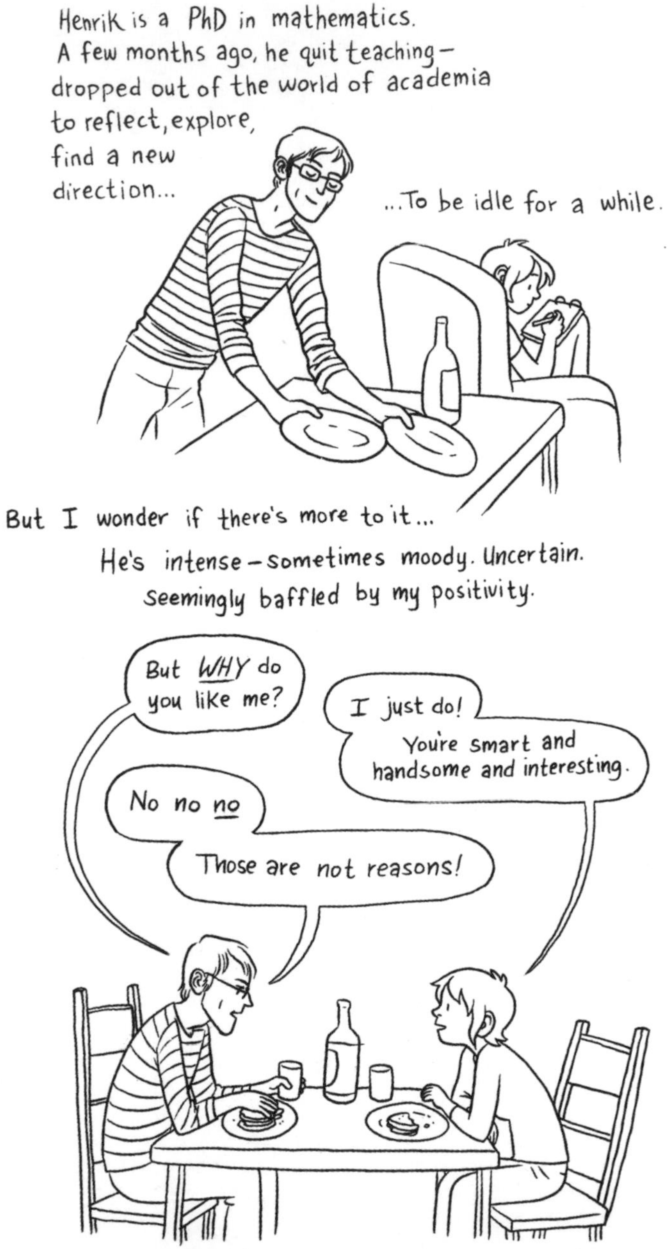
Henrik is a PhD in mathematics.
A few months ago, he quit teaching—dropped out of the world of academia to reflect, explore, find a new direction...
...To be idle for a while.
But I wonder if there's more to it...
He's intense—sometimes moody. Uncertain. Seemingly baffled by my positivity.
But WHY do you like me?
I just do!
You're smart and handsome and interesting.
No no no
Those are not reasons!

This turns into a discussion about cultural classism, educational ubiquity in Western culture, and the disconnect from the reality of human suffering...

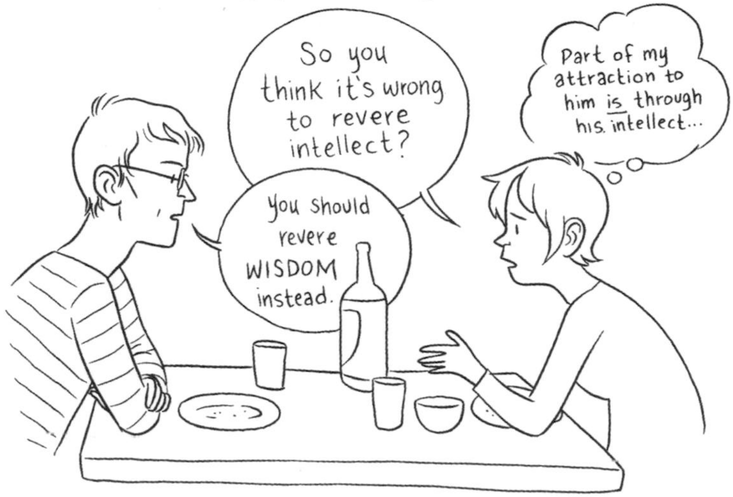
So you think it's wrong to revere intellect?
Part of my attraction to him is through his intellect...
You should revere WISDOM instead.

He's a mathematician! I can't help but be impressed– I failed Algebra 2, *twice*.

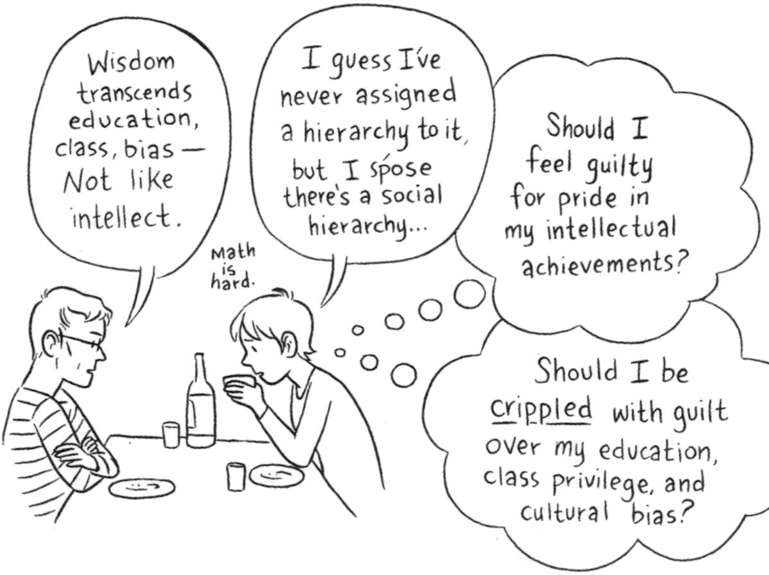
Wisdom transcends education, class, bias — Not like intellect.
I guess I've never assigned a hierarchy to it, but I s'pose there's a social hierarchy...
Math is hard.
Should I feel guilty for pride in my intellectual achievements?
Should I be crippled with guilt over my education, class privilege, and cultural bias?

GUILT

It's not wrong to travel & love and to be silly & lucky, or even to make work about it— it can be *GOOD* & also *MEANINGFUL* to celebrate these things. In this case, guilt is useless.

But guilt can be useful— to drive us to be better, work harder...

TO MOVE FORWARD.

& TO CHECK our PRIVILEGE

Your words are meaningless and invalidated by your privilege.

I CAN IMPROVE!

BUT ←THIS IS ALSO A PROBLEM...

WHITE AS SNOW

SILVER SPOON

I AM LUCKY

I AM AWARE OF THAT LUCK

CAN I EVER BE WISE?

Maybe not, but I work hard.

Yes, I make work about food and art & travel

BUT THERE IS MEANING IN IT

if to no one else but me.

(Perhaps the definition of "unwise")

85

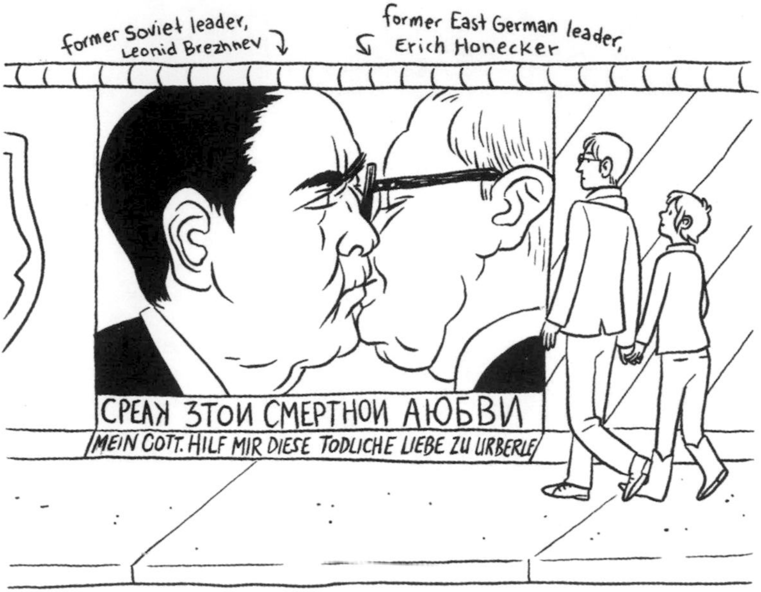
former Soviet leader, Leonid Breznhev
former East German leader, Erich Honecker
СРЕАЖ ЗТОИ СМЕРТНОИ АЮБВИ
MEIN COTT. HILF MIR DIESE TODLICHE LIEBE ZU URBERLE

We go to the segment of the Berlin Wall that remains. It's covered by murals commissioned by artists to celebrate peace, equality, and human rights. It's clever and cool and sad.

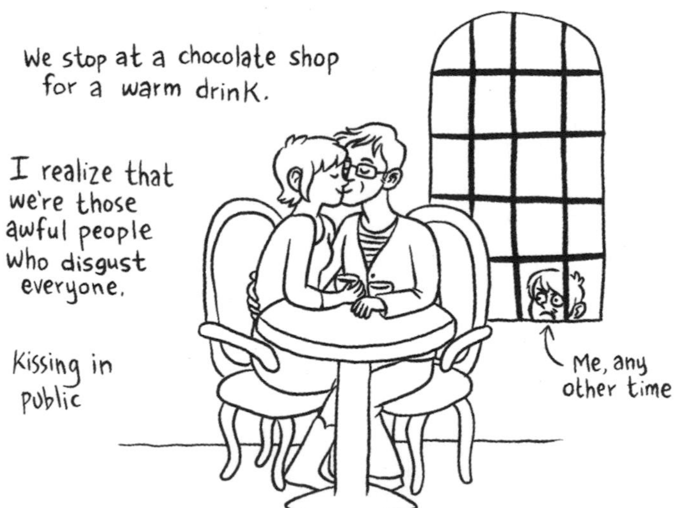
We stop at a chocolate shop for a warm drink.
I realize that we're those awful people who disgust everyone.
Kissing in public
Me, any other time

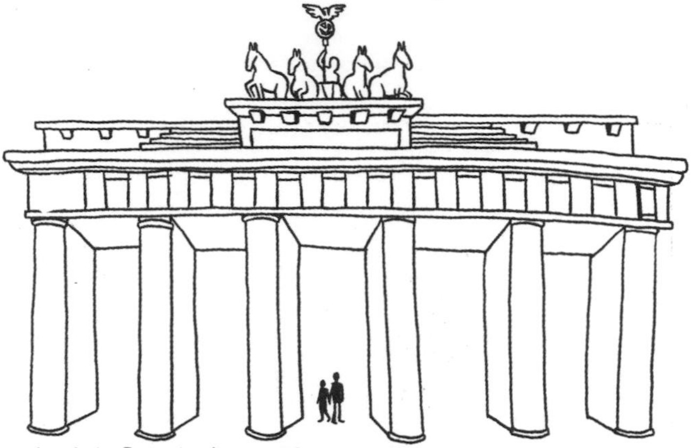

We visit Brandenburger Tor just after the sun sets and it's lit up golden in the dark. It's a beautiful landmark—the ancient entry gate to Berlin.

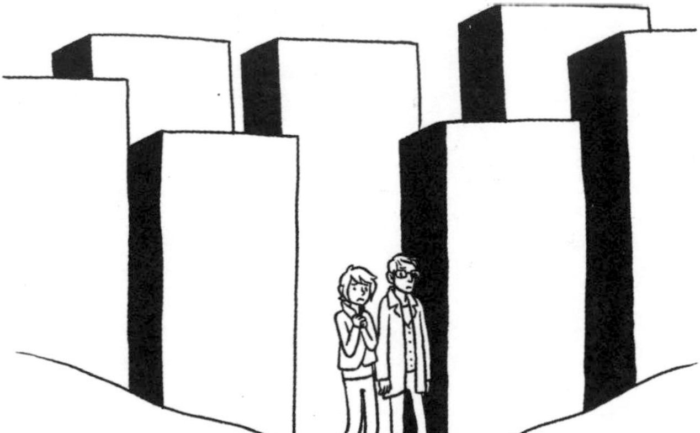

Then we walk through the enormous monument to the murdered Jews of the Holocaust.

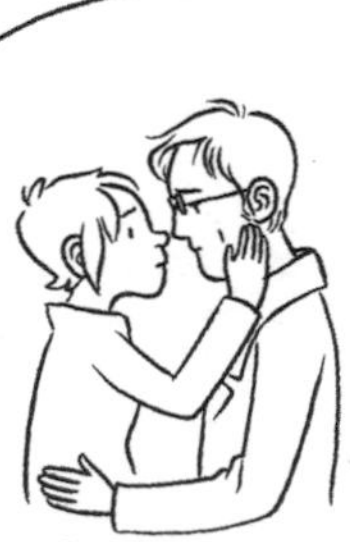

The effect of the field of enormous granite blocks that loom over the sloping paths is sobering and intensely disquieting; like descending into the grave.

All our ancestors were murdered, murderers, complicit to murder, or combating murder. It's intense.

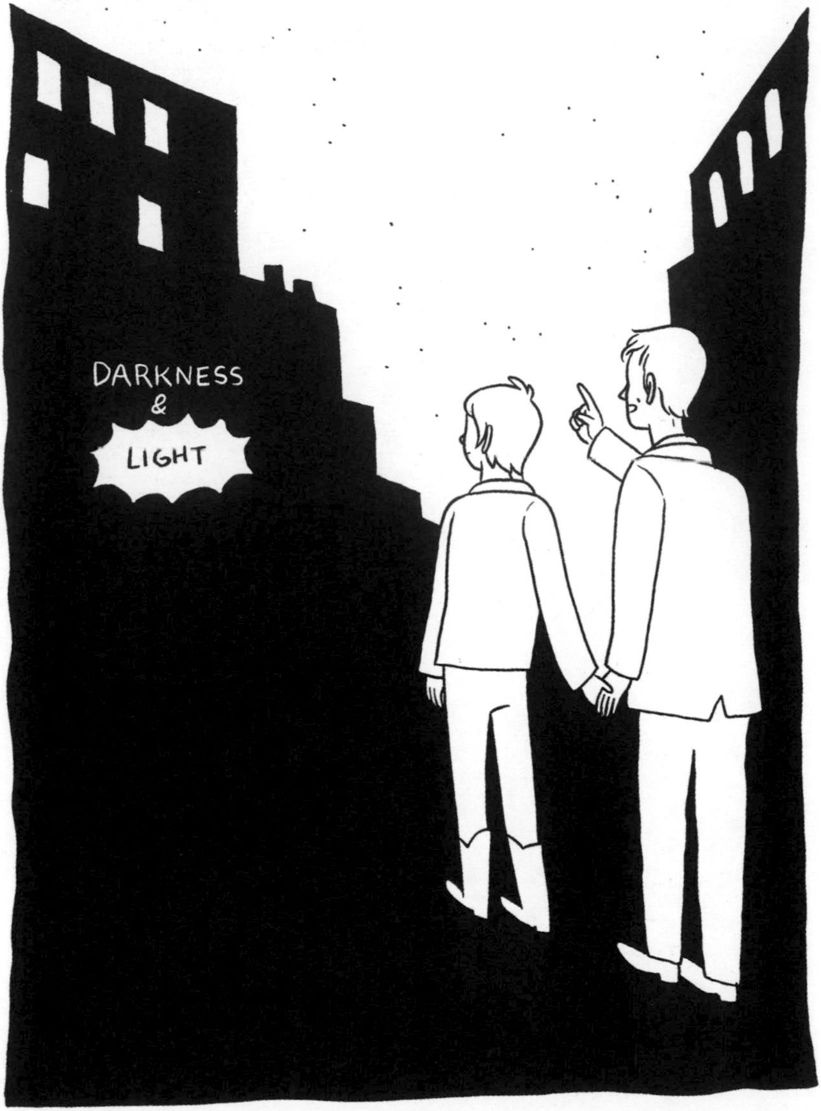
DARKNESS
&
LIGHT

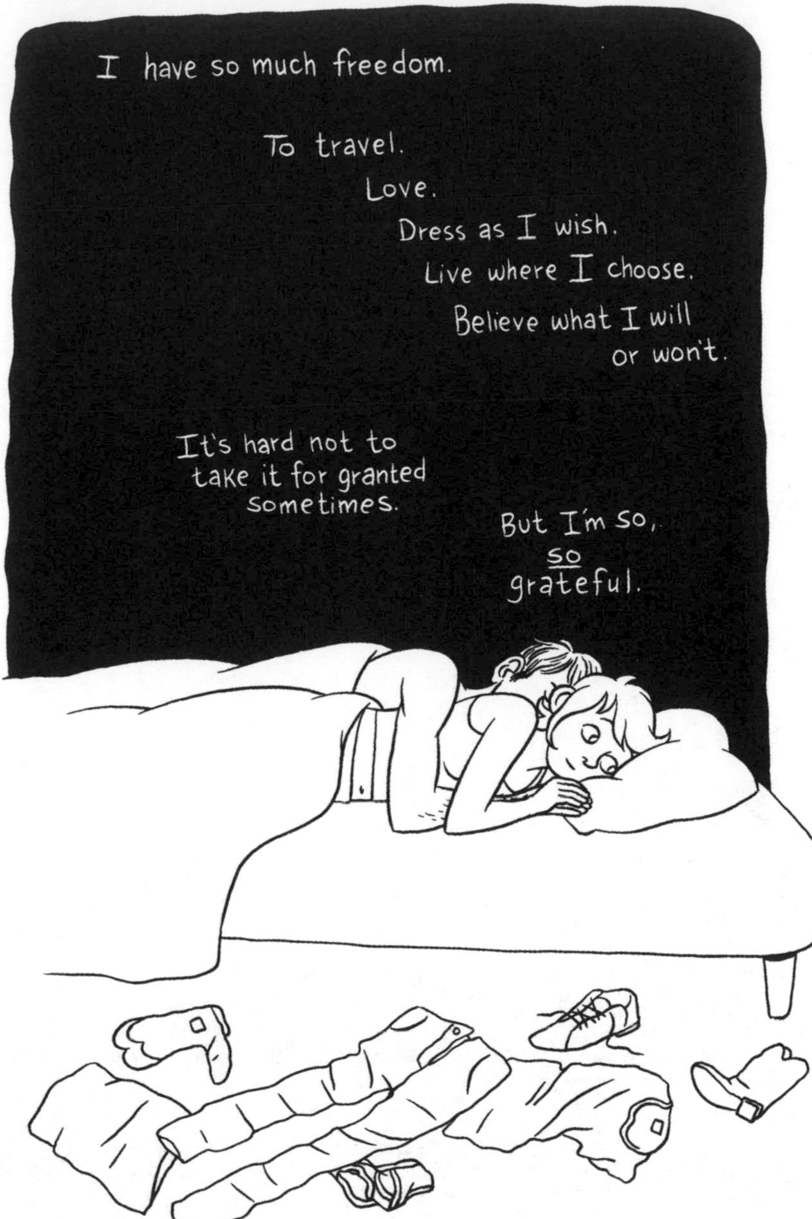
I have so much freedom.
To travel.
Love.
Dress as I wish.
Live where I choose.
Believe what I will or won't.
It's hard not to take it for granted sometimes.
But I'm so, so grateful.

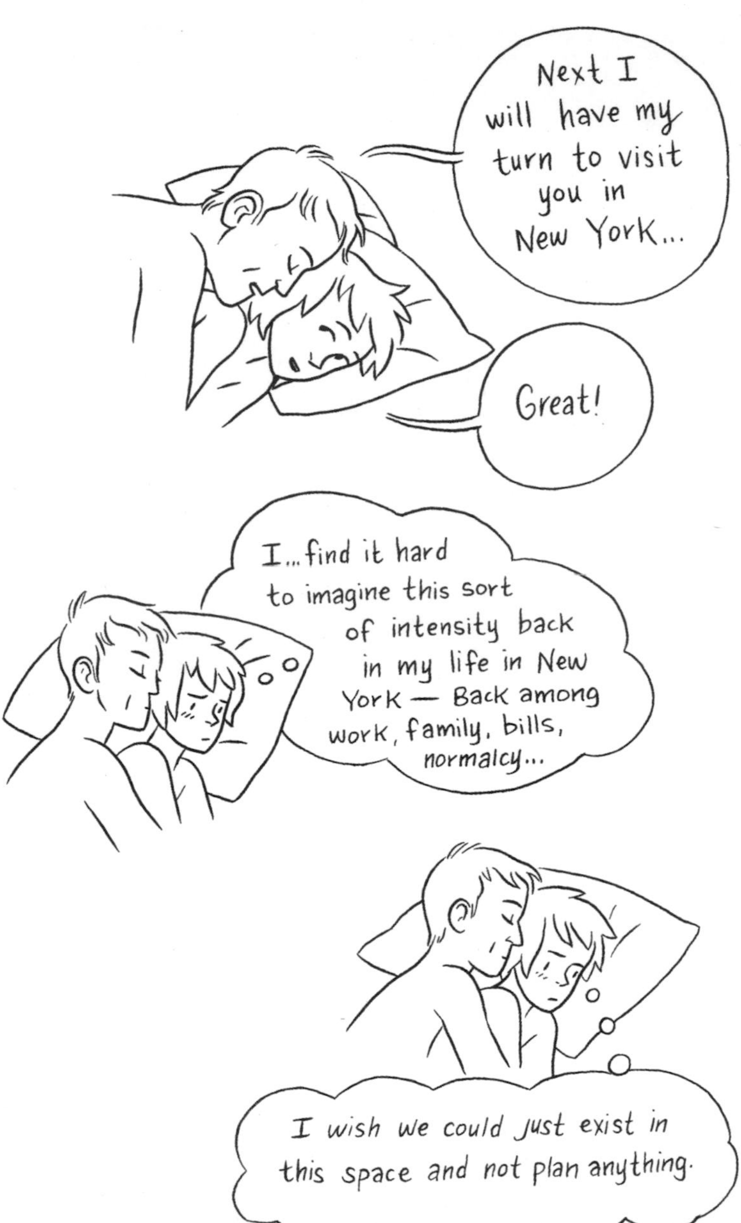
Next I will have my turn to visit you in New York...
Great!
I... find it hard to imagine this sort of intensity back in my life in New York — Back among work, family, bills, normalcy...
I wish we could just exist in this space and not plan anything.

TO BEAUNE, FRANCE

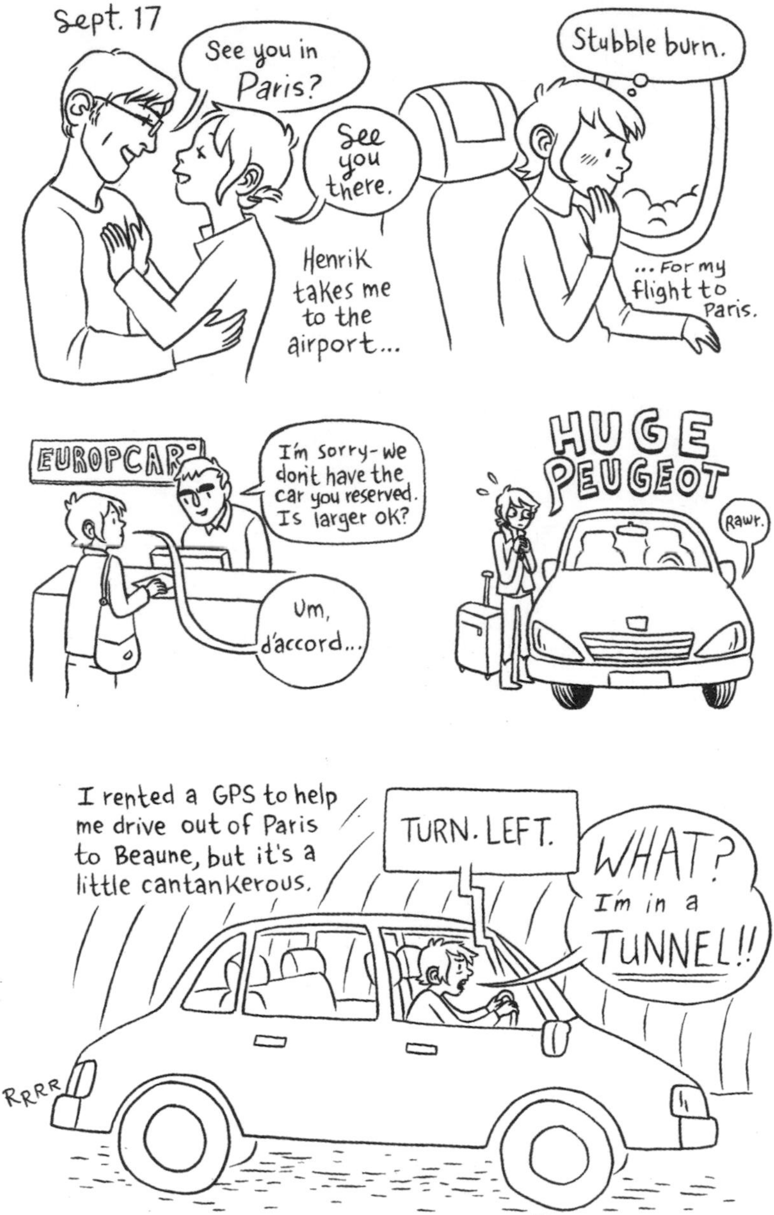
Sept. 17
See you in Paris?
See you there.
Henrik takes me to the airport...
Stubble burn.
...For my flight to Paris.
EUROPCAR
I'm sorry- we don't have the car you reserved. Is larger OK?
Um, d'accord...
HUGE PEUGEOT
Rawr.
I rented a GPS to help me drive out of Paris to Beaune, but it's a little cantankerous.
TURN. LEFT.
WHAT? I'm in a TUNNEL!!
RRRR

Once I get going, the drive is
wonderful.

while I drive through vineyards, I listen to old songs
on French radio and feel amazed at my good luck.

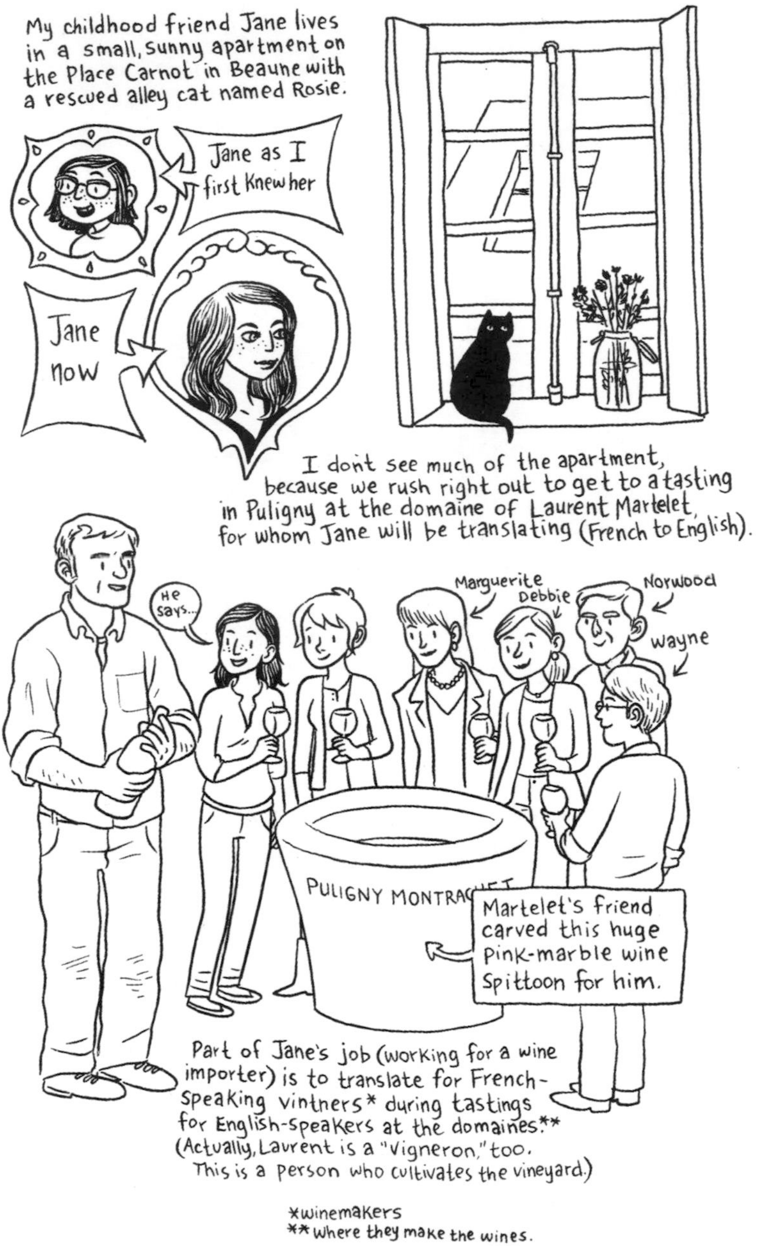
My childhood friend Jane lives in a small, sunny apartment on the Place Carnot in Beaune with a rescued alley cat named Rosie.
Jane as I first Knew her
Jane now
I don't see much of the apartment, because we rush right out to get to a tasting in Puligny at the domaine of Laurent Martelet, for whom Jane will be translating (French to English).
He says...
Marguerite
Debbie
Norwood
wayne
PULIGNY MONTRAC
Martelet's friend carved this huge pink-marble wine spittoon for him.
Part of Jane's job (working for a wine importer) is to translate for French-speaking vintners* during tastings for English-speakers at the domaines.** (Actually, Laurent is a "vigneron," too. This is a person who cultivates the vineyard.)
*winemakers
**Where they make the wines.

AMERICAN★MISHAPS when Greeting in the FRENCH★STYLE

Left/right, or right/left?!

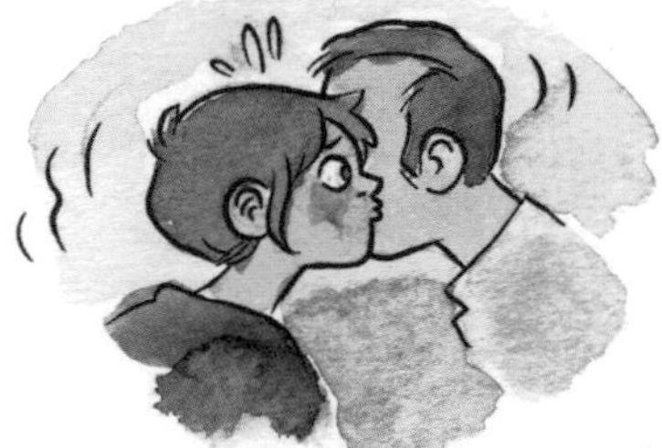

What to do with your hands?

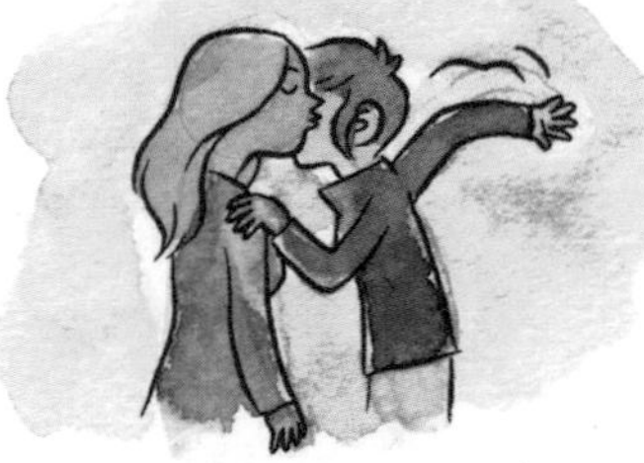

Glasses clink

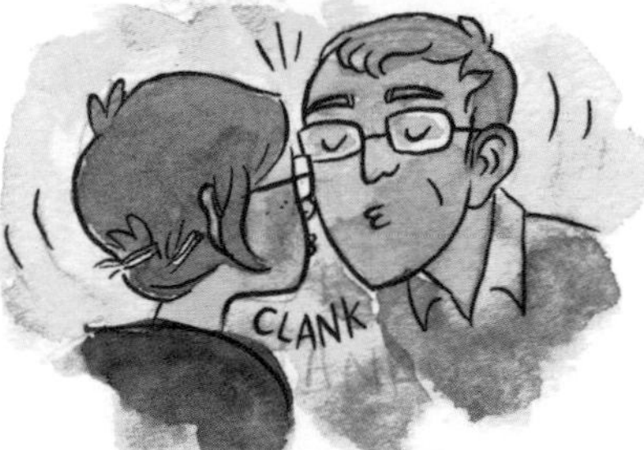
CLANK

Inadvertent and embarrassing "muah" noises

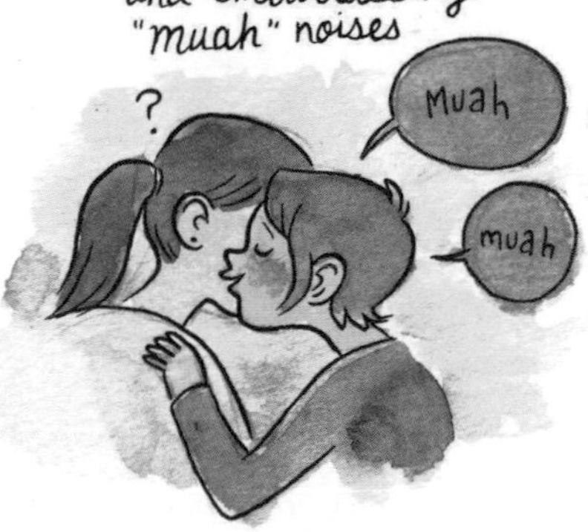
?
Muah
muah

Le Caveau de Puligny

My French comprehension is RUSTY!

Quand uu uuu uu?

Oui! uuuu le muu' pas!

ça uu m uu'!

Afterwards, Jane takes me to a little wine bar and shop nearby, where we taste more wines and meet up with Françoise & Vincent, Jane's host parents from her high school year abroad.

(We sit outside)

Then we go over to where some friends of Jane's who work at a domaine nearby are celebrating the end of the harvest with a little party outside of the domaine's gorgeous house →

Using vinting tools to make a Jacuzzi!

They show us the caves where they age the wines — ancient and dark and chilly and gorgeous.

Jane's cat, Rosie, bats a wine opener
off the table and around the floor.

Wine is a way of life here.

They talk wine
while drinking
wine and all
while making
and selling
and learning
about wine.

Jane says that
most people who
work in wine
tend to drink
too much.

When the wine
is good and free
and everyone is
young and passionate,
it must be
awfully alluring.

Jane is so
beautiful—
She belongs
here, in this
beautiful
place.

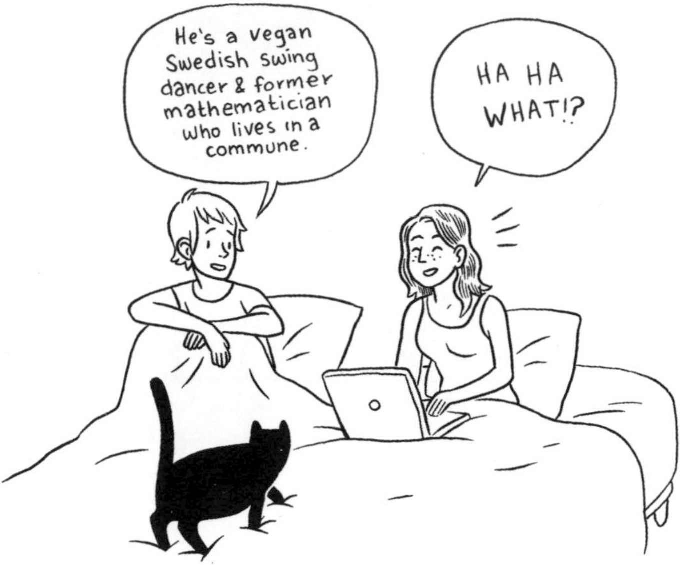
He's a vegan Swedish swing dancer & former mathematician who lives in a commune.
HA HA WHAT!?

It's good to talk about this stuff with someone.
Especially Jane, who UNDERSTANDS.
She's going through some heartbreak of her own.

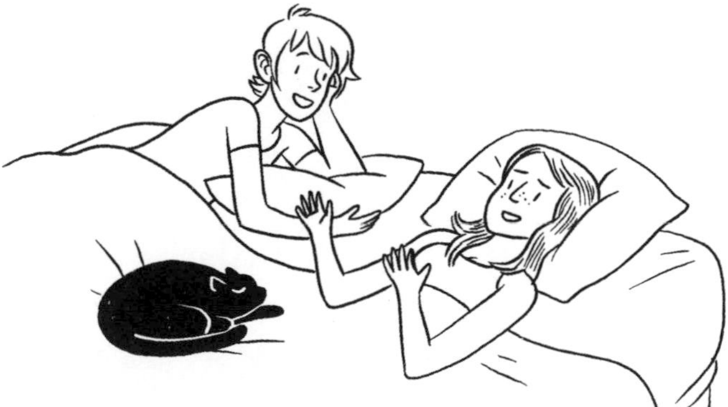

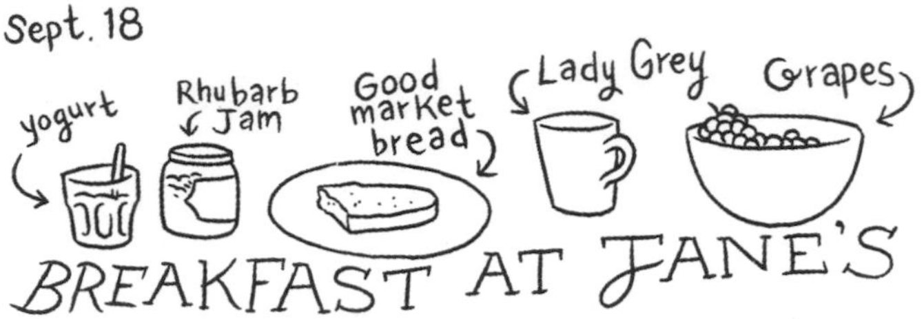
Sept. 18
yogurt
Rhubarb Jam
Good market bread
Lady Grey
Grapes
BREAKFAST AT JANE'S

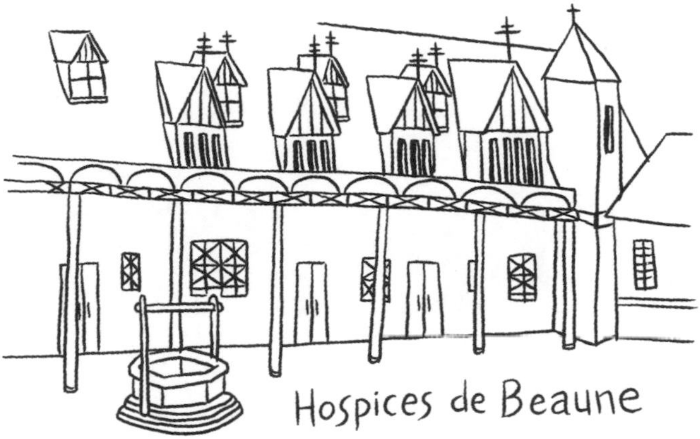
Hospices de Beaune

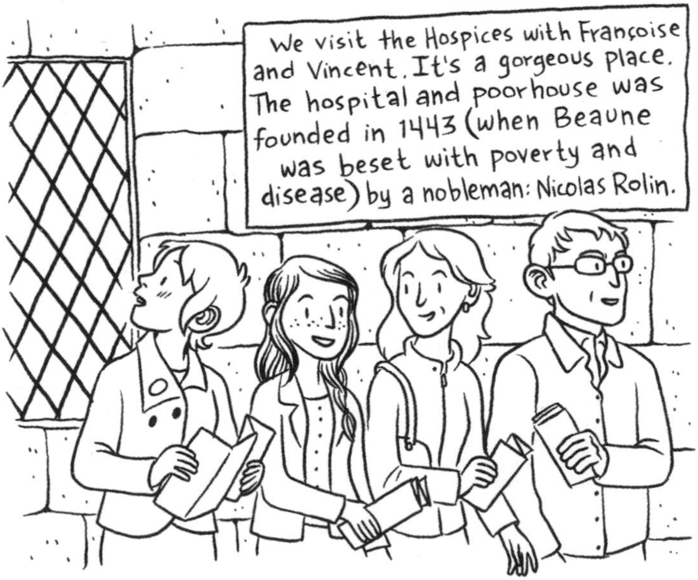
We visit the Hospices with Françoise and Vincent. It's a gorgeous place. The hospital and poorhouse was founded in 1443 (when Beaune was beset with poverty and disease) by a nobleman: Nicolas Rolin.

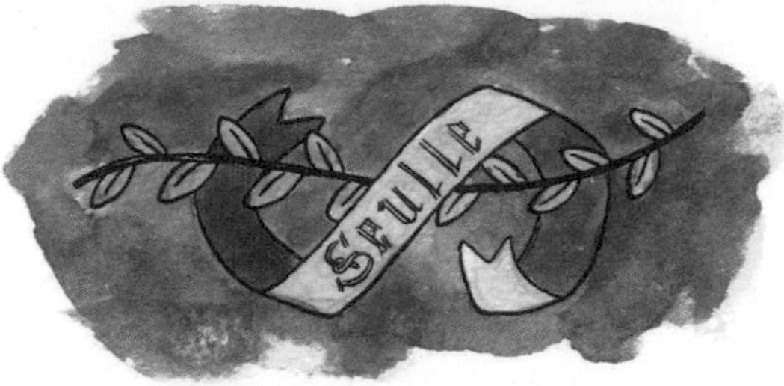
Seulle

Nicolas Rolin specified that designers for the Hospices include this design in the decorative touches. It means "only star" in old French, and was a dedication to his wife, Guigone.

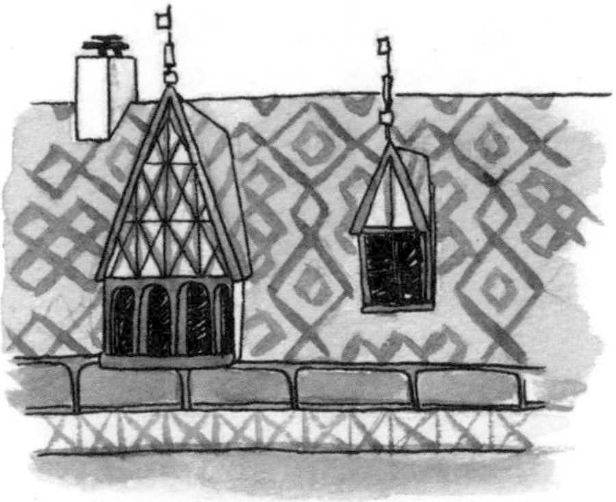

The buildings are famous for the gorgeous tiles on the roof.

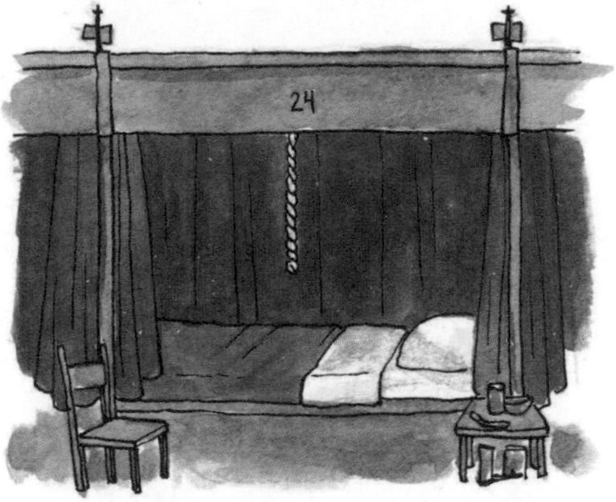
24

The luxurious beds for the sick and poor had beautiful red curtains and a useful rope to help patients sit up.

Each patient had a small collection of pewter bowls and cups. Average people usually had wooden versions. Pewter was luxurious!

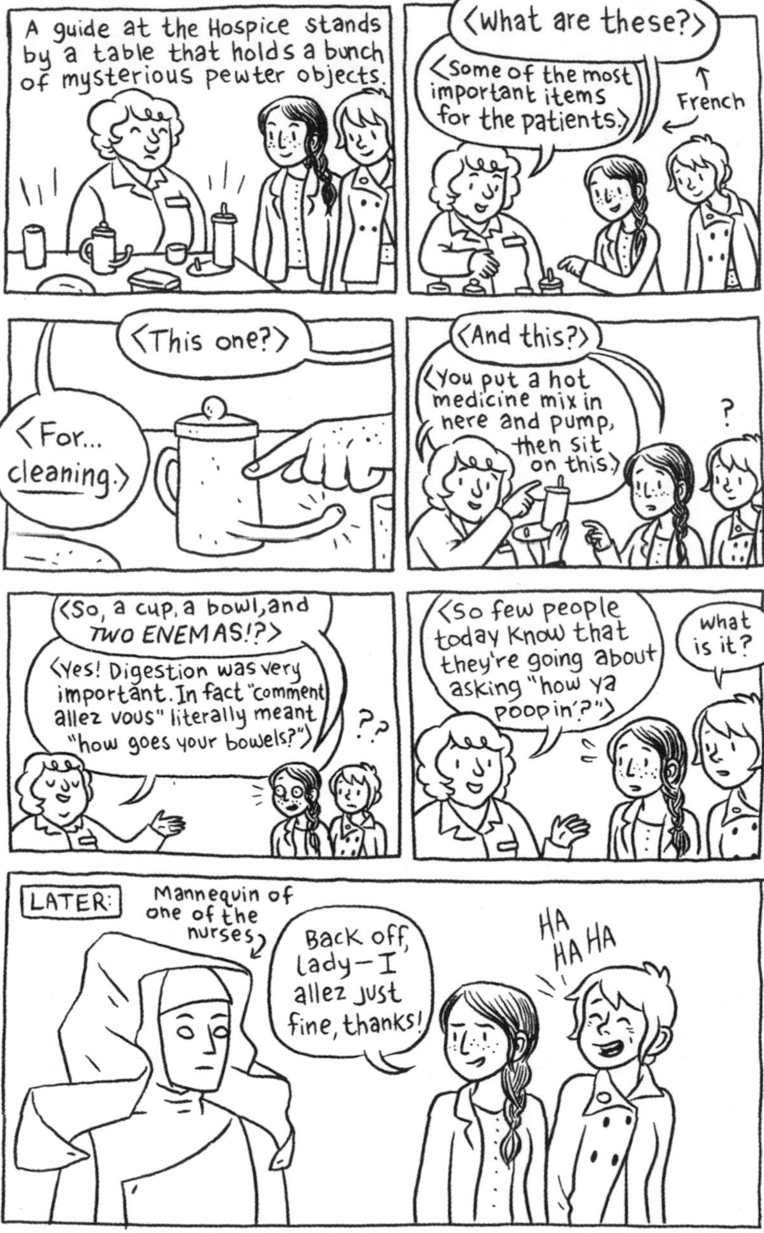

A guide at the Hospice stands by a table that holds a bunch of mysterious pewter objects.
<What are these?>
<Some of the most important items for the patients.>
French
<This one?>
<For... cleaning.>
<And this?>
<You put a hot medicine mix in here and pump, then sit on this.>
?
<So, a cup, a bowl, and TWO ENEMAS!?>
<Yes! Digestion was very important. In fact "comment allez vous" literally meant "how goes your bowels?">
??
<So few people today know that they're going about asking "how ya poopin'?">
what is it?
LATER:
Mannequin of one of the nurses
Back off, lady—I allez just fine, thanks!
HA HA HA

In the Hospice apothecary, beautiful bottles of strange medicines from long ago line the walls.

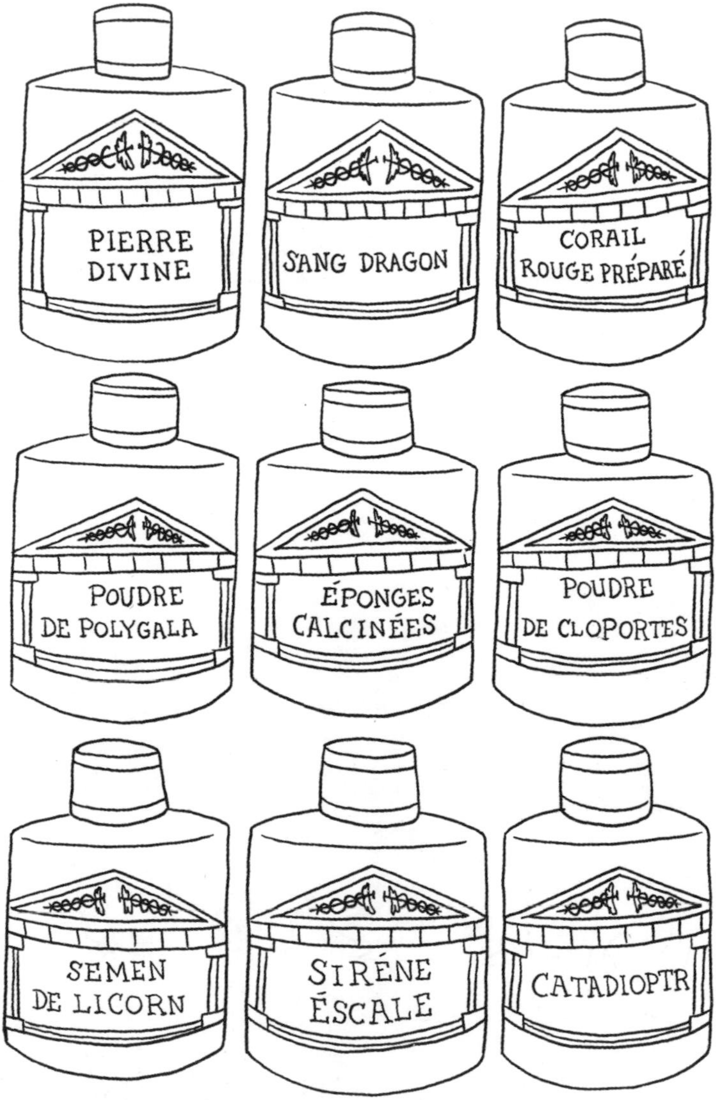

PIERRE DIVINE
SANG DRAGON
CORAIL ROUGE PRÉPARÉ
POUDRE DE POLYGALA
ÉPONGES CALCINÉES
POUDRE DE CLOPORTES
SEMEN DE LICORN
SIRÈNE ÉSCALE
CATADIOPTR

"Engoulant" at l'Hospice.
They mean "throat"
or "swallow," and hold
ceiling beams.

I love the
floor tiles in
the main hall
(Guigone is buried
beneath)

ceule
ceule
ceule
ceule

Tapestries
with the
Hospice
symbols

Sept. 18

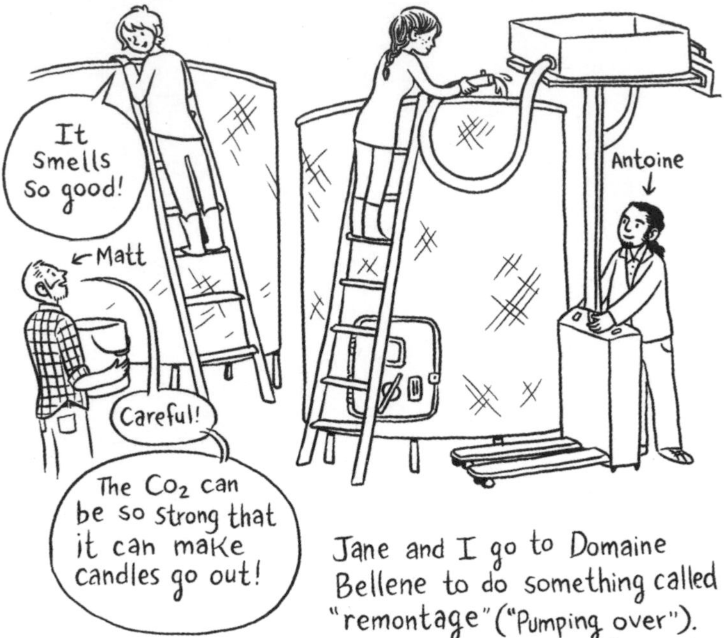
It smells so good!
Matt
Antoine
Careful!
The CO_2 can be so strong that it can make candles go out!

Jane and I go to Domaine Bellene to do something called "remontage" ("Pumping over"). You drain a vat of the fermenting wine from the bottom of the tank and pour it over the top, where the "chapeau" sits (the layer of grape skins and stems), to aerate and mix the wine.

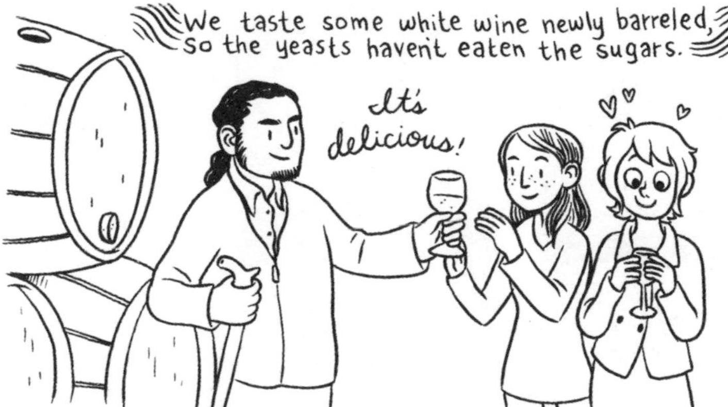
We taste some white wine newly barreled, so the yeasts haven't eaten the sugars.
It's delicious!

Because wines from this area (the Burgundy Region) are so "big" in flavor, they're drunk from *big* glasses, to aerate and "spread out."

Very old wines start to separate a bit, so you can *see* it go a bit clear at the edges.

Then we go to this incredible tasting in the caves at Domaine Pierre Guillemot. Denis

Vincent

We taste lots of amazing wines, including one from 1971!

After the 10th wine, I'm starting to get pretty overwhelmed, even though I'm spitting.

I think part of it is because we've been down in a cave for around *FOUR HOURS*.

After the 20th wine, I feel a bit faint.

Later, Jane tells me that she had similar experiences when she started tasting.

Jane's job in wine has given her the skill to spit wine tastes gracefully.

Pleh

I am less practiced at it...

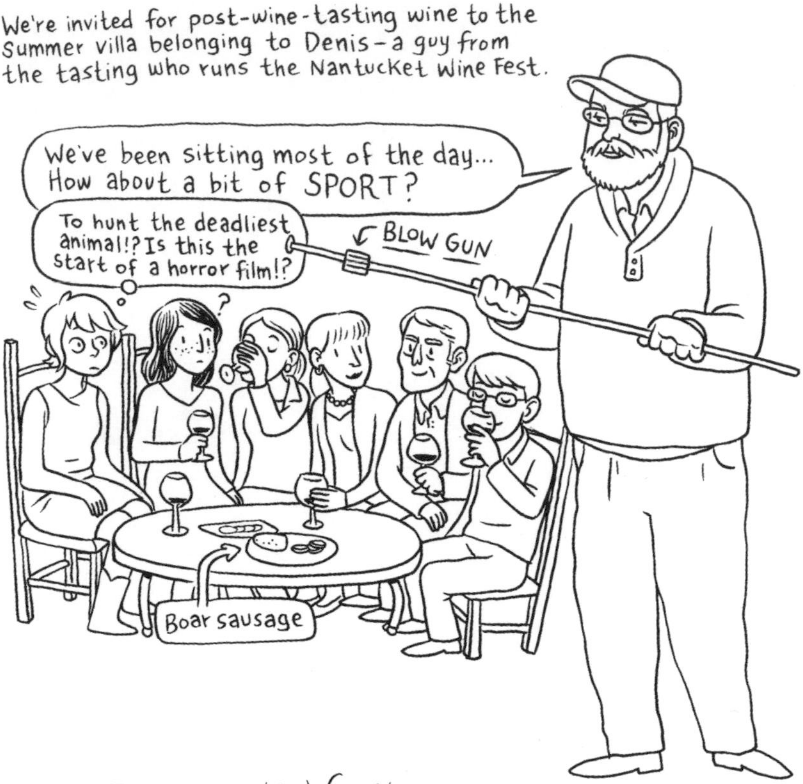
We're invited for post-wine-tasting wine to the Summer villa belonging to Denis – a guy from the tasting who runs the Nantucket Wine Fest.
We've been sitting most of the day... How about a bit of SPORT?
To hunt the deadliest animal!? Is this the start of a horror film!?
BLOW GUN
Boar sausage

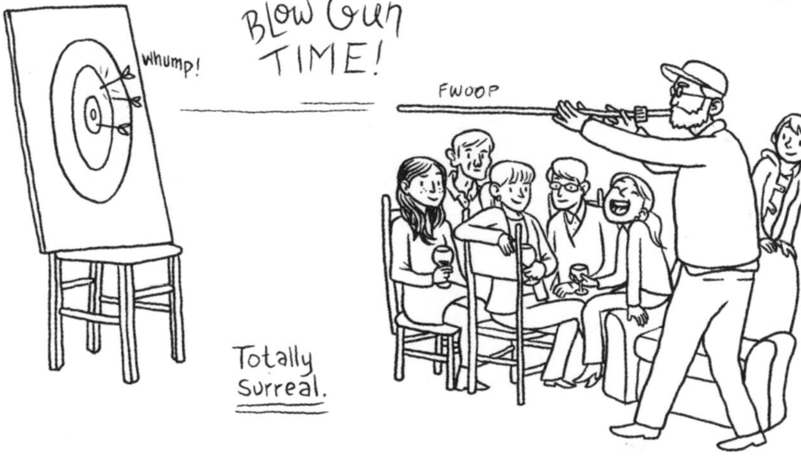
BLOW GUN TIME!
whump!
FWOOP
Totally Surreal.

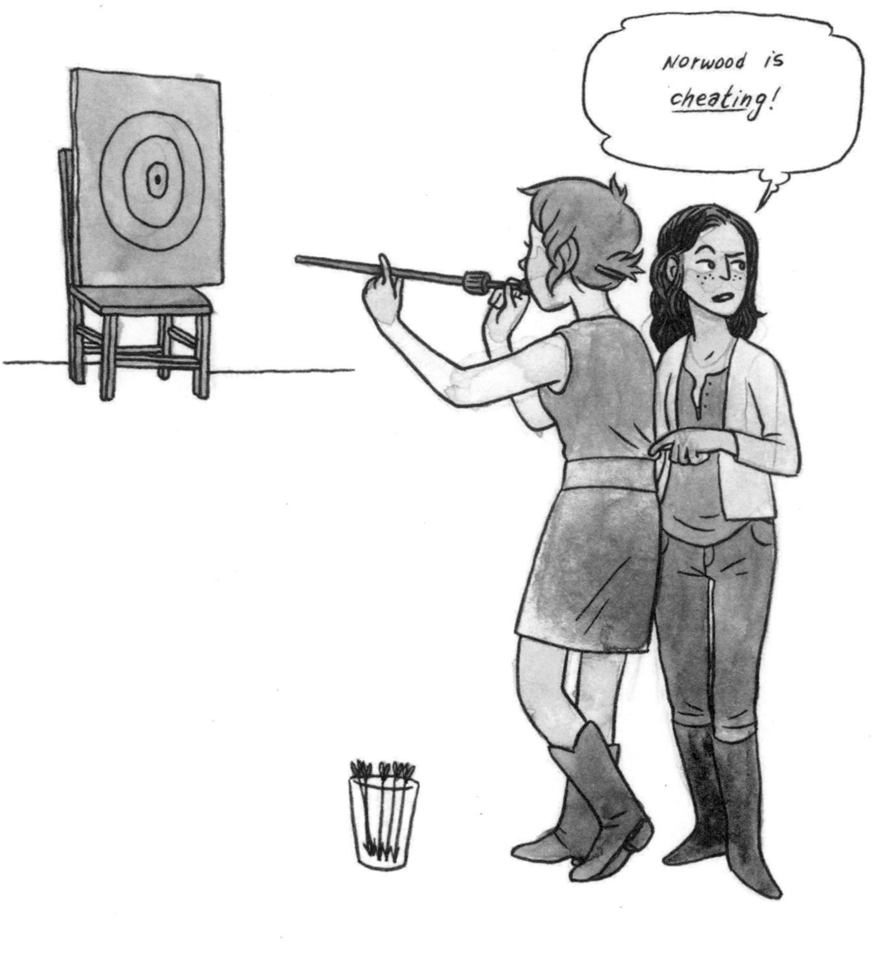
Norwood is cheating!

It's true—He was!

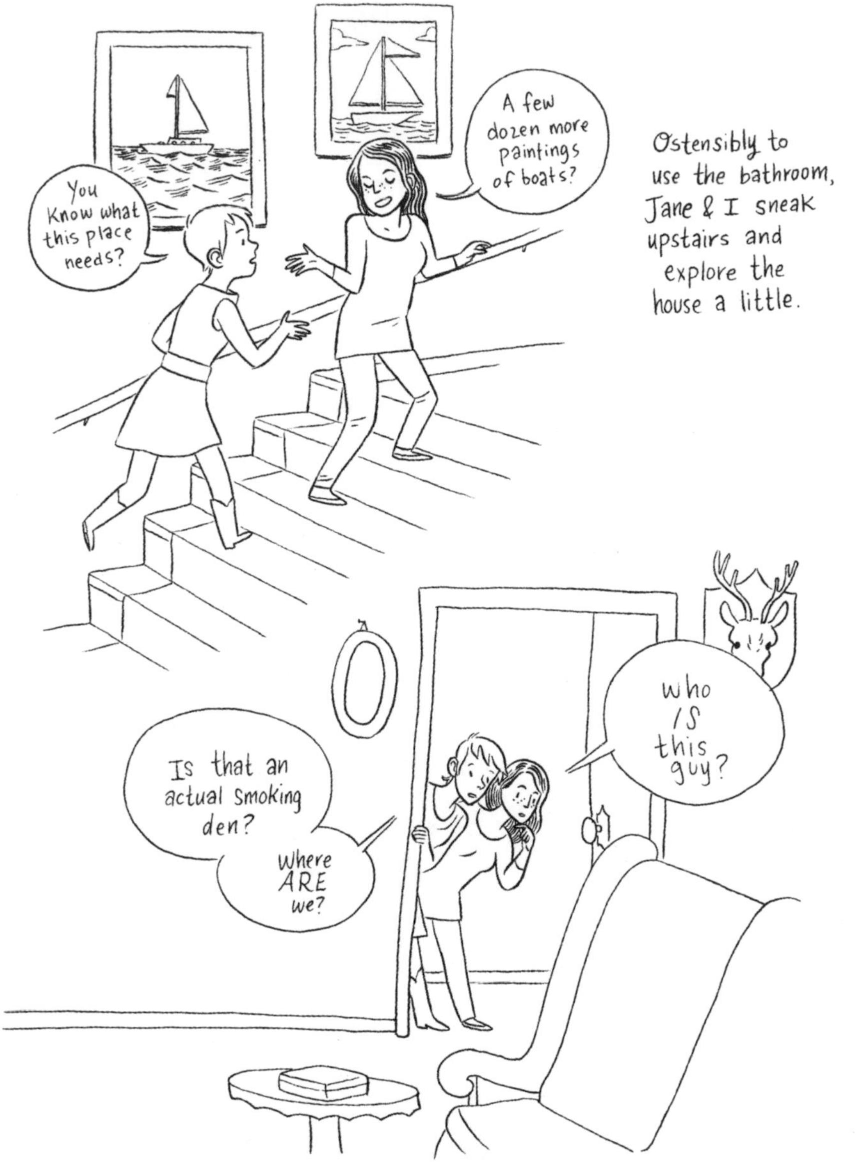
You know what this place needs?
A few dozen more paintings of boats?
Ostensibly to use the bathroom, Jane & I sneak upstairs and explore the house a little.
Is that an actual smoking den?
Where ARE we?
Who IS this guy?

After the others leave, we stay to have a drink with Denis. When we ask him what he does for a living besides organize the Nantucket Wine Fest, he replies:

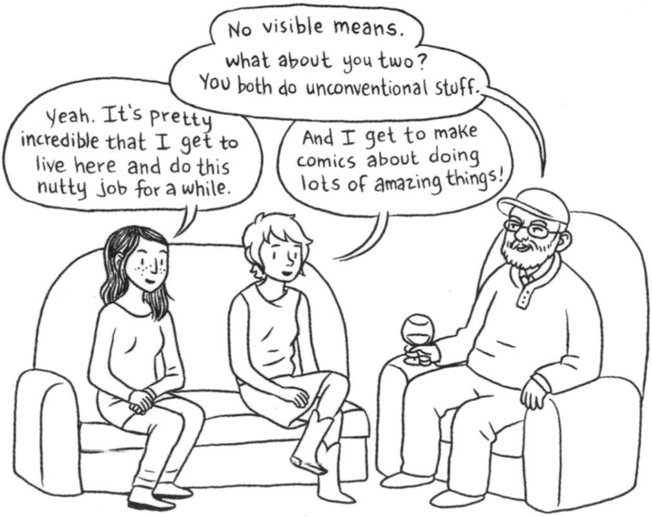
No visible means.
What about you two? You both do unconventional stuff.
Yeah. It's pretty incredible that I get to live here and do this nutty job for a while.
And I get to make comics about doing lots of amazing things!

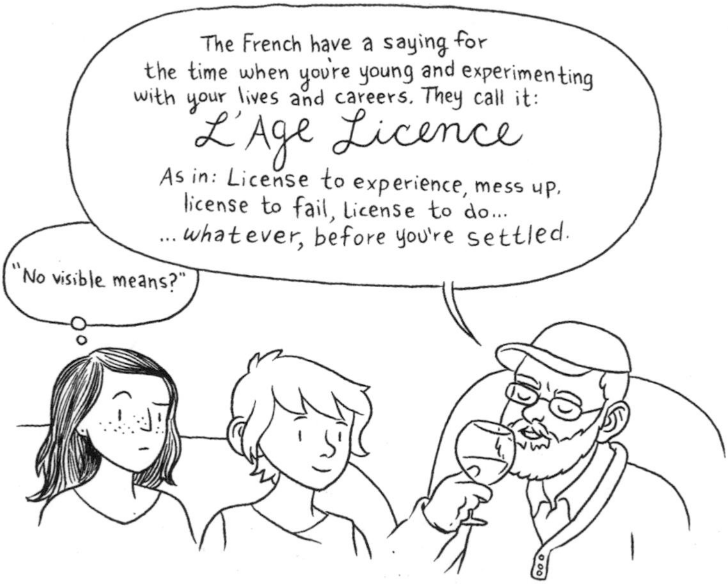
The French have a saying for the time when you're young and experimenting with your lives and careers. They call it:
L'Age Licence
As in: License to experience, mess up, license to fail, license to do... ...whatever, before you're settled.
"No visible means?"

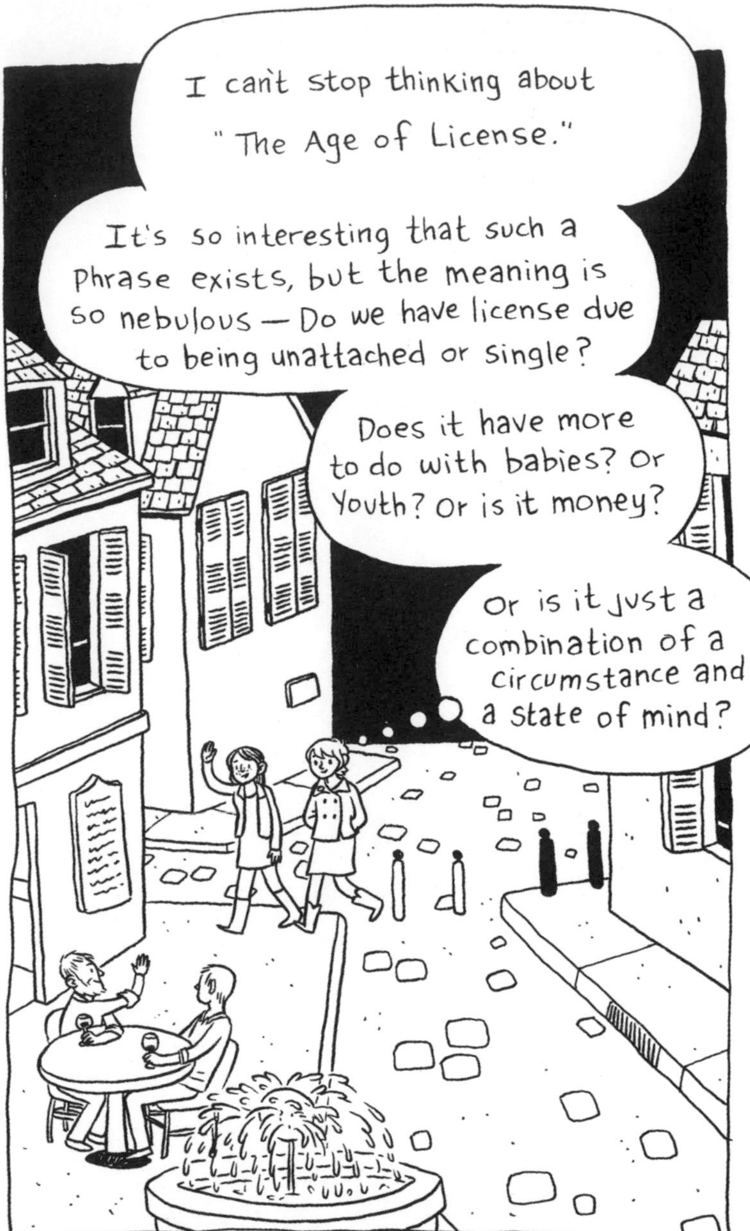
I can't stop thinking about "The Age of License."
It's so interesting that such a phrase exists, but the meaning is so nebulous — Do we have license due to being unattached or single?
Does it have more to do with babies? Or Youth? Or is it money?
Or is it just a combination of a circumstance and a state of mind?

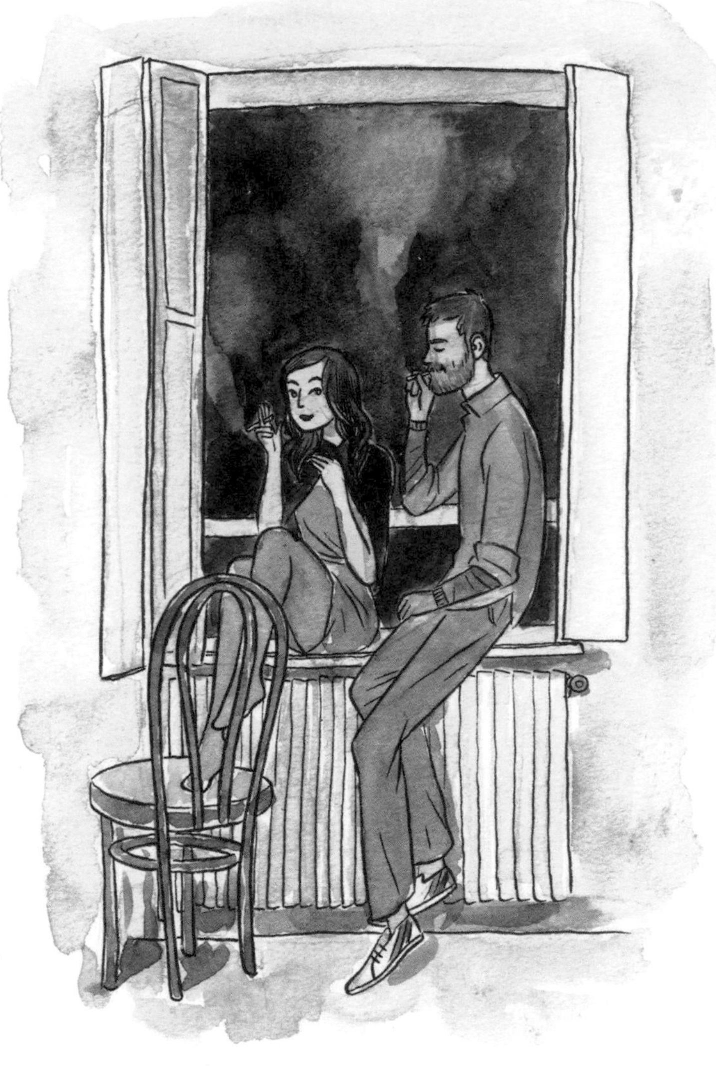

We run into some friends of Jane's on our way home,
so they come back to Jane's place for a chat and drink.

Looking up old friends online

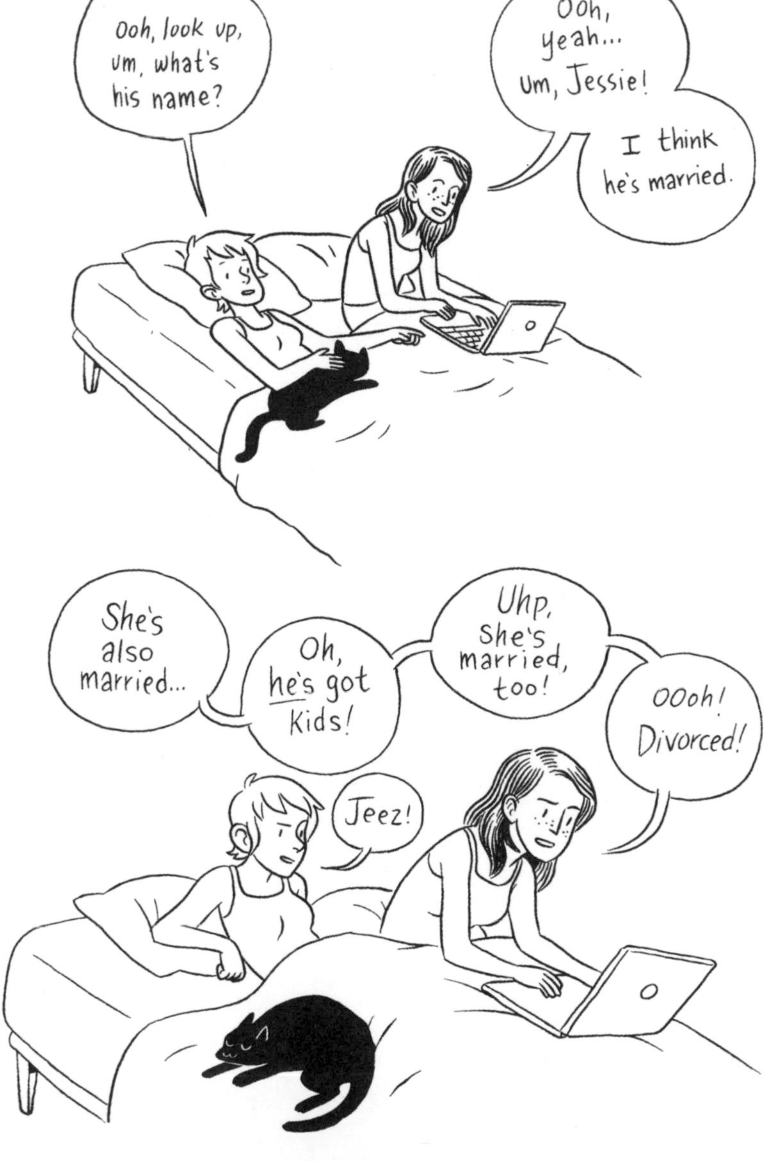
Ooh, look up, um, what's his name?
Ooh, yeah... Um, Jessie!
I think he's married.
She's also married...
Oh, he's got Kids!
Uhp, she's married, too!
OOoh! Divorced!
Jeez!

TO
LYON

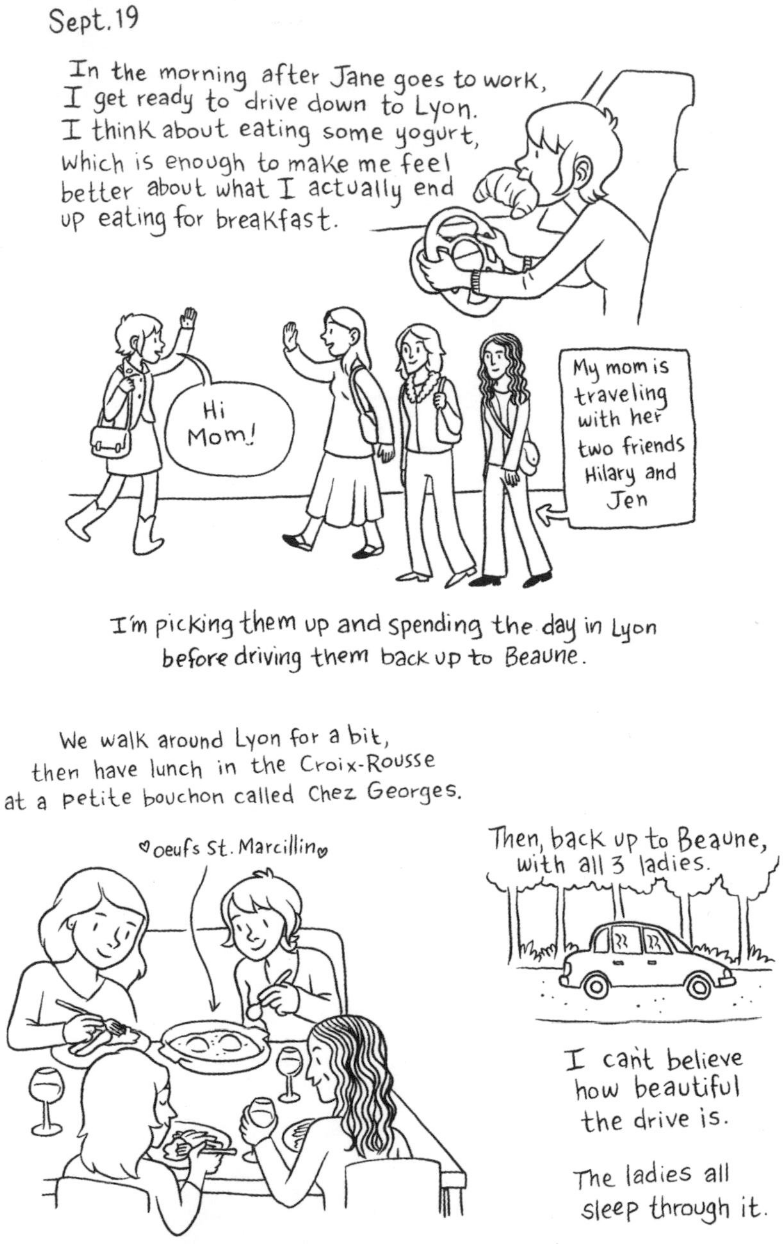
Sept. 19
In the morning after Jane goes to work, I get ready to drive down to Lyon. I think about eating some yogurt, which is enough to make me feel better about what I actually end up eating for breakfast.
Hi Mom!
My mom is traveling with her two friends Hilary and Jen
I'm picking them up and spending the day in Lyon before driving them back up to Beaune.
We walk around Lyon for a bit, then have lunch in the Croix-Rousse at a petite bouchon called Chez Georges.
oeufs St. Marcillin
Then, back up to Beaune, with all 3 ladies.
I can't believe how beautiful the drive is.
The ladies all sleep through it.

In the window of a ballet supply
shop in Lyon's La Croix-Rousse

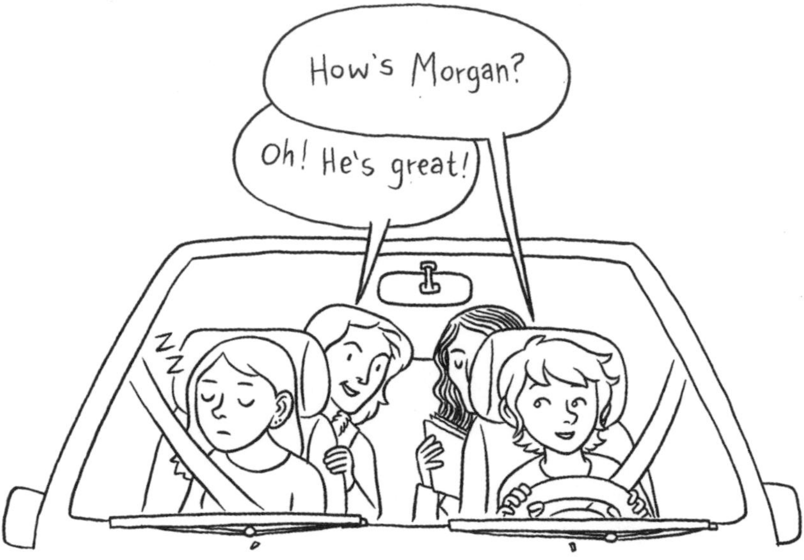
How's Morgan?
Oh! He's great!

(Morgan, Hilary's son, and I were close when we were kids)

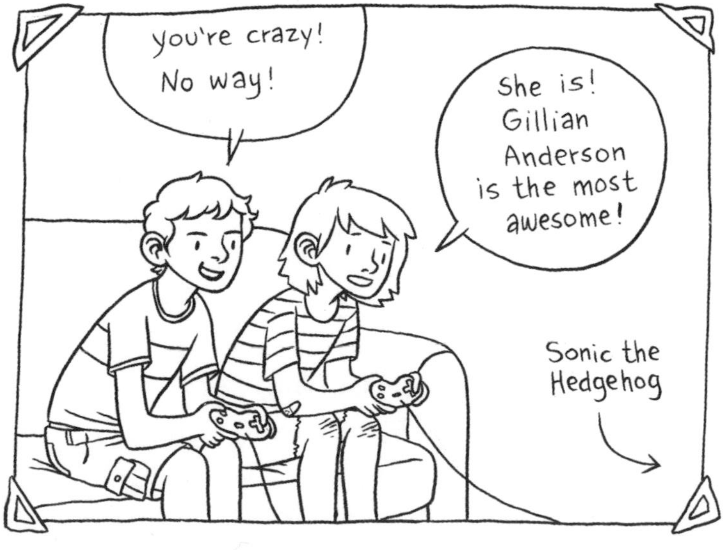
you're crazy! No way!
She is! Gillian Anderson is the most awesome!
Sonic the Hedgehog

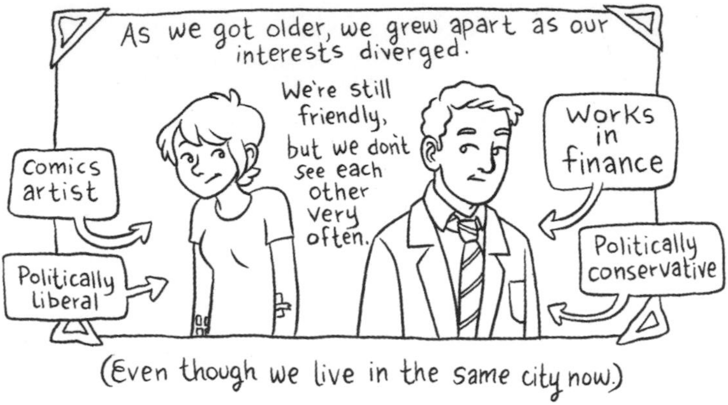
As we got older, we grew apart as our interests diverged.
We're still friendly, but we don't see each other very often.
Comics artist
Politically liberal
Works in finance
Politically conservative
(Even though we live in the same city now.)

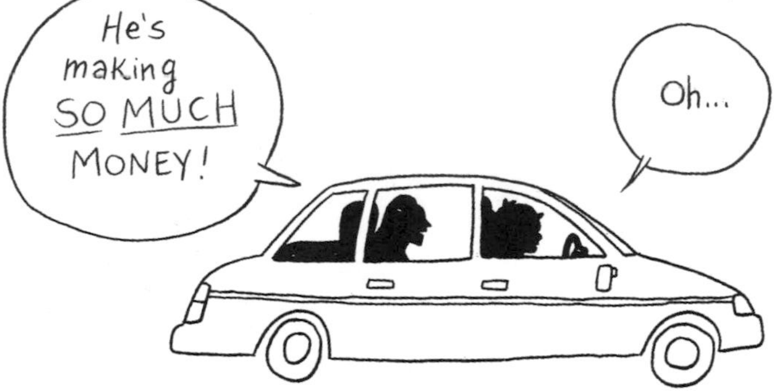
He's making SO MUCH MONEY!
Oh...

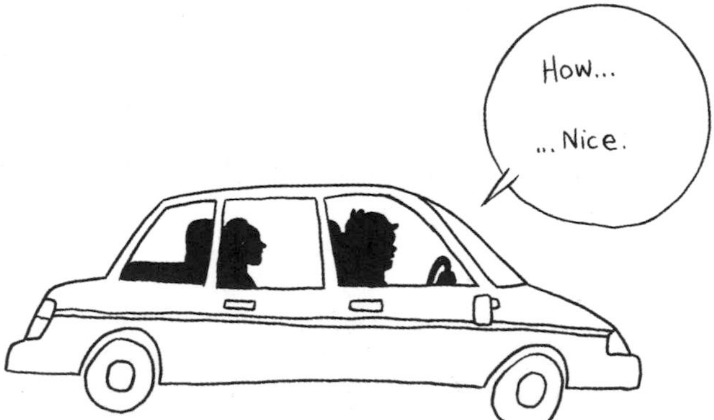
How...
... Nice.

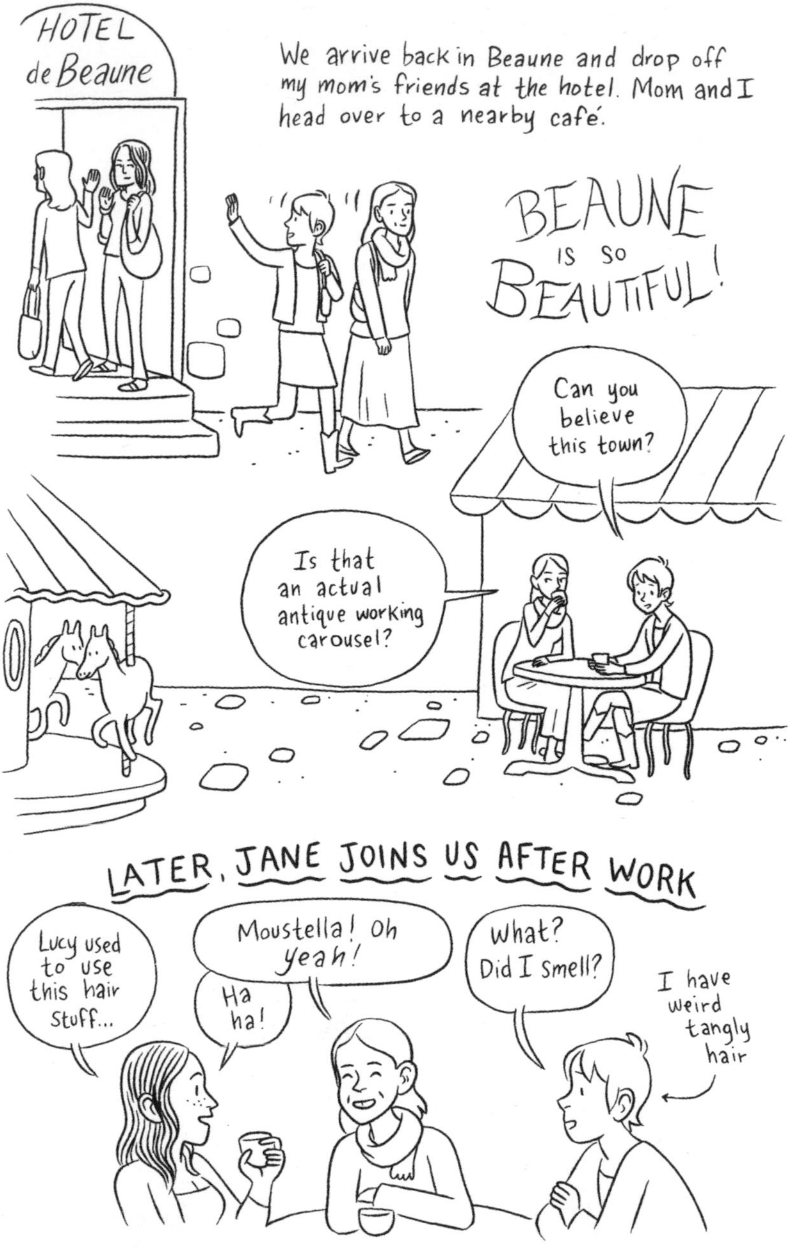
HOTEL de Beaune
We arrive back in Beaune and drop off my mom's friends at the hotel. Mom and I head over to a nearby café.
BEAUNE IS SO BEAUTIFUL!
Can you believe this town?
Is that an actual antique working carousel?
LATER, JANE JOINS US AFTER WORK
Lucy used to use this hair stuff...
Moustella! Oh yeah!
Ha ha!
What? Did I smell?
I have weird tangly hair

We go to dinner at Bistro Au Bord de L'eau with Mom's friends & Jane, on Jane's recommendation.

Cheese
Paté
Toast
Greens

After dinner, we check out the kitchen through windows in the dining room.

dessert chef

Sept. 20

The Next Day

We go for brunch at Chez Montrachet
(a little restaurant & B&B outside of town).
We eat outside
in the sun.

Afterwards, we're set to head out of town,
but first we stop by Jane's work for...

...A few parting gifts!

Like 5 bottles of awesome local wine

(She gets a lot of great wine through work — It's good to work in wine!)

TO ANGOULÊME & ROYAN

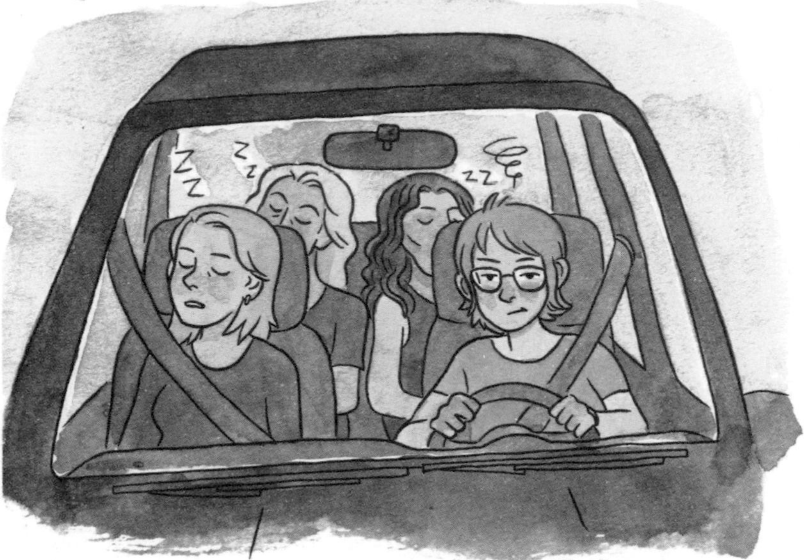

ZZZ
ZZ
ZZZ

I didn't realize that I'd be chauffeuring
3 sleepers all aross France...

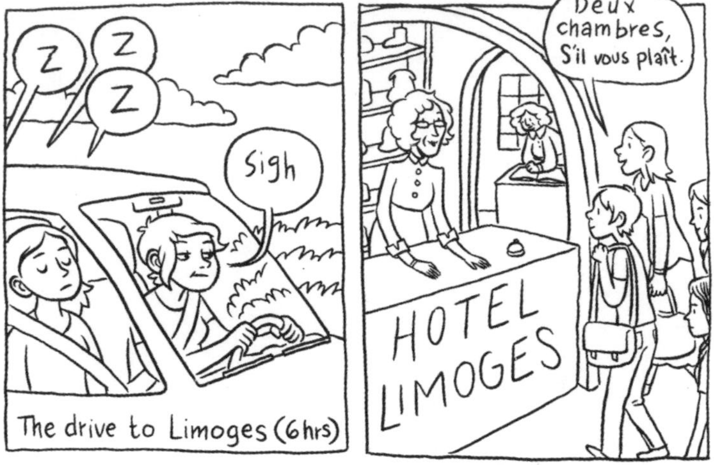
Z
Z
Z
Sigh
The drive to Limoges (6hrs)
Deux chambres, S'il vous plaît.
HOTEL LIMOGES

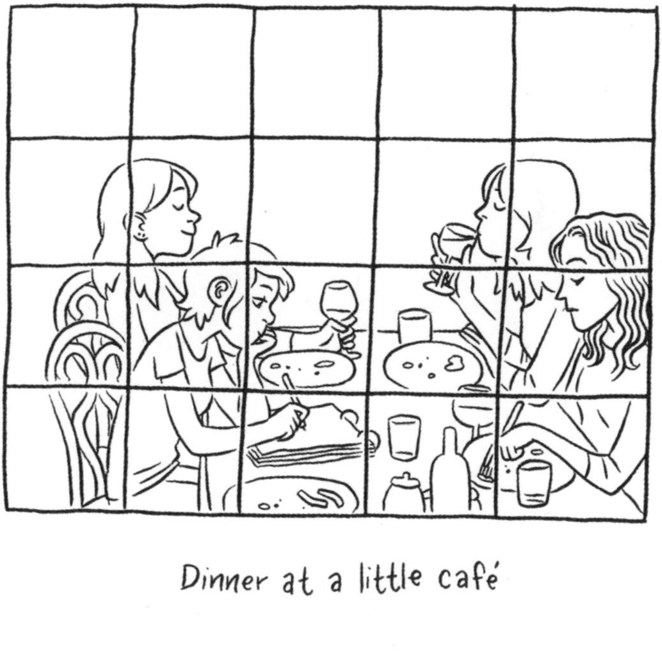

Dinner at a little café

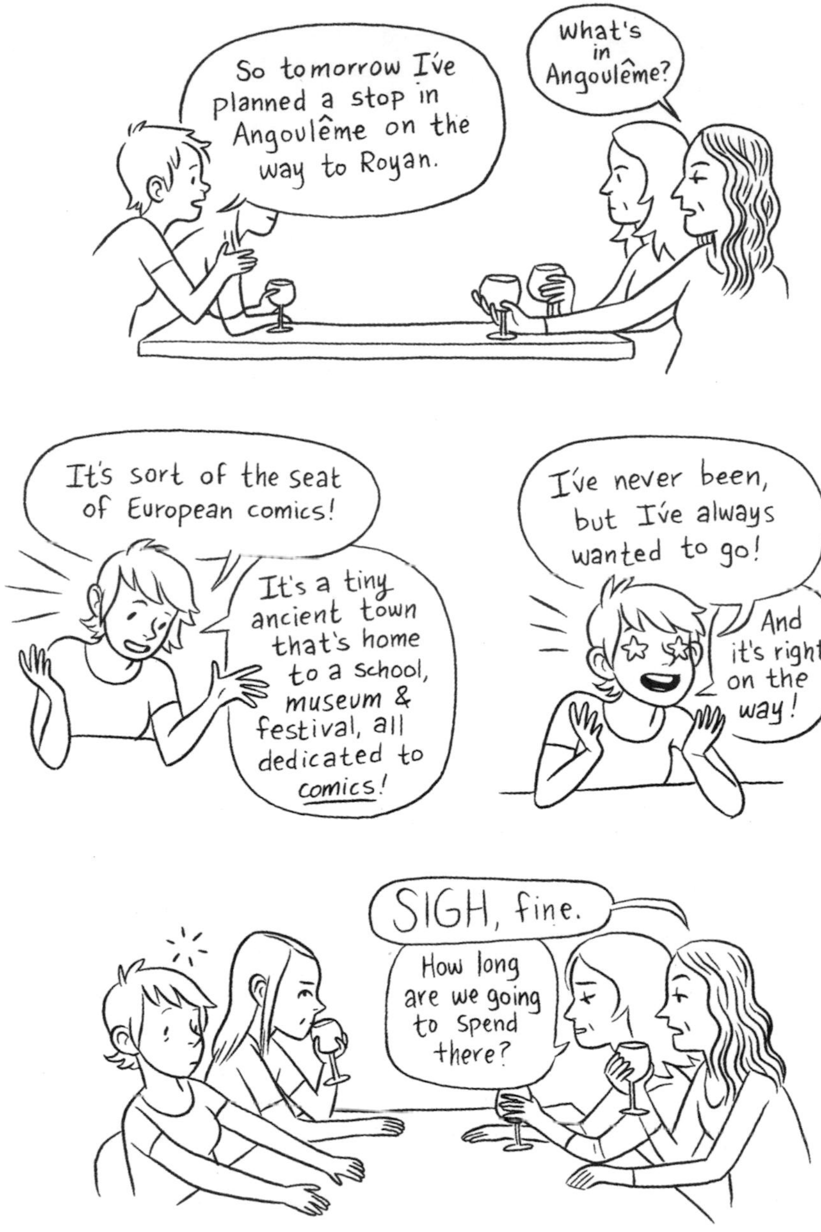
So tomorrow I've planned a stop in Angoulême on the way to Royan.
What's in Angoulême?
It's sort of the seat of European comics!
It's a tiny ancient town that's home to a school, museum & festival, all dedicated to comics!
I've never been, but I've always wanted to go!
And it's right on the way!
SIGH, fine.
How long are we going to spend there?

Sept. 21

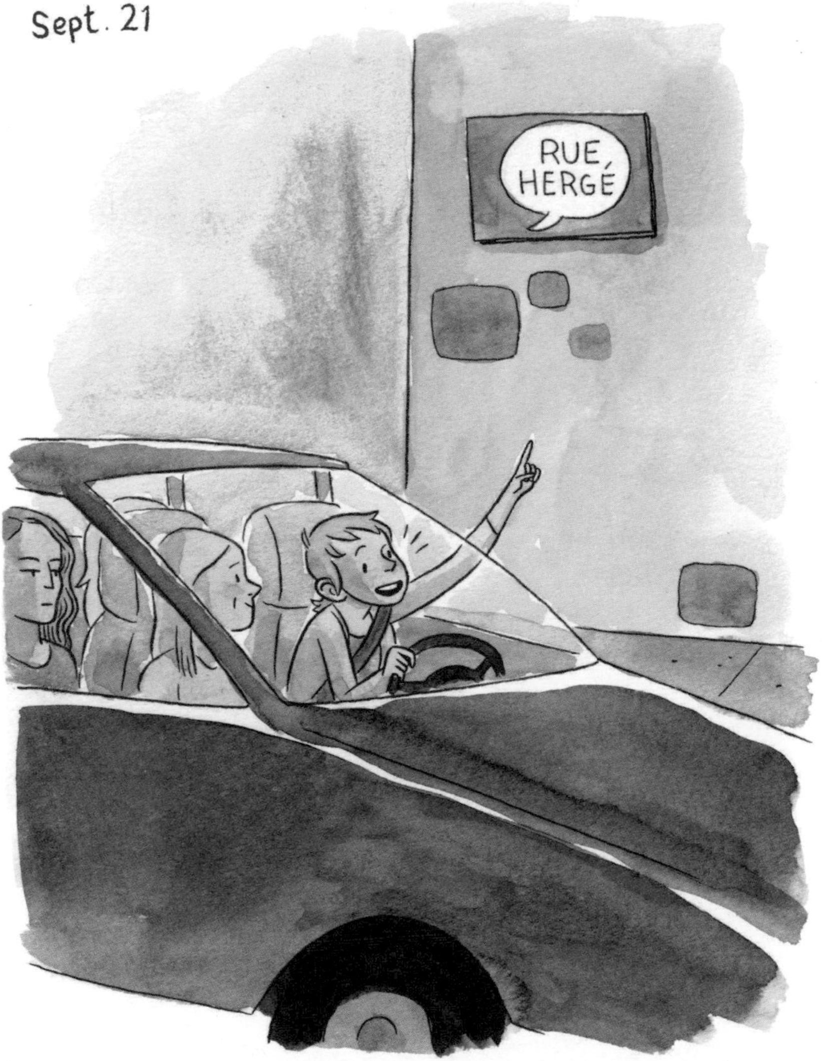
RUE HERGÉ

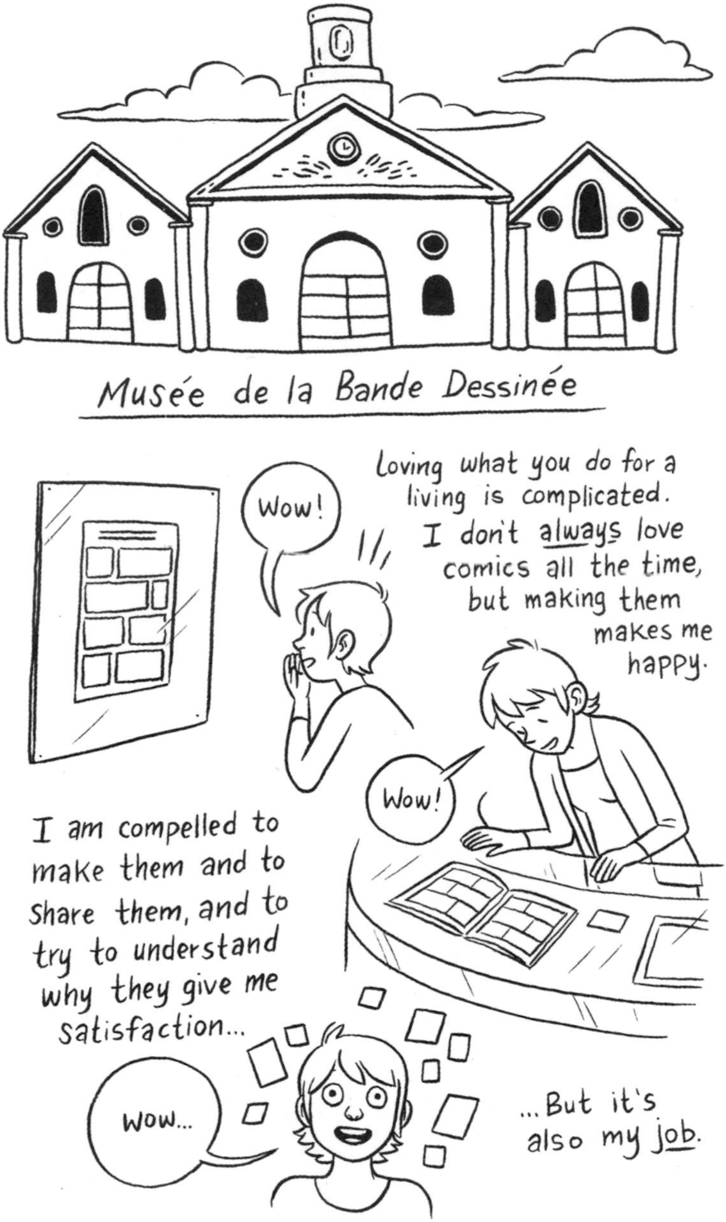
Musée de la Bande Dessinée
Loving what you do for a living is complicated. I don't always love comics all the time, but making them makes me happy.
Wow!
Wow!
I am compelled to make them and to share them, and to try to understand why they give me satisfaction...
Wow...
...But it's also my job.

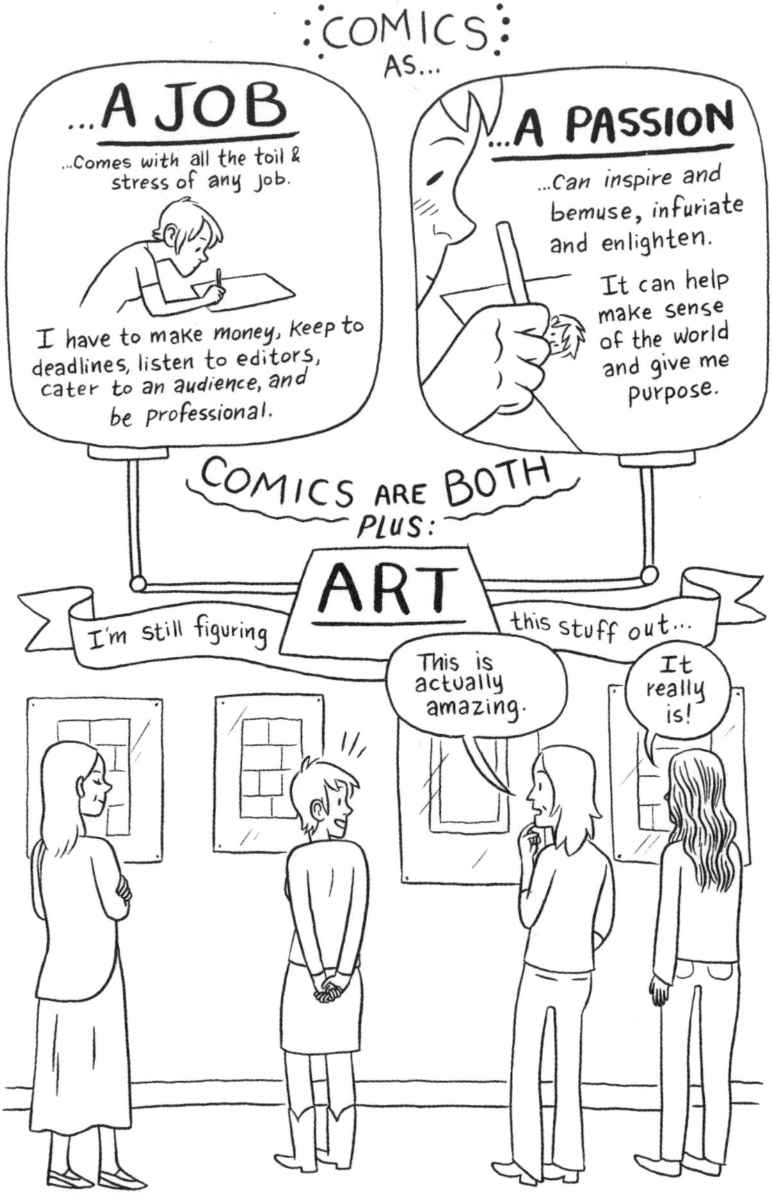
COMICS
AS...
...A JOB
...Comes with all the toil & stress of any job.
I have to make money, keep to deadlines, listen to editors, cater to an audience, and be professional.
...A PASSION
...Can inspire and bemuse, infuriate and enlighten.
It can help make sense of the world and give me purpose.
COMICS ARE BOTH
PLUS:
ART
I'm still figuring this stuff out...
This is actually amazing.
It really is!

Lunch with Mom

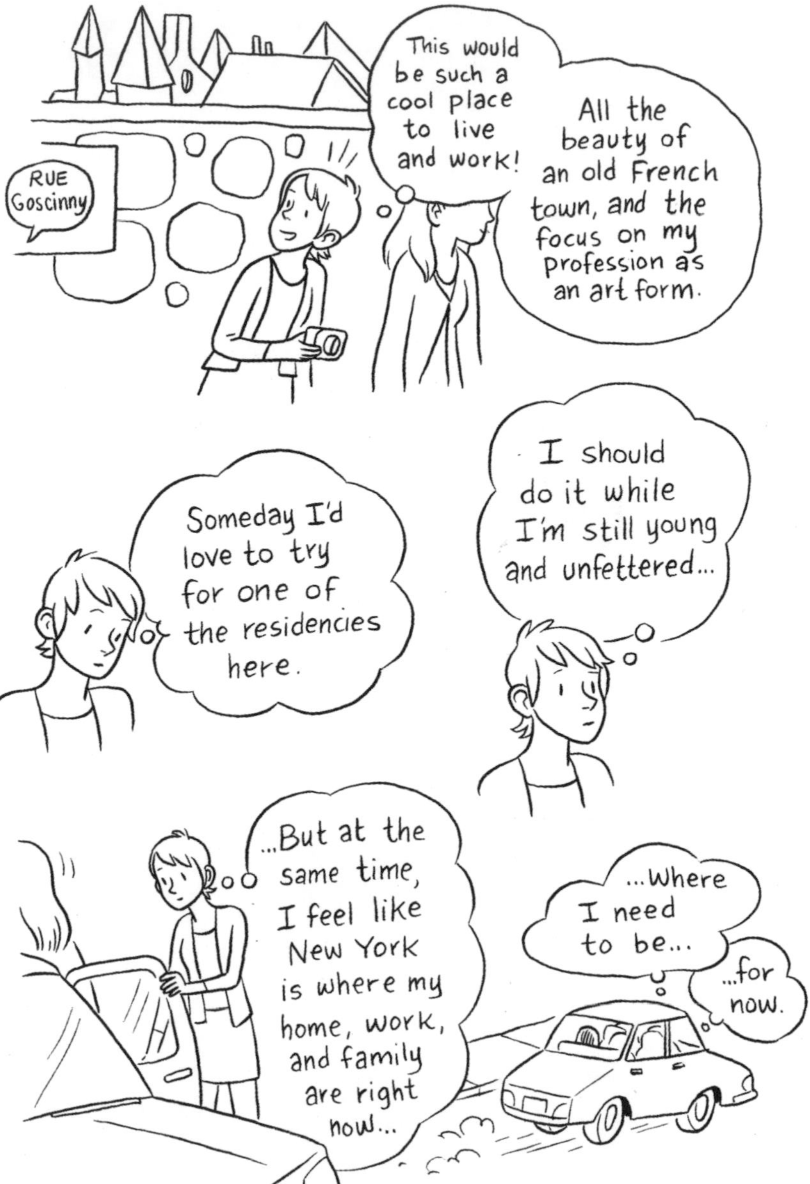
RUE Goscinny
This would be such a cool place to live and work!
All the beauty of an old French town, and the focus on my profession as an art form.
Someday I'd love to try for one of the residencies here.
I should do it while I'm still young and unfettered...
...But at the same time, I feel like New York is where my home, work, and family are right now...
...Where I need to be...
...for now.

Royan, France

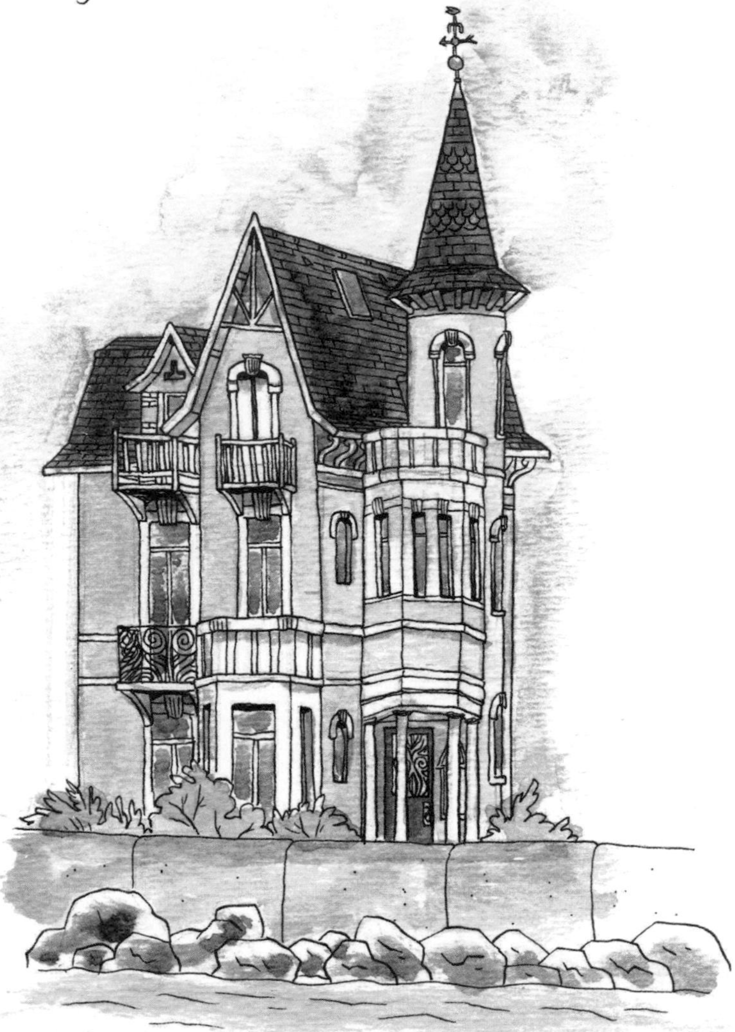

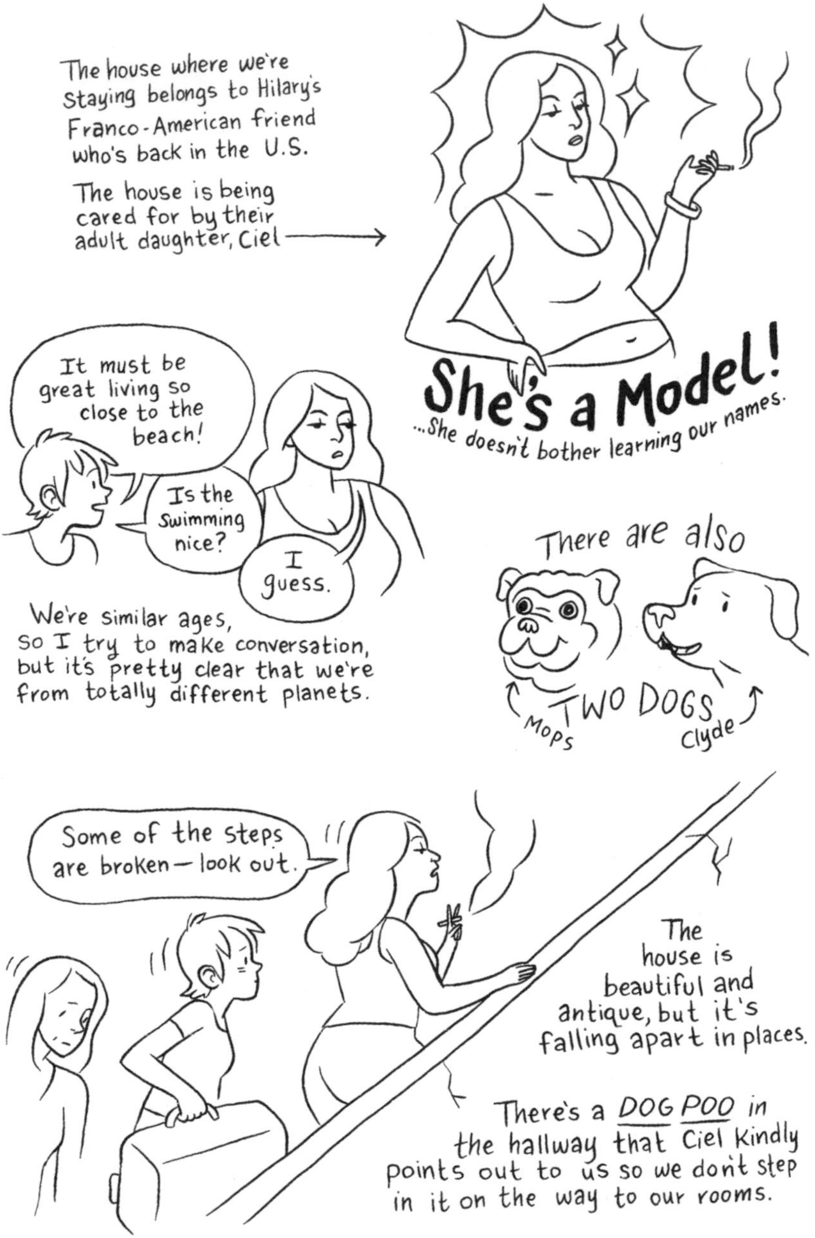
The house where we're staying belongs to Hilary's Franco-American friend who's back in the U.S.
The house is being cared for by their adult daughter, Ciel
She's a Model!
...She doesn't bother learning our names.
It must be great living so close to the beach!
Is the swimming nice?
I guess.
We're similar ages, so I try to make conversation, but it's pretty clear that we're from totally different planets.
There are also
TWO DOGS
Mops
Clyde
Some of the steps are broken — look out.
The house is beautiful and antique, but it's falling apart in places.
There's a DOG POO in the hallway that Ciel kindly points out to us so we don't step in it on the way to our rooms.

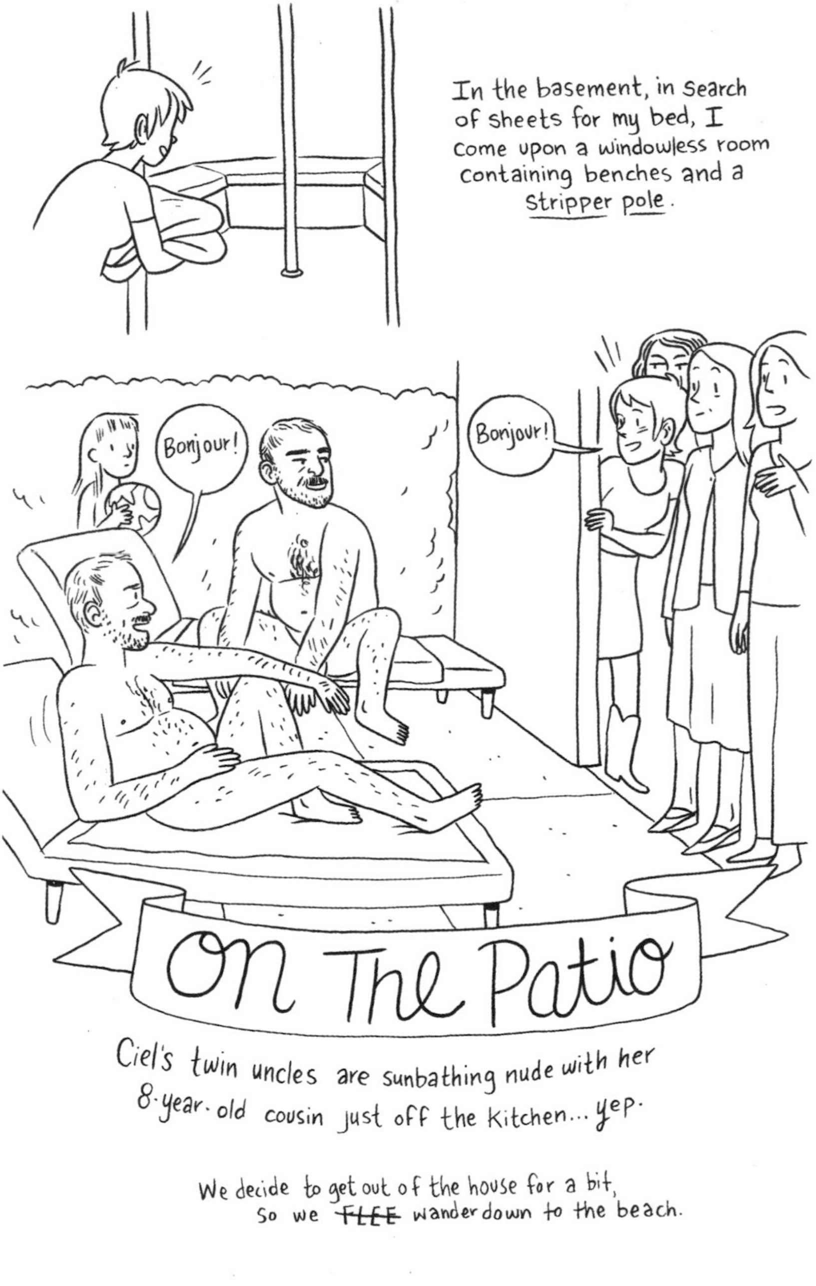
In the basement, in search of sheets for my bed, I come upon a windowless room containing benches and a stripper pole.
Bonjour!
Bonjour!
On The Patio
Ciel's twin uncles are sunbathing nude with her 8-year-old cousin just off the kitchen... yep.
We decide to get out of the house for a bit, so we ~~FLEE~~ wander down to the beach.

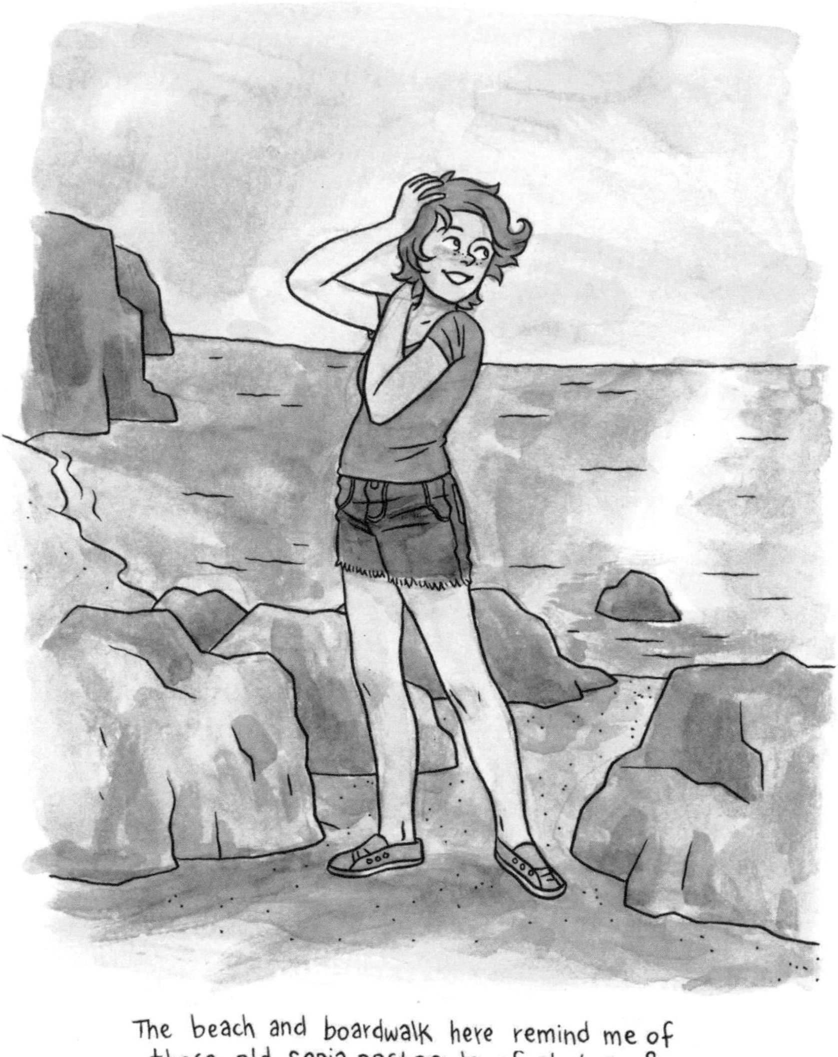

The beach and boardwalk here remind me of those old sepia postcards of photos of shorelines and vacationers from the 1930s.

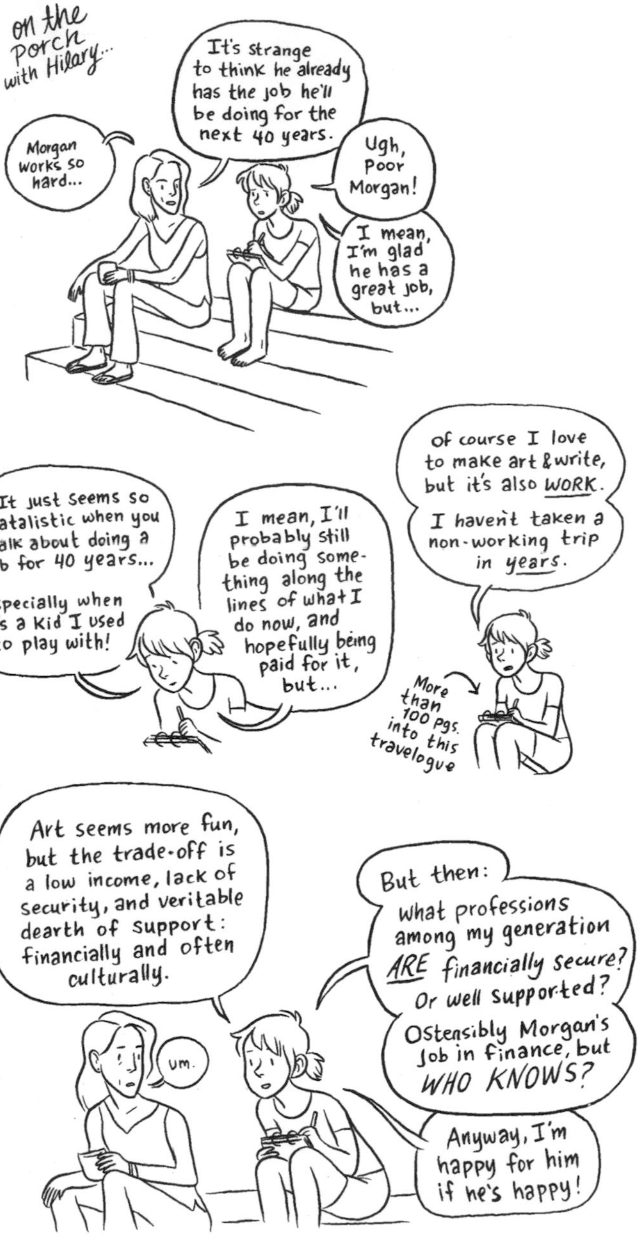
on the porch with Hilary...
Morgan works so hard...
It's strange to think he already has the job he'll be doing for the next 40 years.
Ugh, Poor Morgan!
I mean, I'm glad he has a great job, but...
...It just seems so fatalistic when you talk about doing a job for 40 years...
Especially when it's a kid I used to play with!
I mean, I'll probably still be doing something along the lines of what I do now, and hopefully being paid for it, but...
Of course I love to make art & write, but it's also WORK.
I haven't taken a non-working trip in years.
More than 100 pgs. into this travelogue
Art seems more fun, but the trade-off is a low income, lack of security, and veritable dearth of support: financially and often culturally.
um.
But then:
What professions among my generation ARE financially secure? Or well supported?
Ostensibly Morgan's job in finance, but WHO KNOWS?
Anyway, I'm happy for him if he's happy!

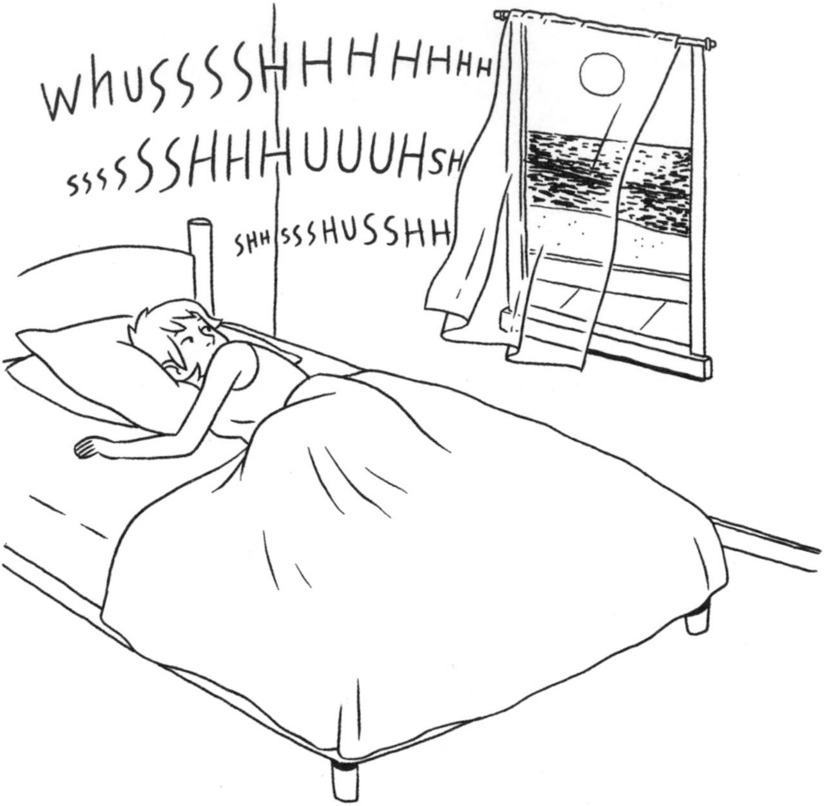
whusssssHHHHHHH
ssssSSHHHUUUHsh
SHHsssHUSSHH

The ocean noise through the window sounds like the soft susurrus of sleeping breath.

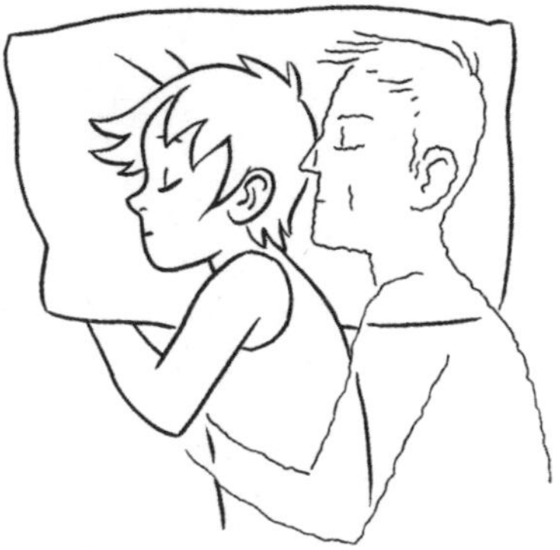

My mind conjures a warm sleeping form beside me.

I'm meeting Henrik in Paris in a few days, to spend some time before I fly home.

Clyde

Mops

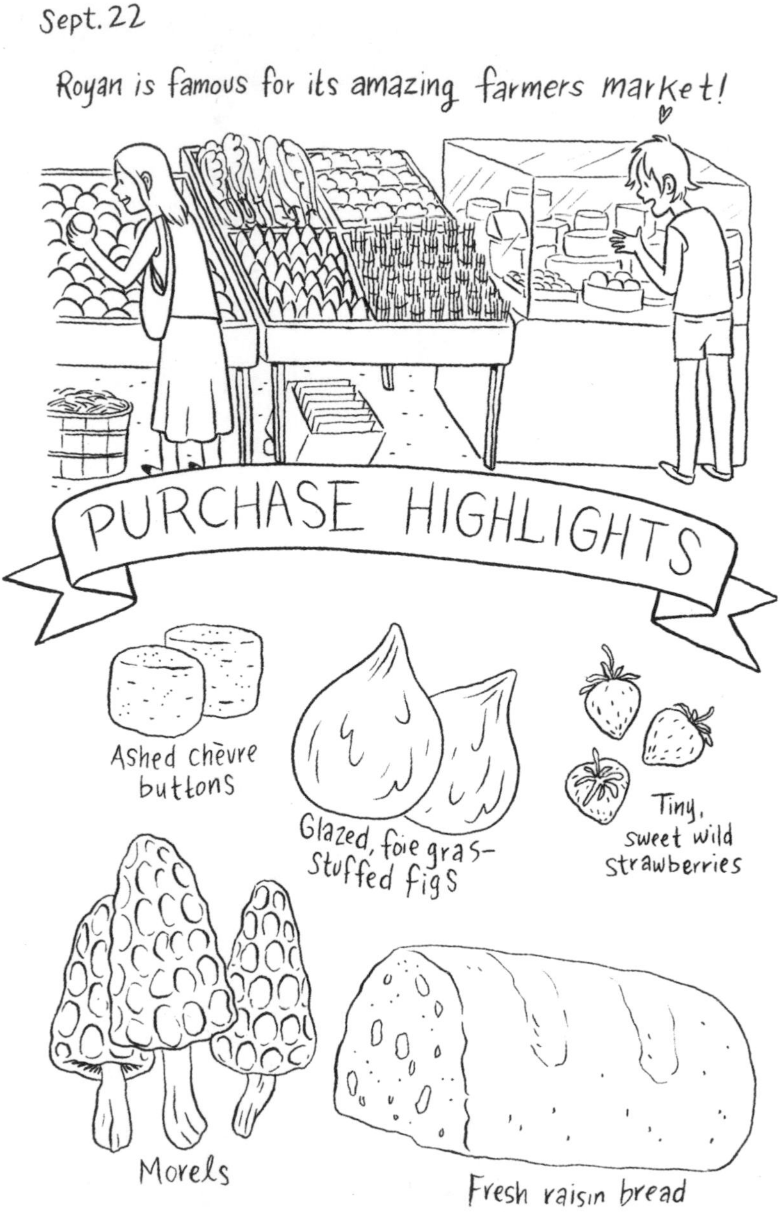
Sept. 22
Royan is famous for its amazing farmers market!
PURCHASE HIGHLIGHTS
Ashed chèvre buttons
Glazed, foie gras-stuffed figs
Tiny, sweet wild strawberries
Morels
Fresh raisin bread

also...

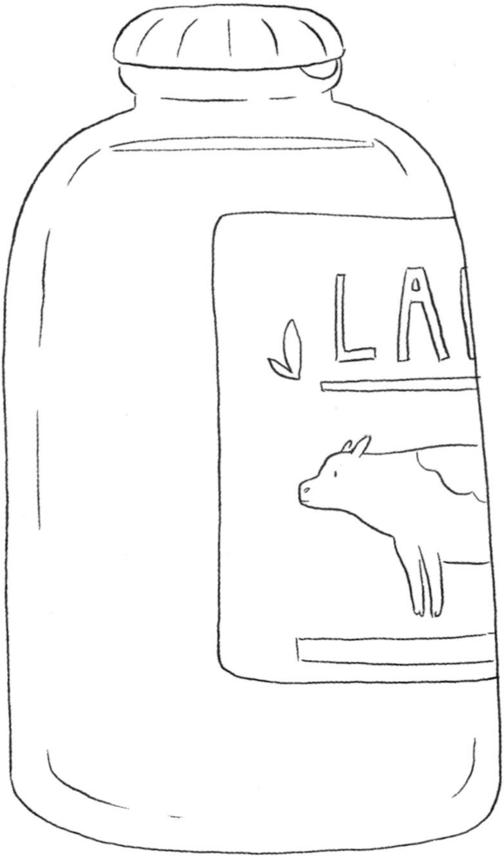
LA

My favorite!

Spotted at the market.
Me, someday?

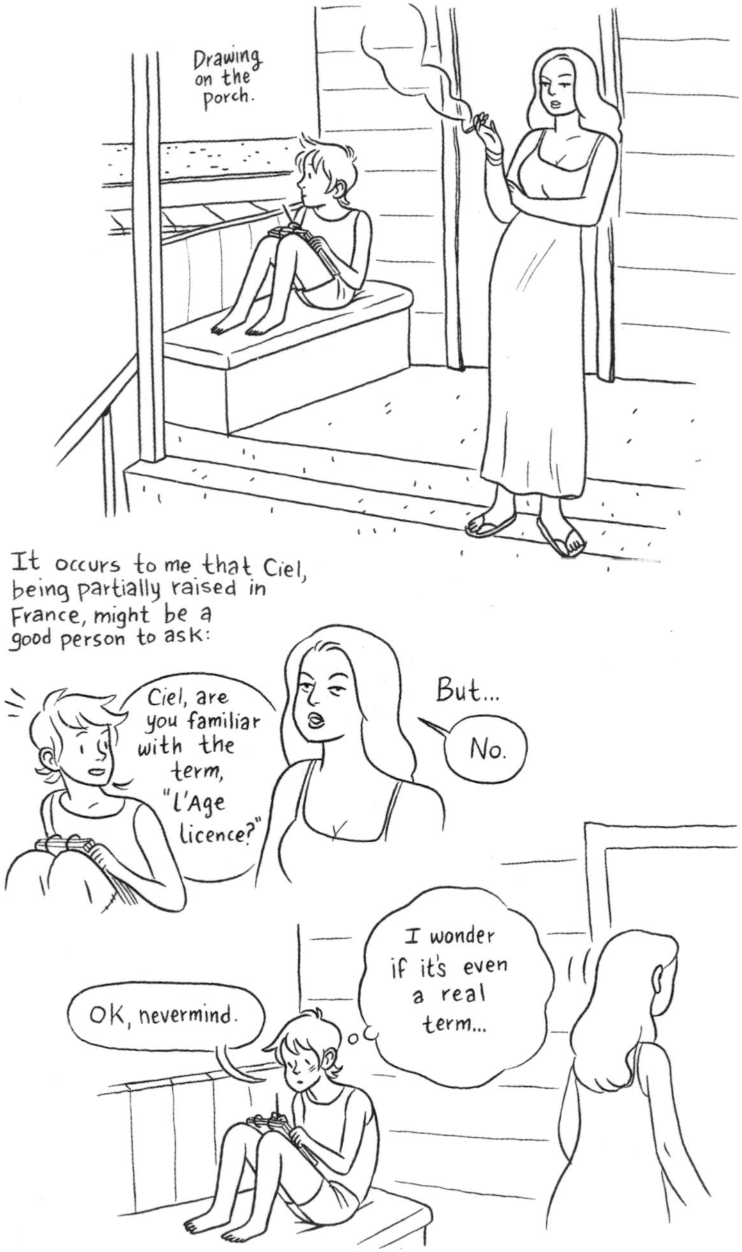
Drawing on the porch.
It occurs to me that Ciel, being partially raised in France, might be a good person to ask:
Ciel, are you familiar with the term, "L'Age licence?"
No.
But...
OK, nevermind.
I wonder if it's even a real term...

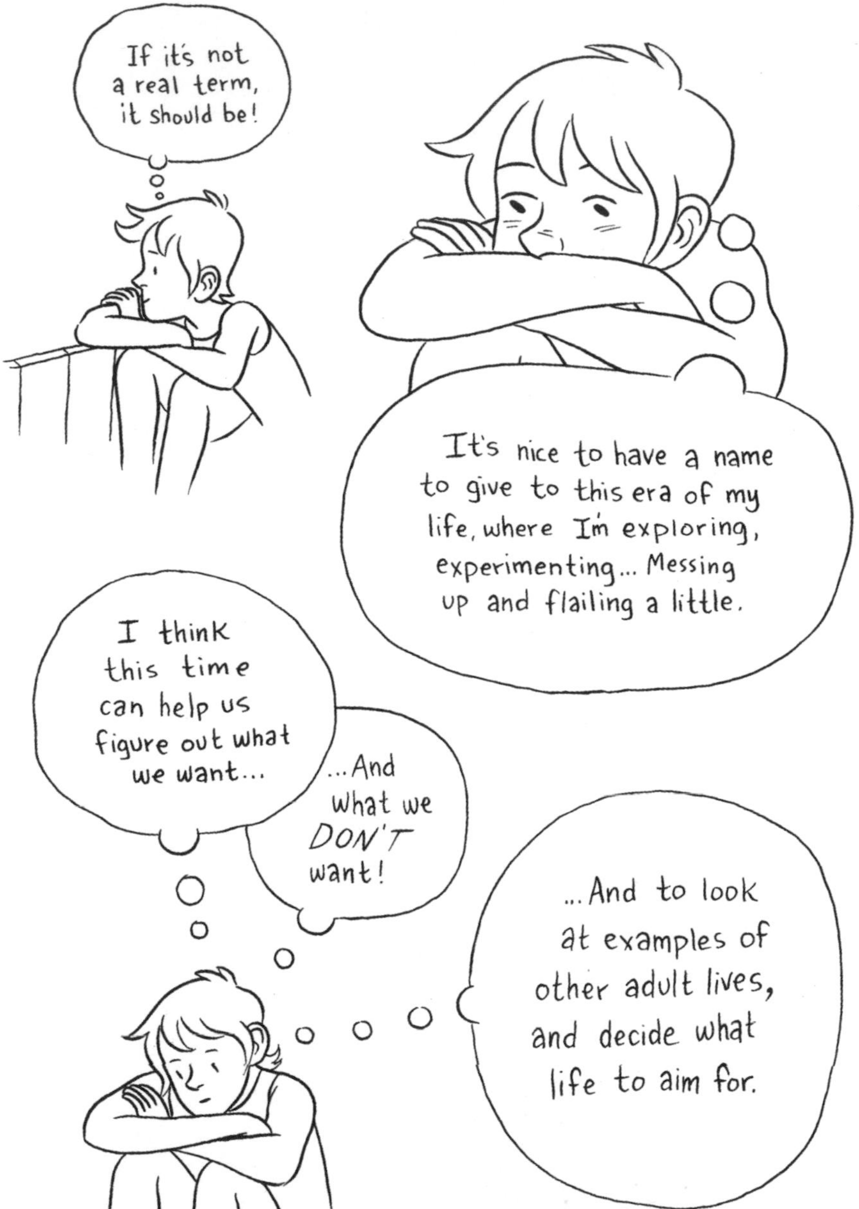
If it's not a real term, it should be!
It's nice to have a name to give to this era of my life, where I'm exploring, experimenting... Messing up and flailing a little.
I think this time can help us figure out what we want...
...And what we DON'T want!
...And to look at examples of other adult lives, and decide what life to aim for.

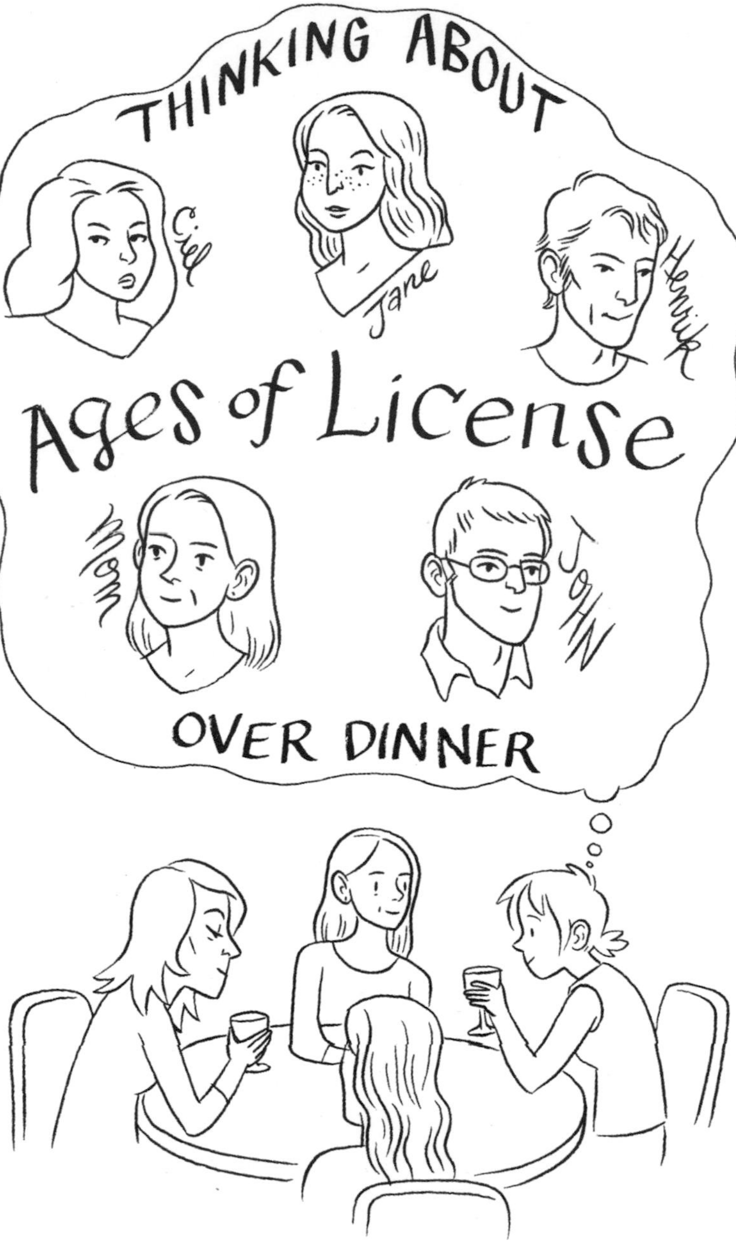
THINKING ABOUT
Ciel
Jane
Henrik
Ages of License
Mom
JOHN
OVER DINNER

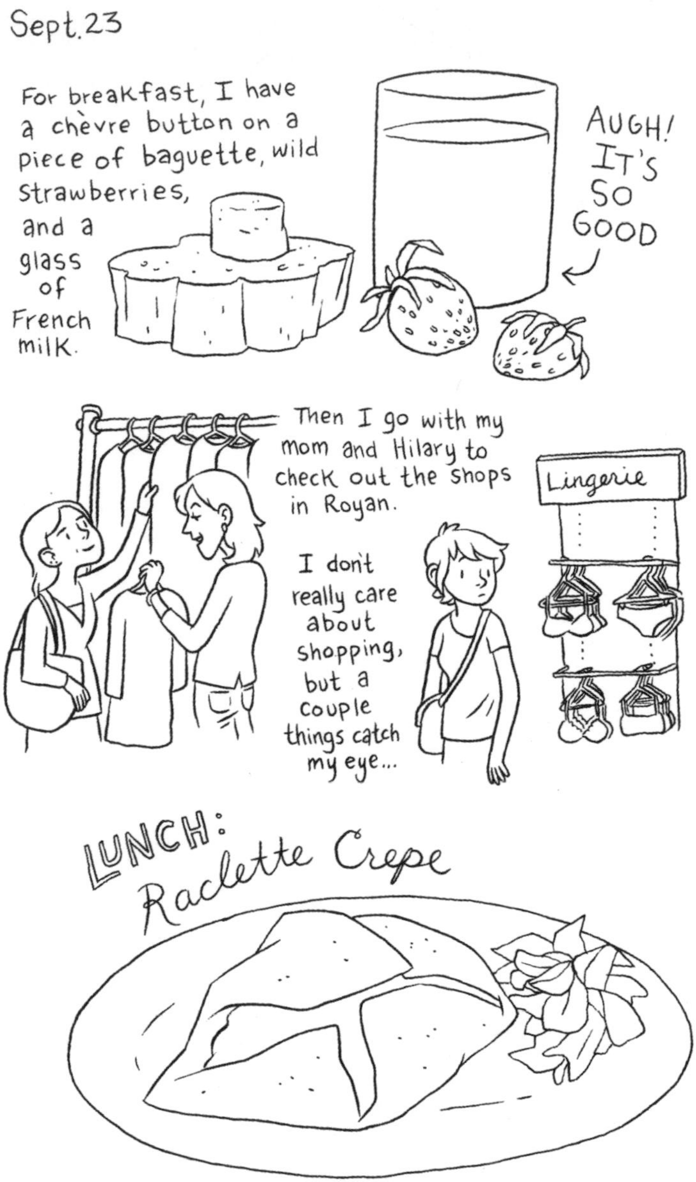
Sept.23
For breakfast, I have a chèvre button on a piece of baguette, wild strawberries, and a glass of French milk.
AUGH! IT'S SO GOOD
Then I go with my mom and Hilary to check out the shops in Royan.
Lingerie
I don't really care about shopping, but a couple things catch my eye...
LUNCH: Raclette Crepe

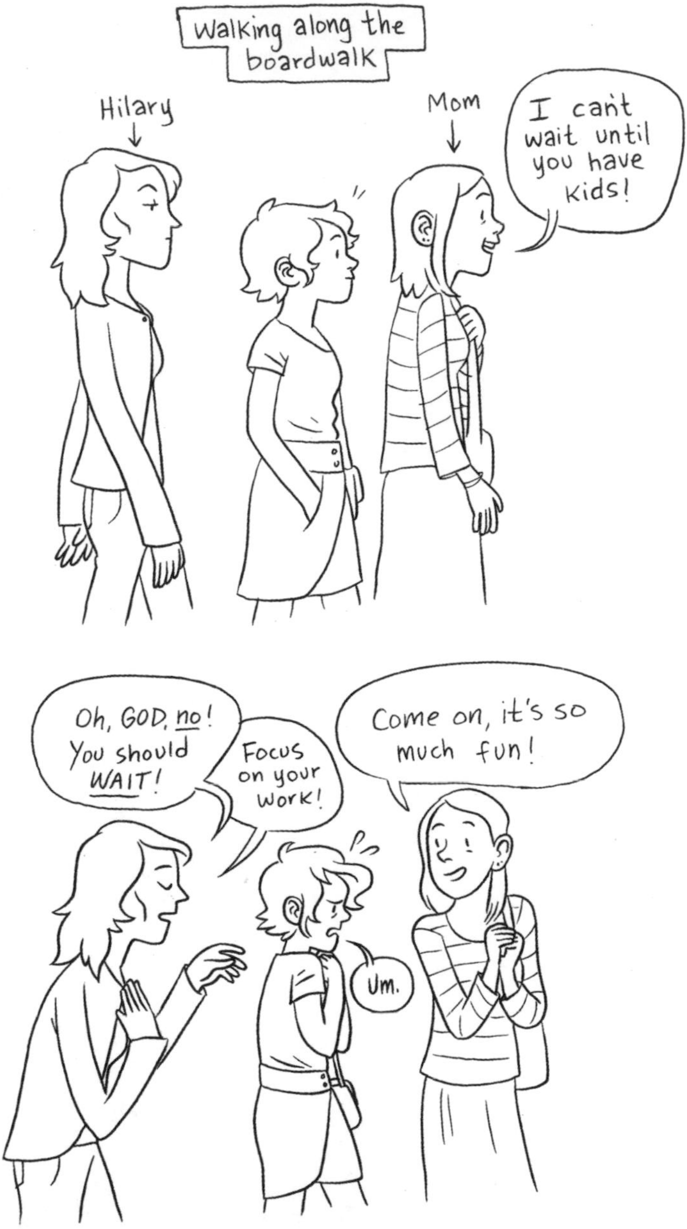
Walking along the boardwalk
Hilary
Mom
I can't wait until you have kids!
Oh, GOD, no! You should WAIT!
Focus on your work!
Come on, it's so much fun!
Um.

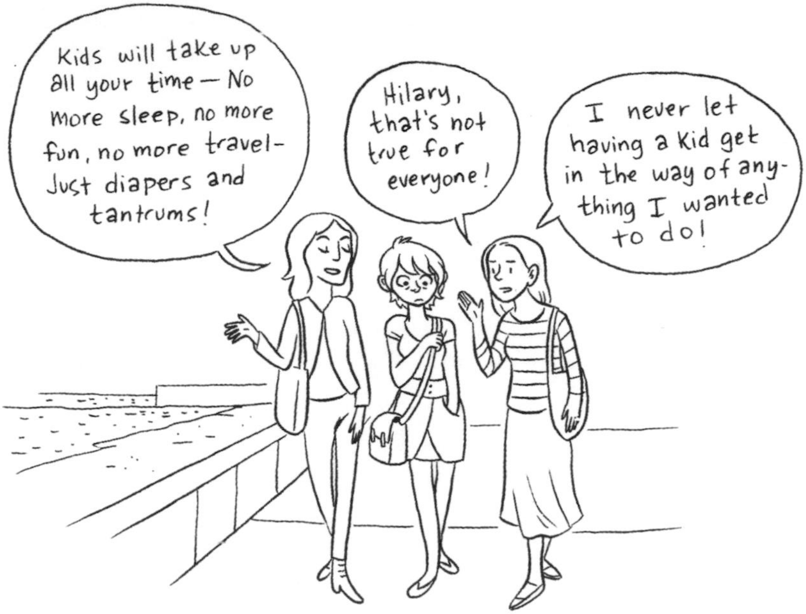
Kids will take up all your time — No more sleep, no more fun, no more travel- Just diapers and tantrums!
Hilary, that's not true for everyone!
I never let having a kid get in the way of anything I wanted to do!

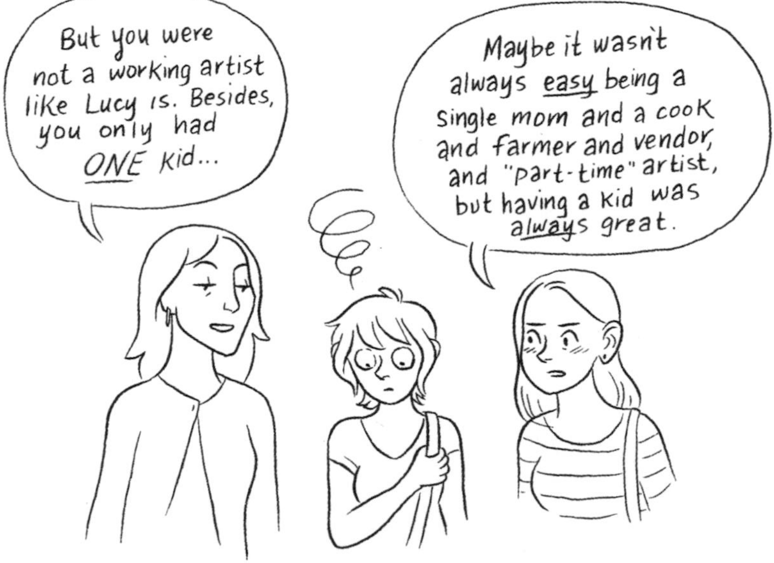
But you were not a working artist like Lucy is. Besides, you only had ONE kid...
Maybe it wasn't always easy being a single mom and a cook and farmer and vendor, and "part-time" artist, but having a kid was always great.

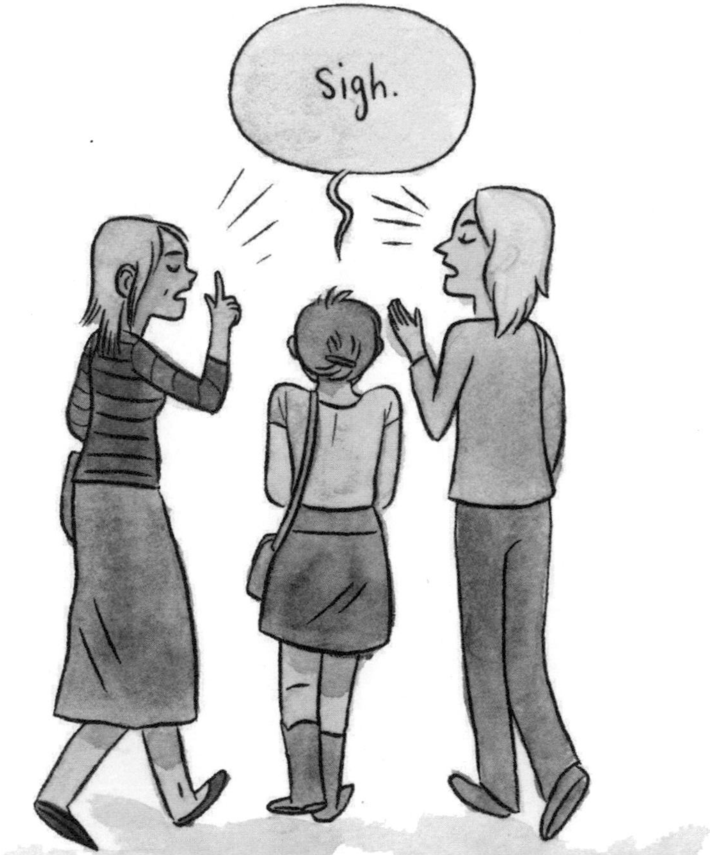
Sigh.

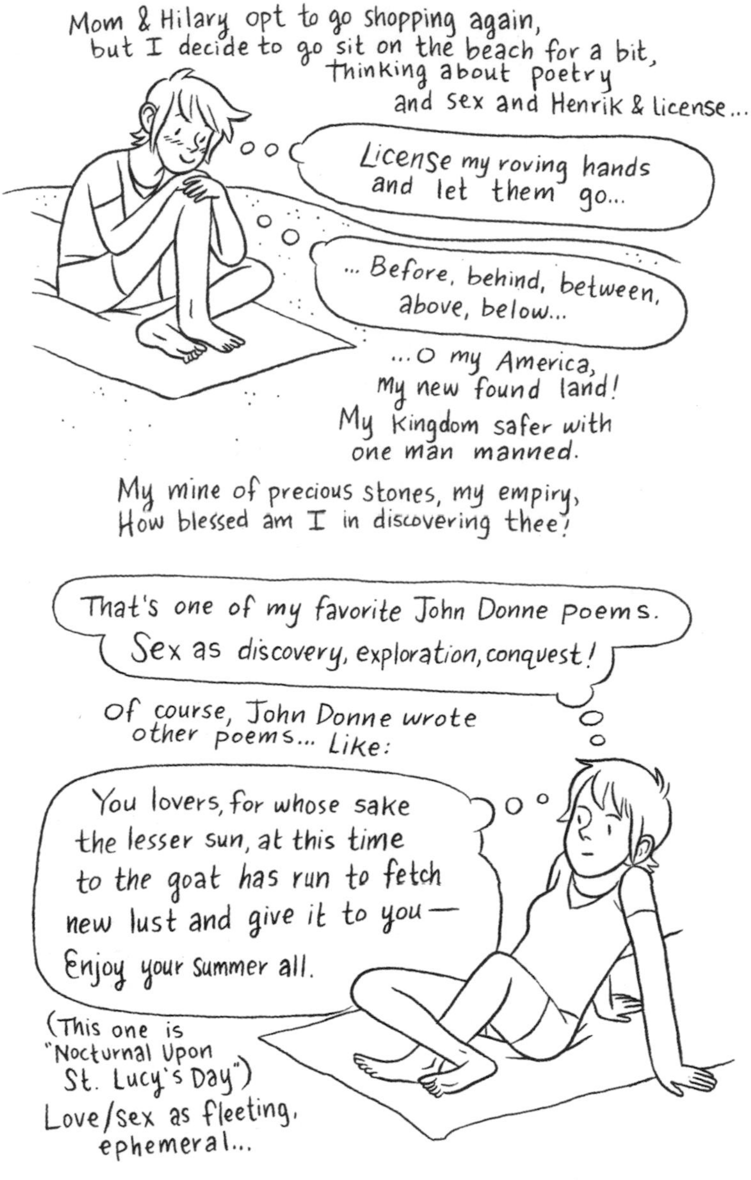
Mom & Hilary opt to go shopping again, but I decide to go sit on the beach for a bit, thinking about poetry and sex and Henrik & license...
License my roving hands and let them go...
... Before, behind, between, above, below...
...O my America, my new found land!
My Kingdom safer with one man manned.
My mine of precious stones, my empiry, How blessed am I in discovering thee!
That's one of my favorite John Donne poems. Sex as discovery, exploration, conquest!
Of course, John Donne wrote other poems... Like:
You lovers, for whose sake the lesser sun, at this time to the goat has run to fetch new lust and give it to you— Enjoy your summer all.
(This one is "Nocturnal Upon St. Lucy's Day")
Love/sex as fleeting, ephemeral...

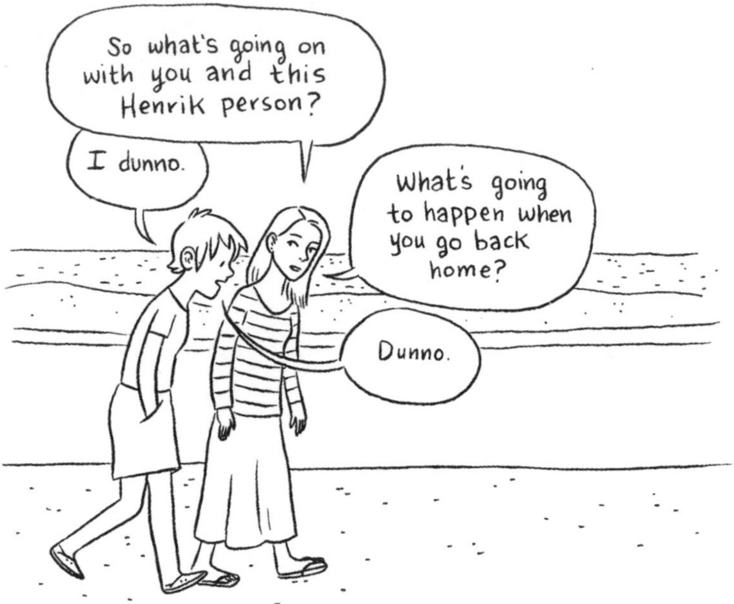
So what's going on with you and this Henrik person?
I dunno.
What's going to happen when you go back home?
Dunno.

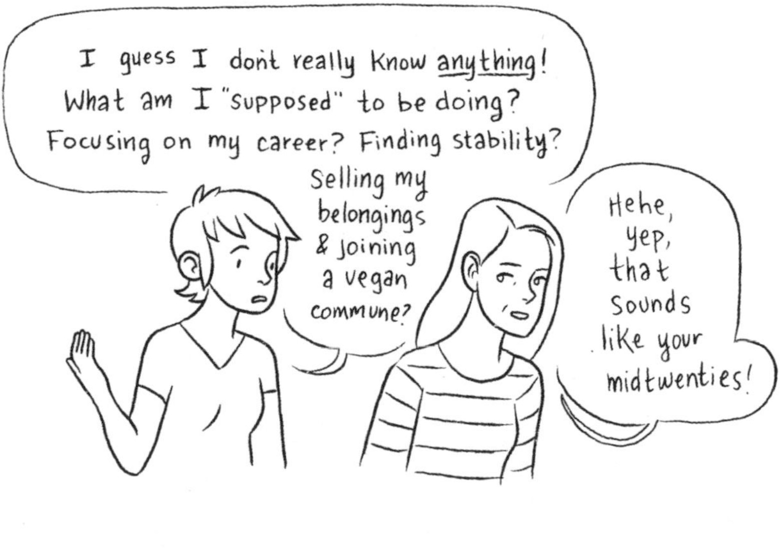
I guess I don't really know anything! What am I "supposed" to be doing? Focusing on my career? Finding stability?
Selling my belongings & joining a vegan commune?
Hehe, yep, that sounds like your midtwenties!

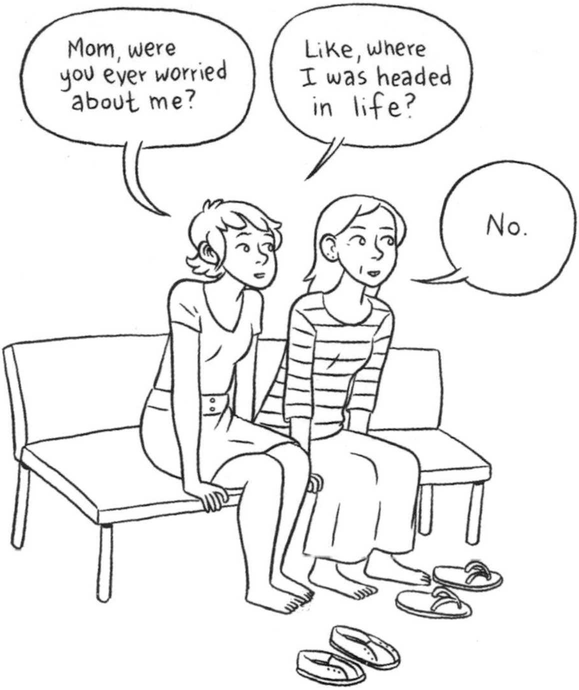
Mom, were you ever worried about me?
Like, where I was headed in life?
No.

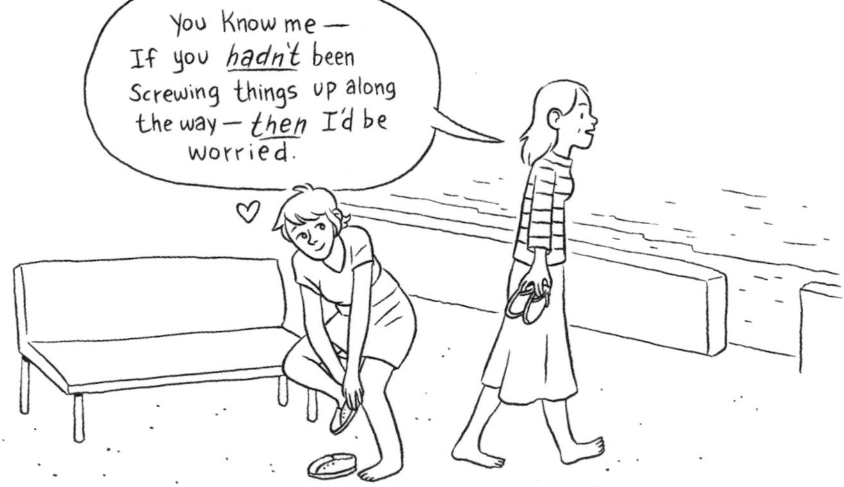
You Know me— If you hadn't been Screwing things up along the way—then I'd be worried.

Sept. 24

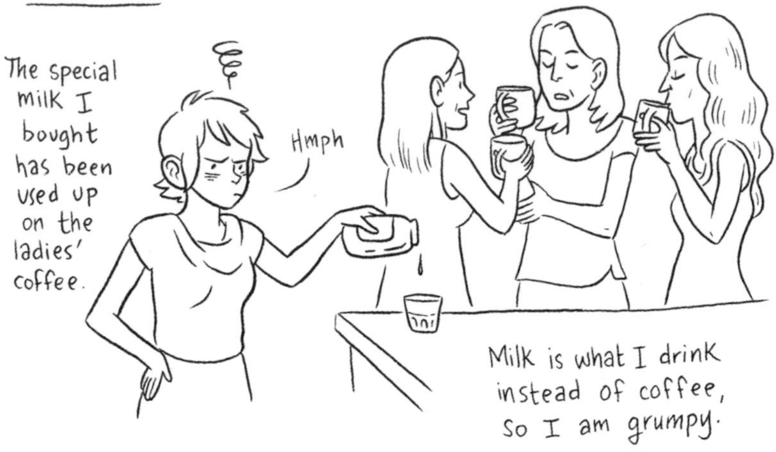
The special milk I bought has been used up on the ladies' coffee.
Hmph
Milk is what I drink instead of coffee, so I am grumpy.

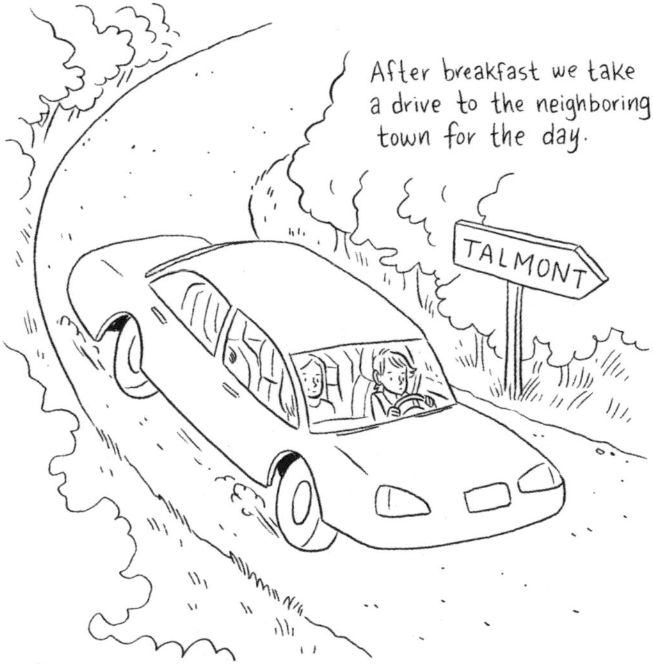
After breakfast we take a drive to the neighboring town for the day.
TALMONT

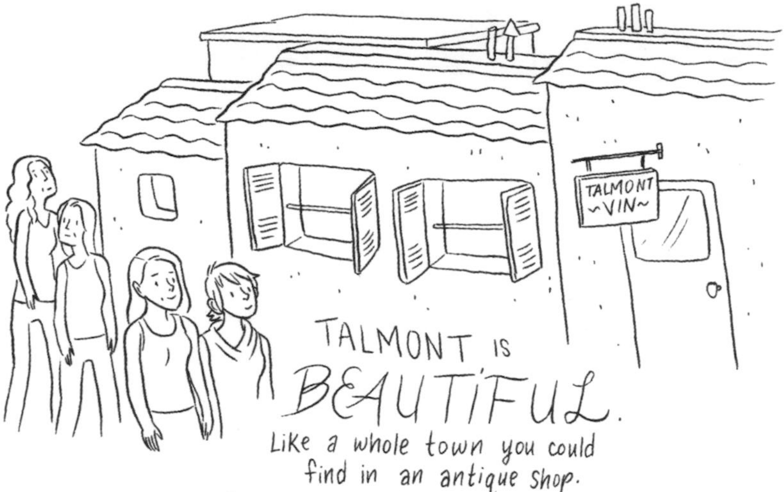
TALMONT ~VIN~
TALMONT IS BEAUTIFUL.
Like a whole town you could find in an antique shop.

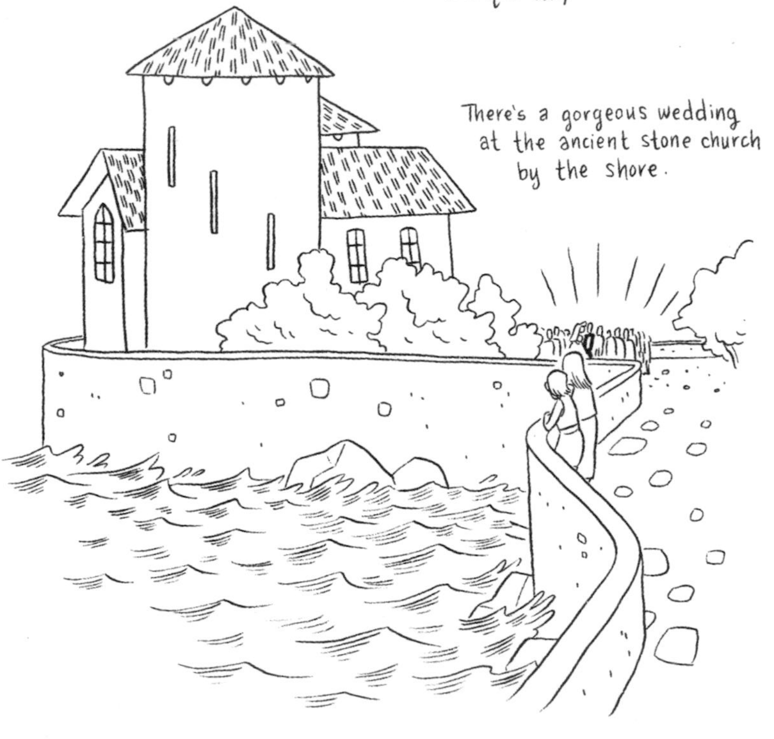
There's a gorgeous wedding at the ancient stone church by the shore.

Mussels!

Chocolate tart encased
in fluffy spun sugar

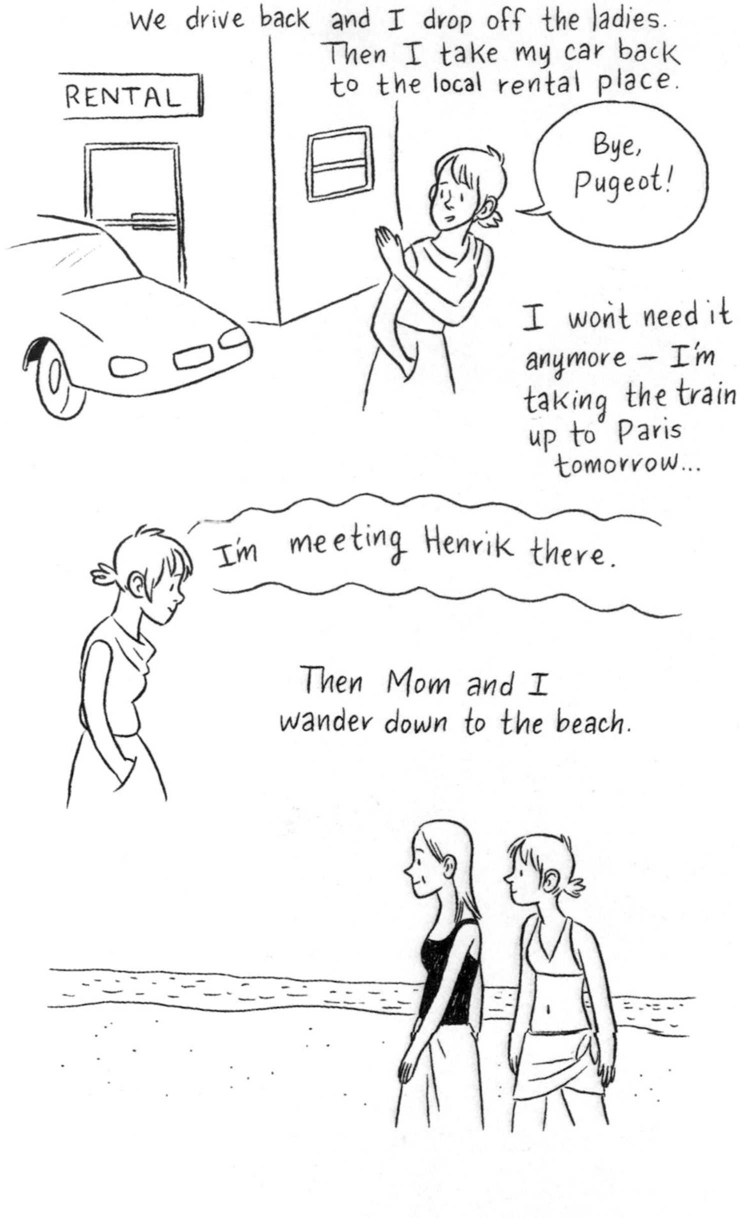
We drive back and I drop off the ladies.
Then I take my car back to the local rental place.
RENTAL
Bye, Pugeot!
I won't need it anymore – I'm taking the train up to Paris tomorrow...
I'm meeting Henrik there.
Then Mom and I wander down to the beach.

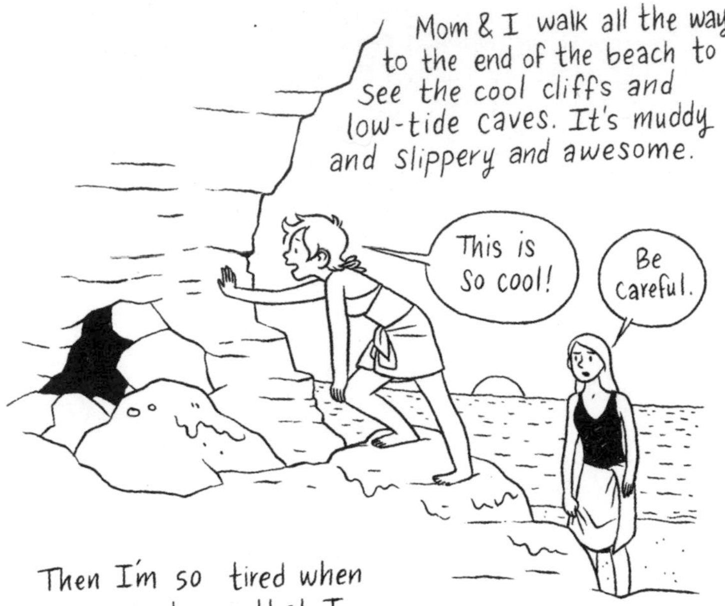
Mom & I walk all the way to the end of the beach to see the cool cliffs and low-tide caves. It's muddy and slippery and awesome.
This is so cool!
Be careful.

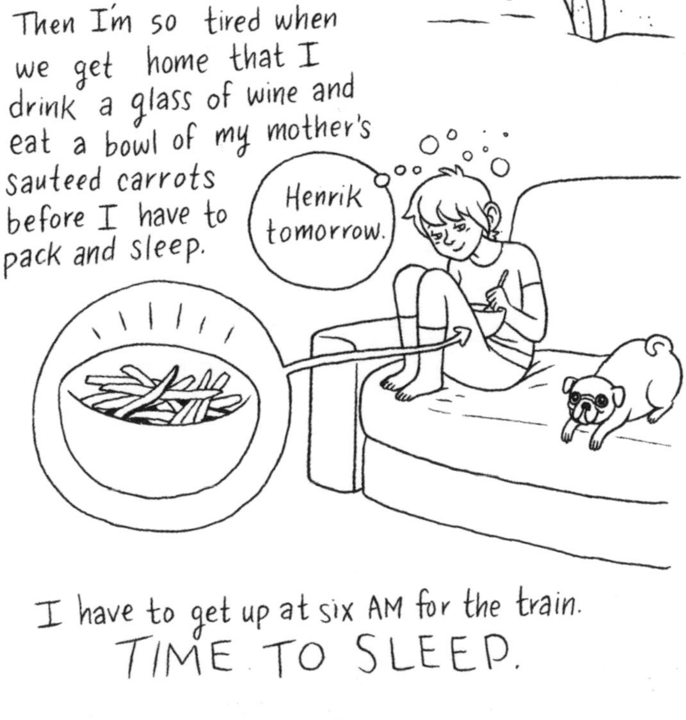
Then I'm so tired when we get home that I drink a glass of wine and eat a bowl of my mother's sauteed carrots before I have to pack and sleep.
Henrik tomorrow.
I have to get up at six AM for the train.
TIME TO SLEEP.

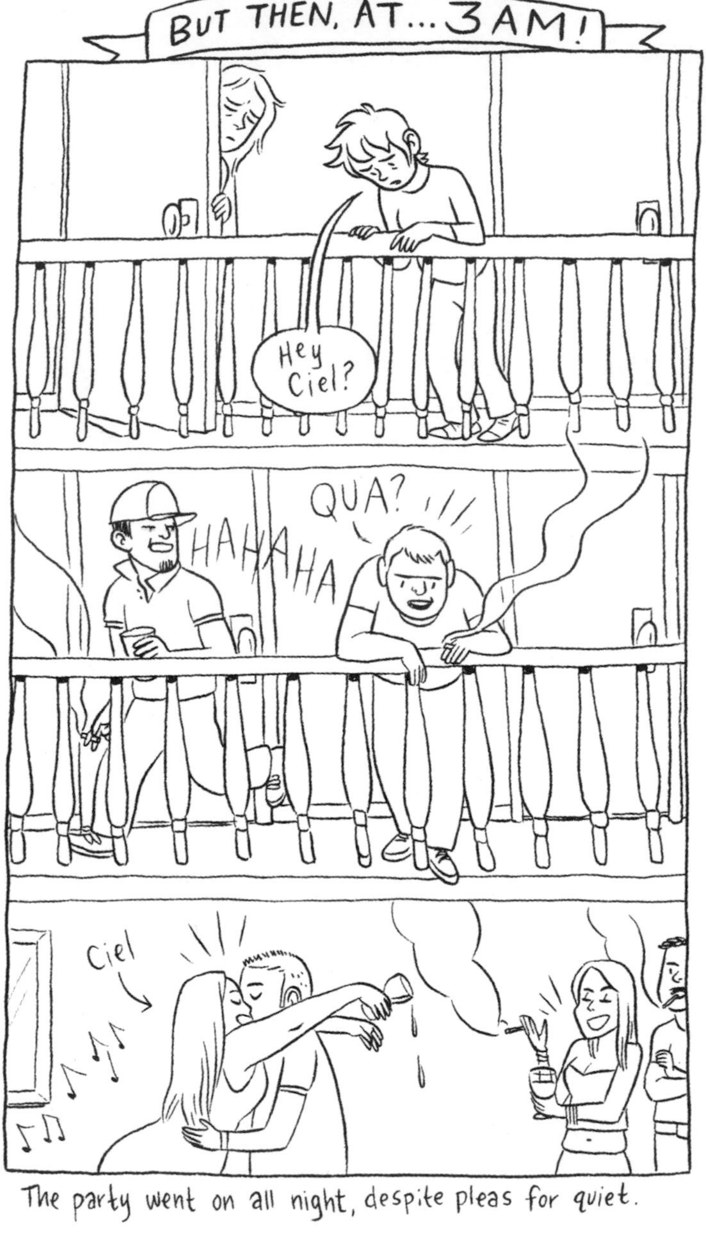
BUT THEN, AT... 3 AM!
Hey Ciel?
QUA?
HAHAHAHA
Ciel
The party went on all night, despite pleas for quiet.

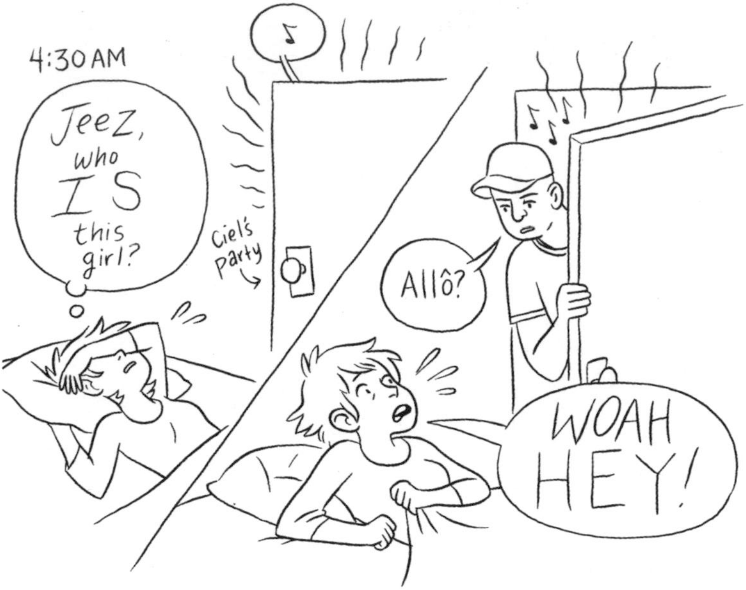
4:30 AM
Jeez, who IS this girl?
Ciel's party
Allô?
WOAH HEY!

4 more burst-ins later, it was time to get up.

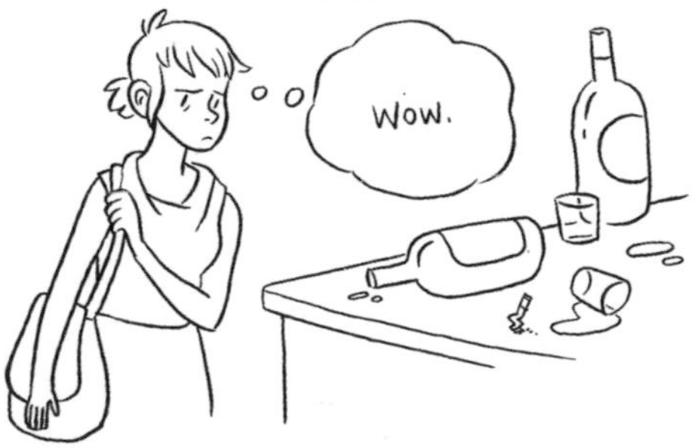
Ciel and her friends have stolen & drunk all the wine that Jane gave us.
The house is trashed.
Wow.

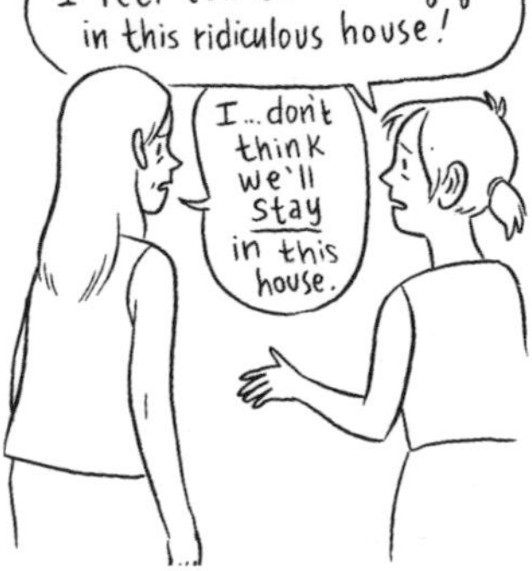
Mom gets up to walk me to the train station.
I feel terrible leaving you in this ridiculous house!
I... don't think we'll stay in this house.

PARIS

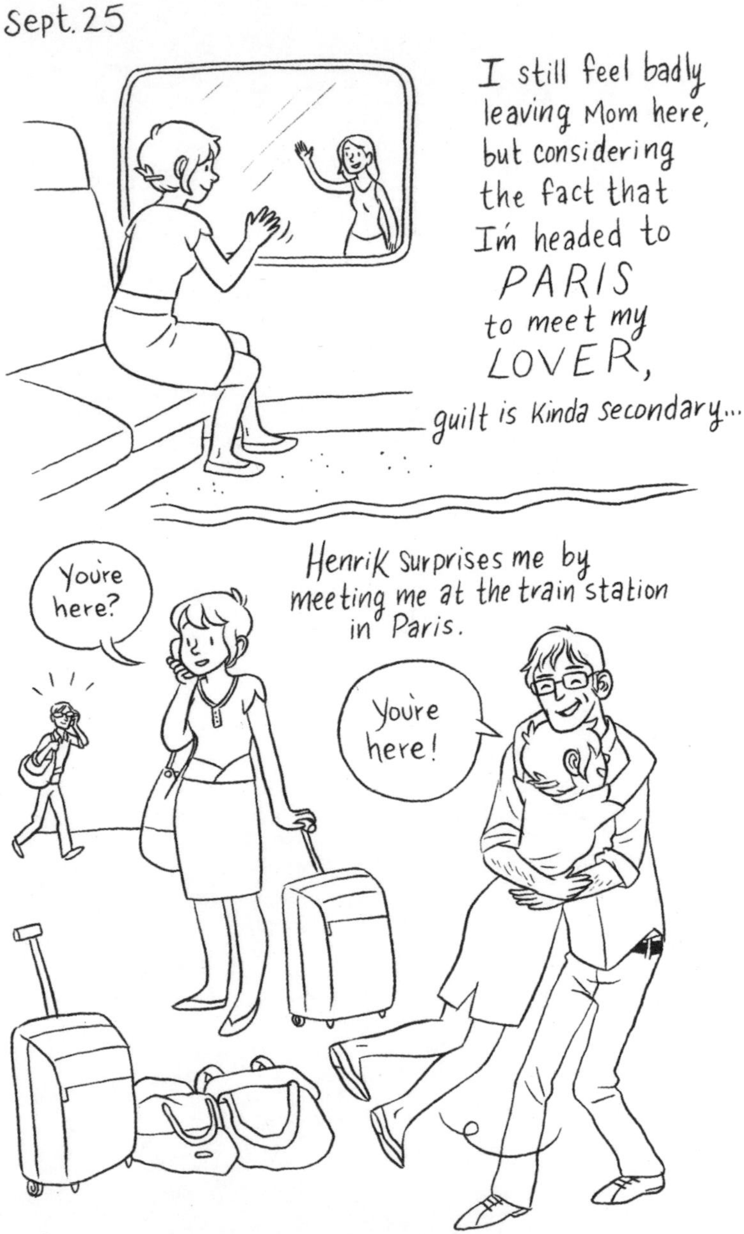
Sept. 25
I still feel badly leaving Mom here, but considering the fact that I'm headed to PARIS to meet my LOVER, guilt is kinda secondary...
Henrik surprises me by meeting me at the train station in Paris.
You're here?
You're here!

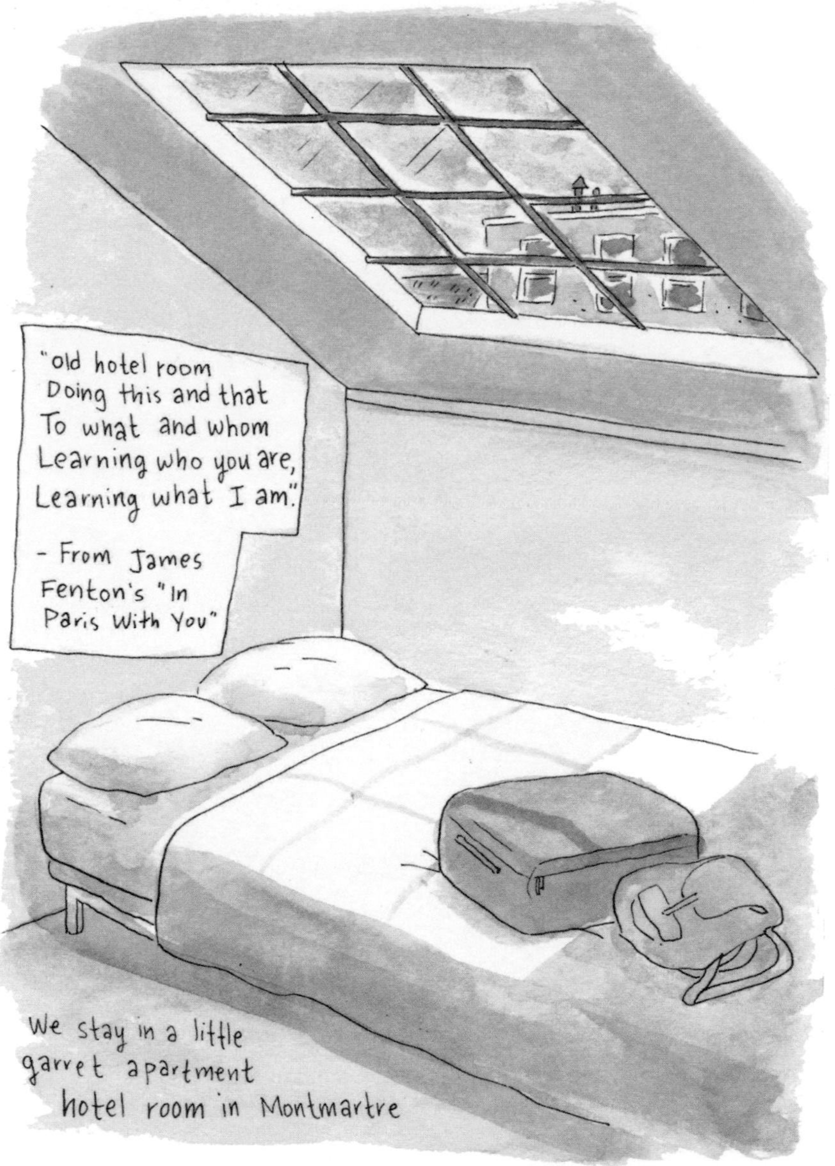
"old hotel room
Doing this and that
To what and whom
Learning who you are,
Learning what I am".
- From James
Fenton's "In
Paris With You"
We stay in a little
garret apartment
hotel room in Montmartre

We walk through the Marais

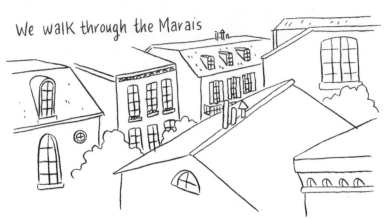

I keep thinking of a poem by James Fenton that I love:

"In Paris With You."

"I'm in Paris with the slightest thing you do.
I'm in Paris with your eyes, your mouth,
In Paris with...
all points south.
Am I embarrassing you?
I'm in Paris with you."

Dinner at La Potager du Marais, a cozy little vegan place I track down.

It's strange to eat vegan in <u>Paris</u> of all places — land of butter, cream & meat!

We walk through Cimetière de Montmartre — a favorite of mine, due to the generations of inbred cemetery cats that live there!

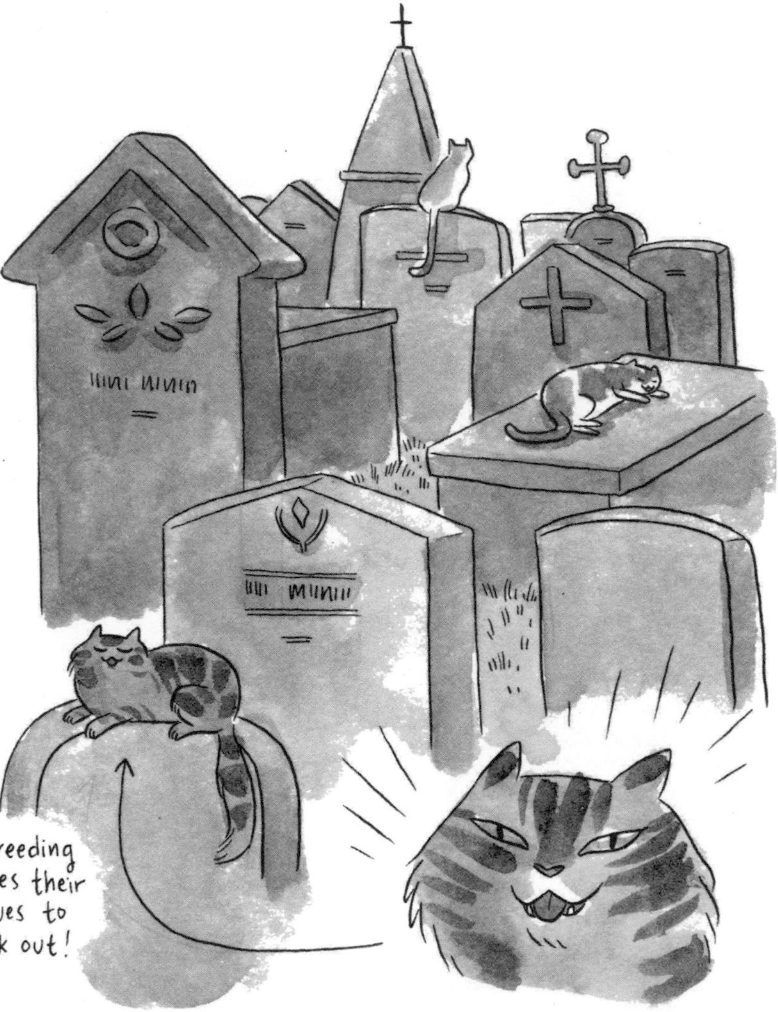
Inbreeding causes their tongues to stick out!

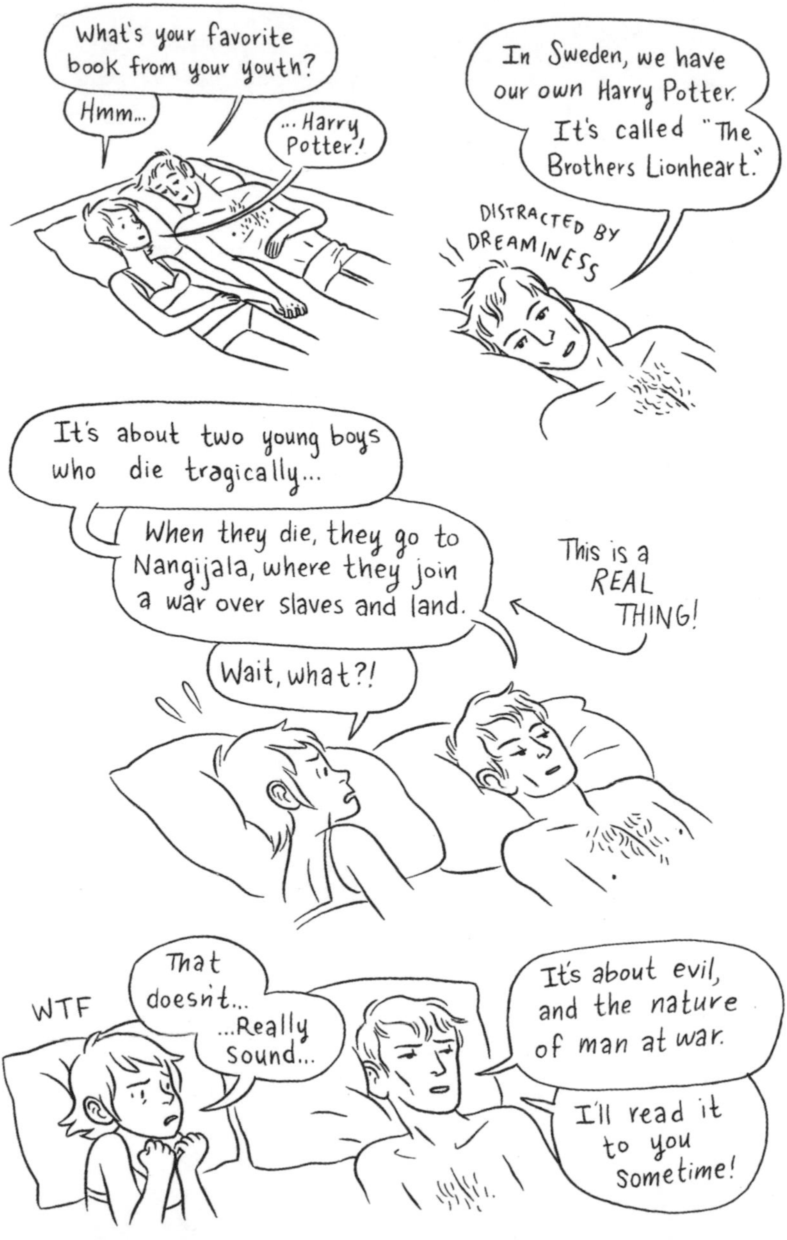
What's your favorite book from your youth?
Hmm...
...Harry Potter!
In Sweden, we have our own Harry Potter. It's called "The Brothers Lionheart."
DISTRACTED BY DREAMINESS
It's about two young boys who die tragically...
When they die, they go to Nangijala, where they join a war over slaves and land.
This is a REAL THING!
Wait, what?!
WTF
That doesn't...
...Really sound...
It's about evil, and the nature of man at war.
I'll read it to you sometime!

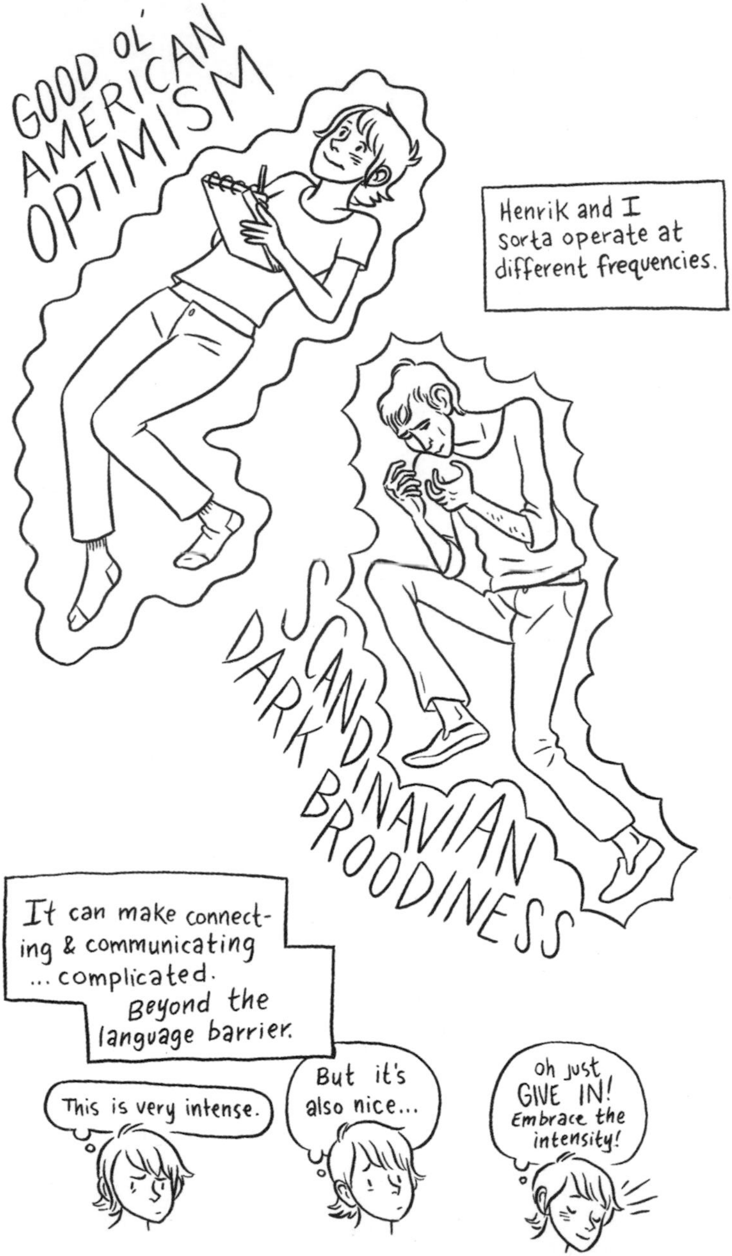
GOOD OL' AMERICAN OPTIMISM
Henrik and I sorta operate at different frequencies.
SCANDINAVIAN DARK BROODINESS
It can make connecting & communicating ... complicated. Beyond the language barrier.
This is very intense.
But it's also nice...
Oh just GIVE IN! Embrace the intensity!

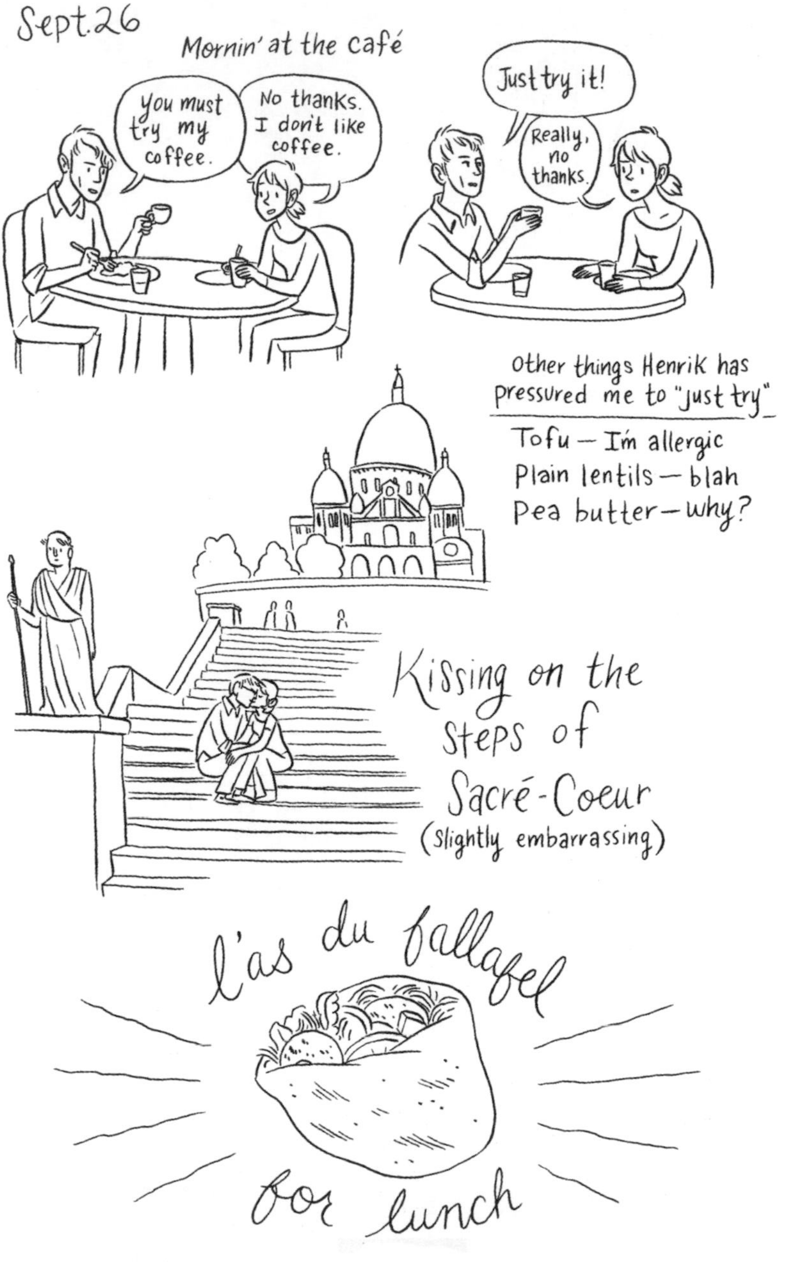
Sept. 26
Mornin' at the café
You must try my coffee.
No thanks. I don't like coffee.
Just try it!
Really, no thanks.
Other things Henrik has pressured me to "just try"
Tofu — I'm allergic
Plain lentils — blah
Pea butter — why?
Kissing on the steps of Sacré-Coeur (slightly embarrassing)
l'as du fallafel for lunch

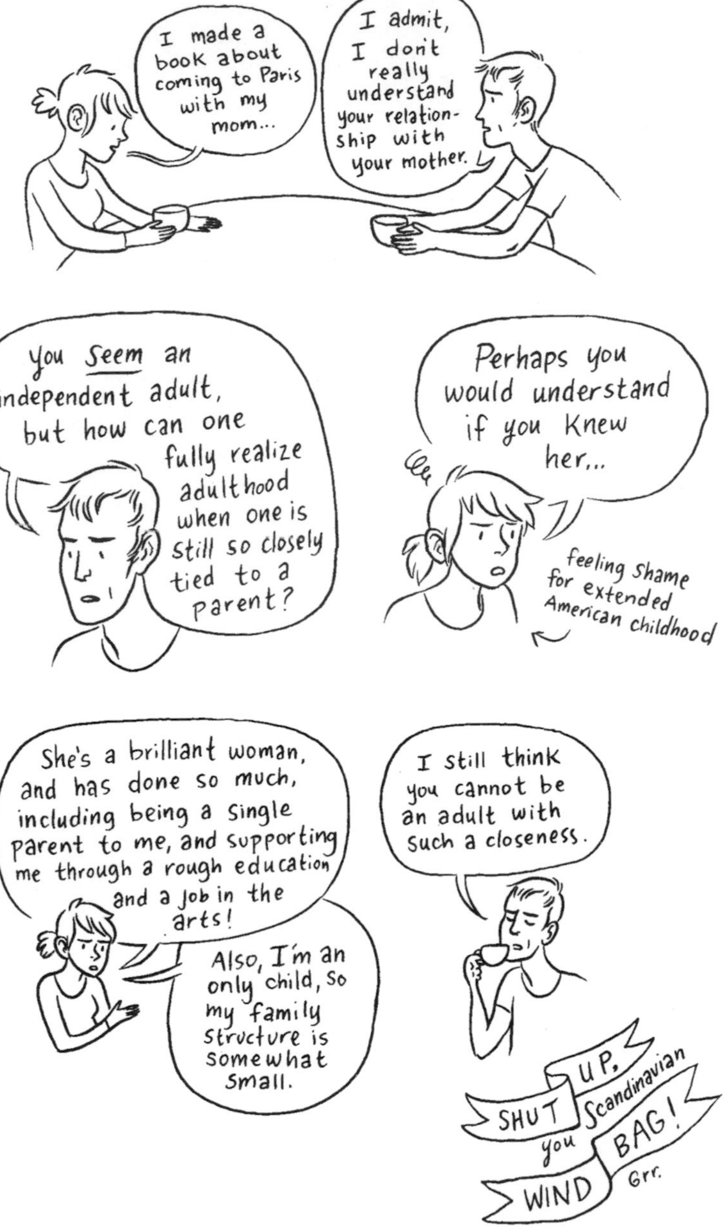
I made a book about coming to Paris with my mom...
I admit, I don't really understand your relationship with your mother.
You seem an independent adult, but how can one fully realize adulthood when one is still so closely tied to a parent?
Perhaps you would understand if you knew her...
feeling shame for extended American childhood
She's a brilliant woman, and has done so much, including being a single parent to me, and supporting me through a rough education and a job in the arts!
Also, I'm an only child, so my family structure is somewhat small.
I still think you cannot be an adult with such a closeness.
SHUT UP, you Scandinavian WIND BAG!
Grr.

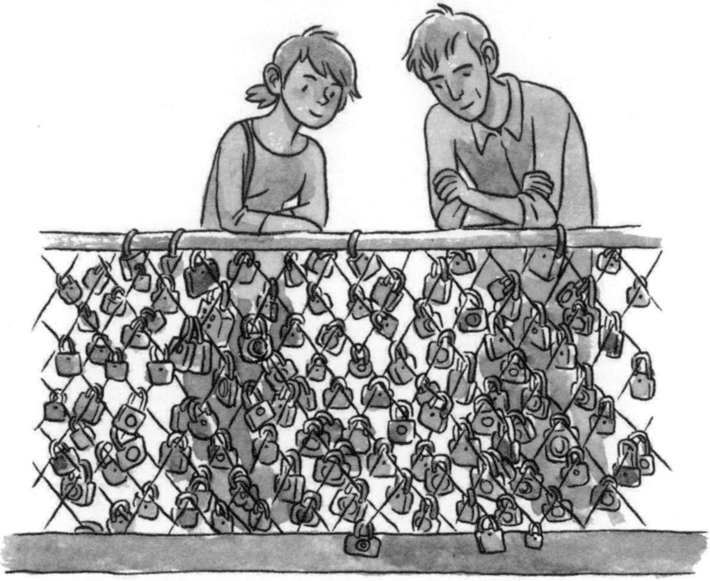

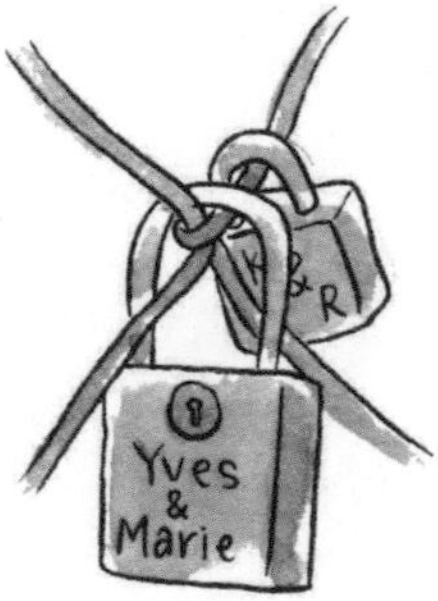
Yves
&
Marie

We pause on the Pont Louis Philipe to admire the hundreds of locks attached to the bridge and inscribed with names of couples who placed them there as a symbol of the permanence of their bond... Every few months, the city clips them off & throws them away.

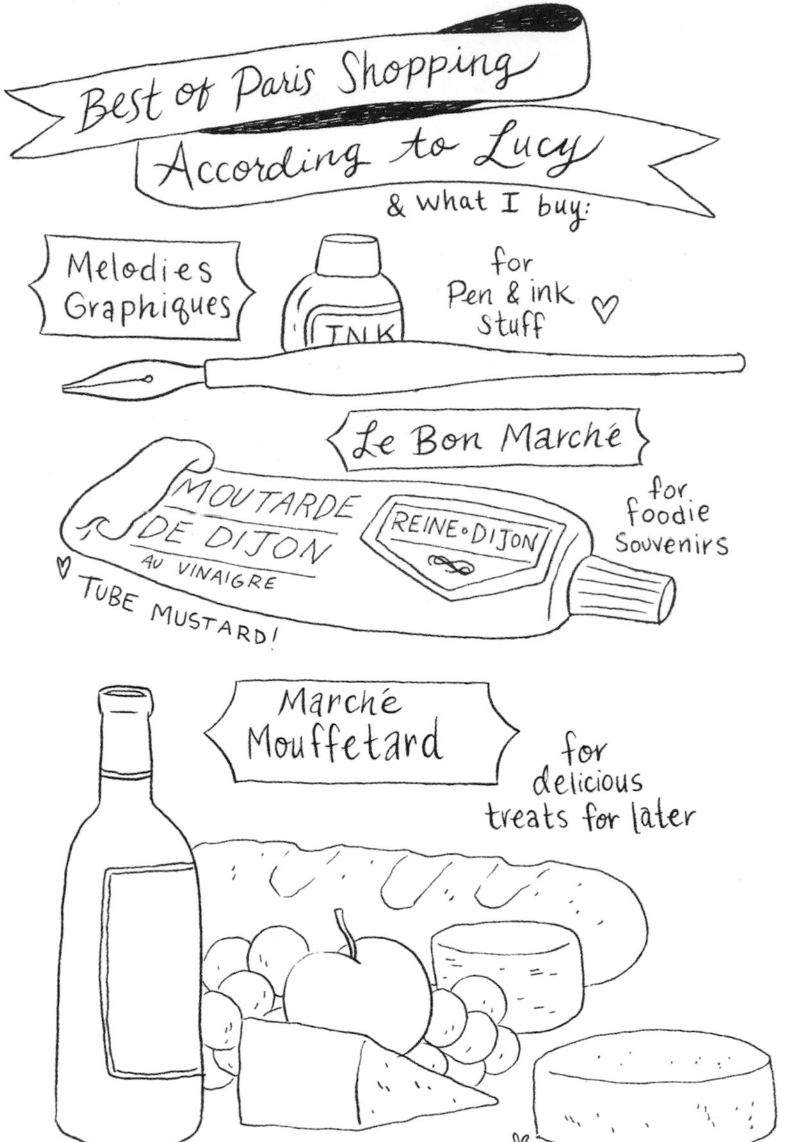
Best of Paris Shopping
According to Lucy
& what I buy:
Melodies Graphiques
INK
for Pen & ink stuff
Le Bon Marché
MOUTARDE DE DIJON
AU VINAIGRE
REINE • DIJON
for foodie Souvenirs
TUBE MUSTARD!
Marché Mouffetard
for delicious treats for later
Chocolate fondant

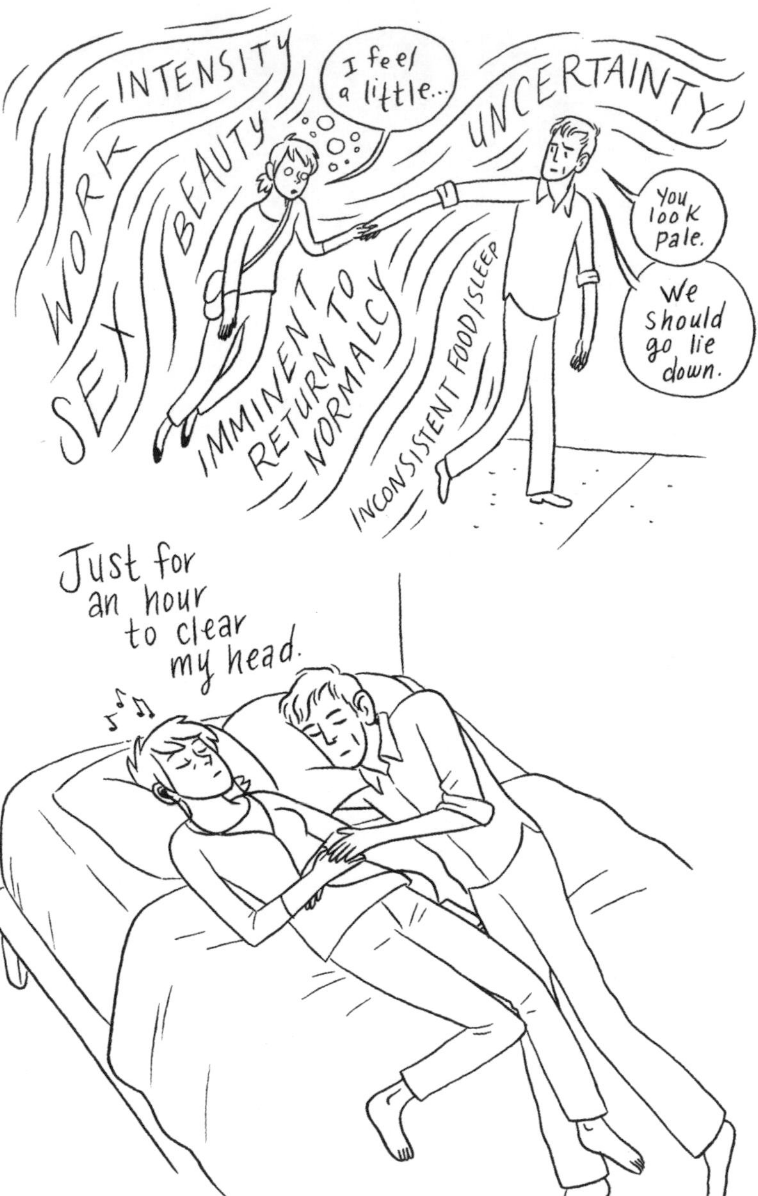
WORK
INTENSITY
SEX
BEAUTY
I feel a little...
IMMINENT RETURN TO NORMALCY
INCONSISTENT FOOD/SLEEP
UNCERTAINTY
You look pale.
We should go lie down.
Just for an hour to clear my head.

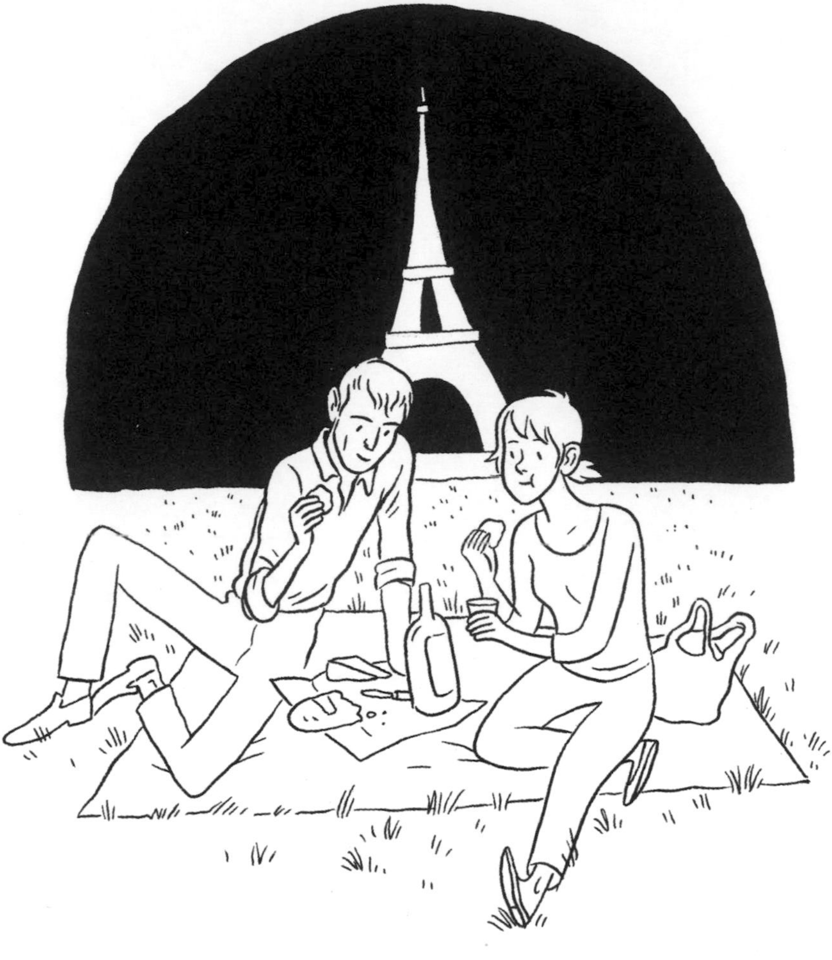

Midnight picnic
by the Eiffel Tower

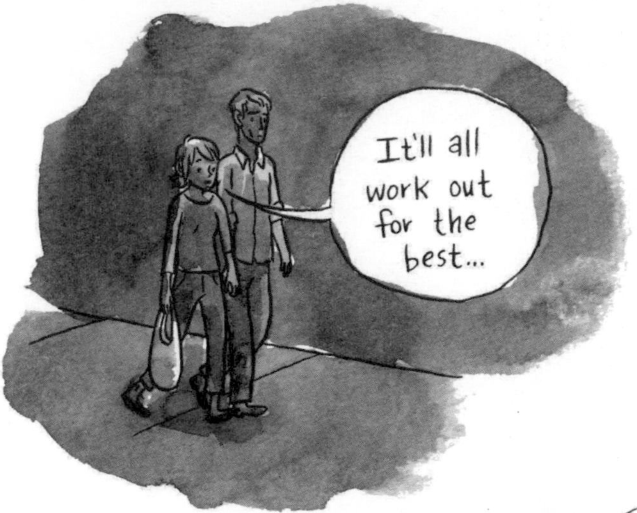
It'll all work out for the best...

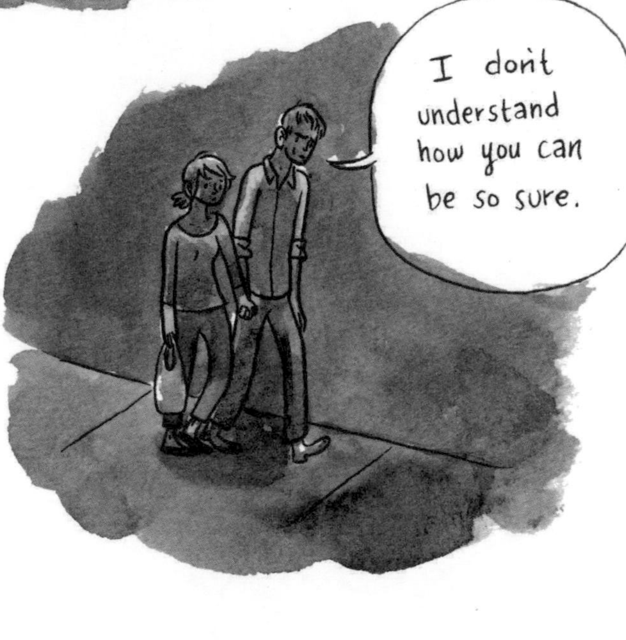
I don't understand how you can be so sure.

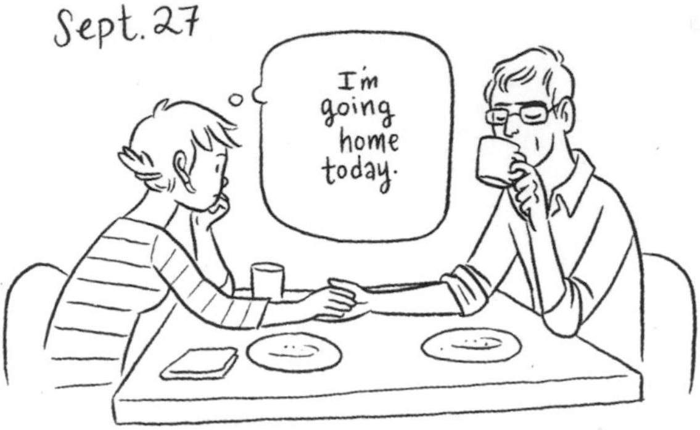
Sept. 27
I'm going home today.

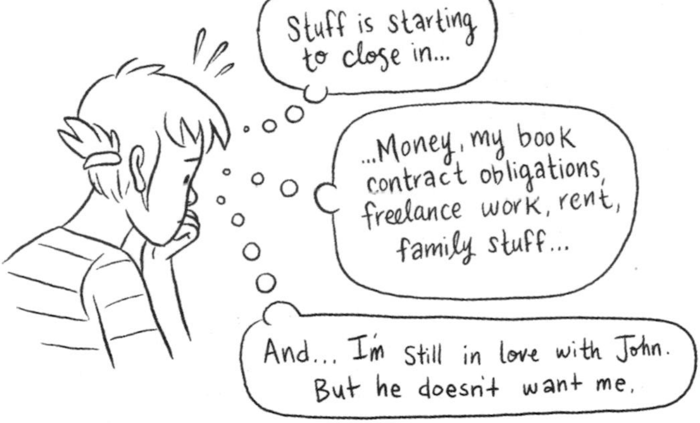
Stuff is starting to close in...
...Money, my book contract obligations, freelance work, rent, family stuff...
And... I'm still in love with John. But he doesn't want me.

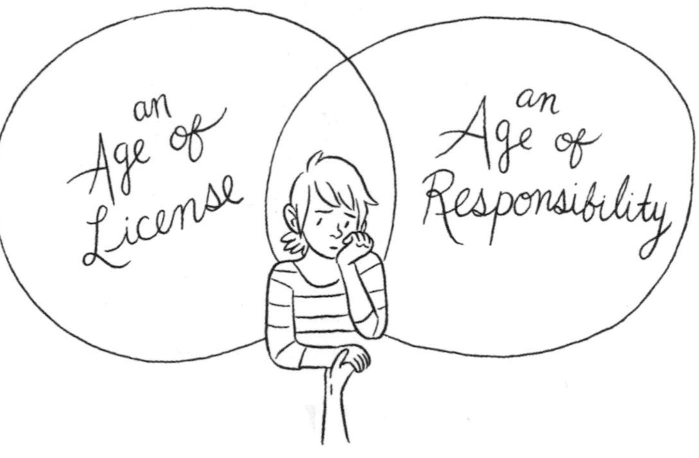
an Age of License
an Age of Responsibility

Part of me
already knows...

...This won't last...

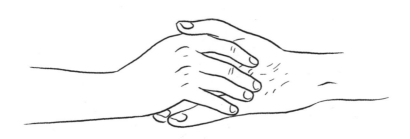

...It can't.

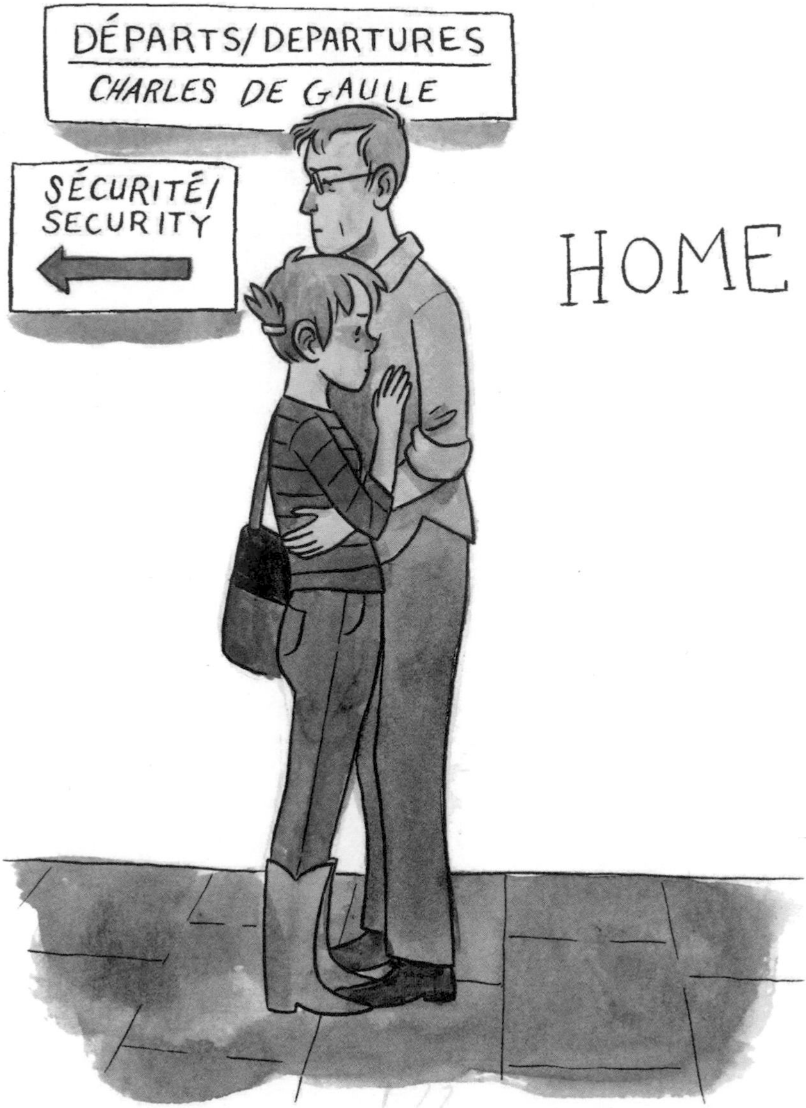

HOME

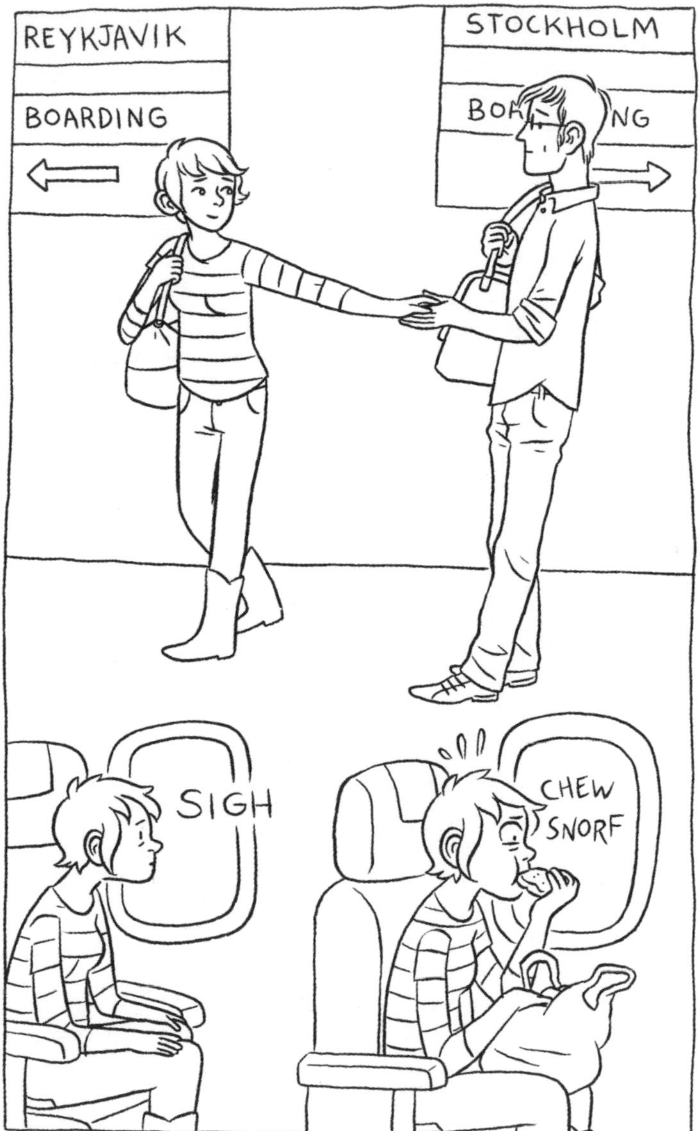
REYKJAVIK
BOARDING
STOCKHOLM
BOA NG
SIGH
CHEW
SNORF

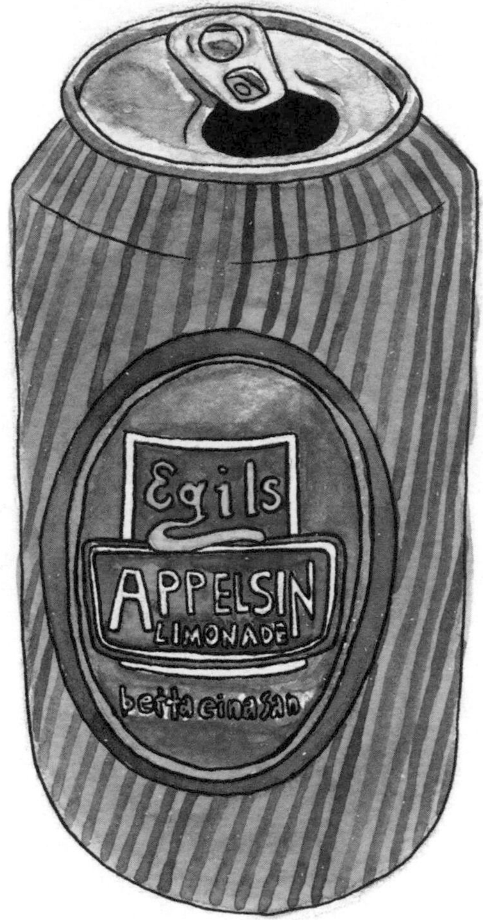
Egils
APPELSIN
LIMONADE
berta einasan

I ordered this on the plane because I thought it was Apfelschorle, or at least lemonade, but it's inexplicably ORANGE SODA.

What day is it anymore?

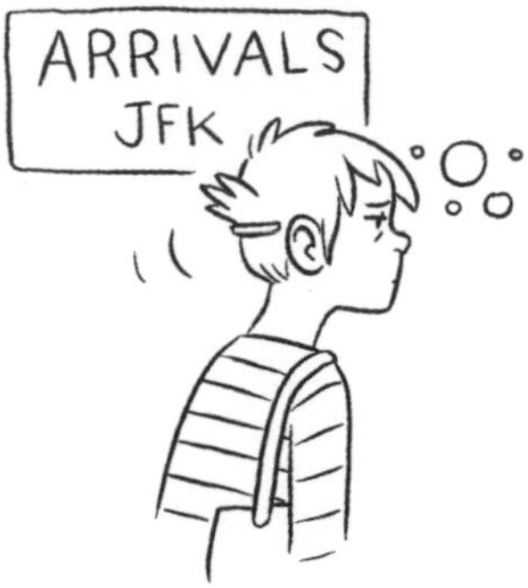
ARRIVALS
JFK

6 HOURS LATER

I feel raw.

Everything is loud & ugly.

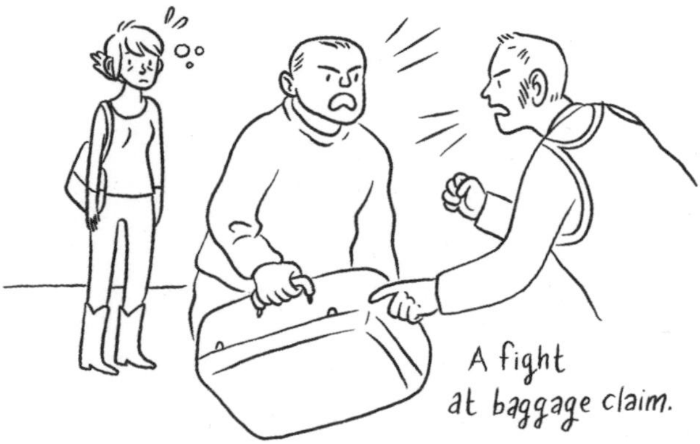

A fight at baggage claim.

Subway...

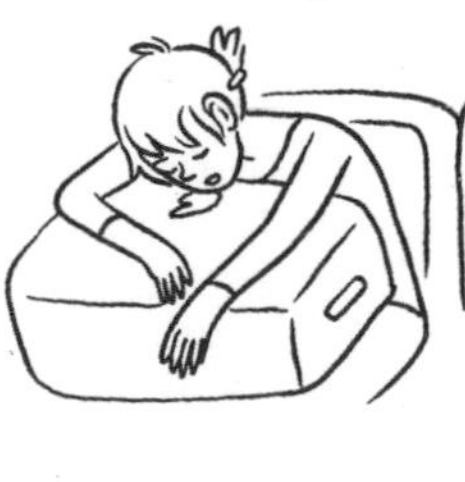

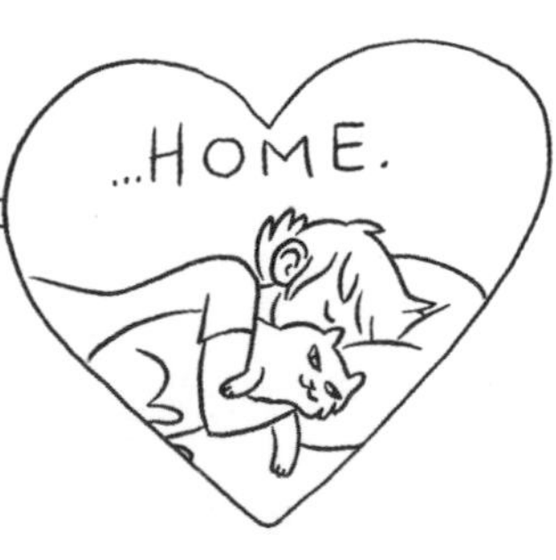
...HOME.

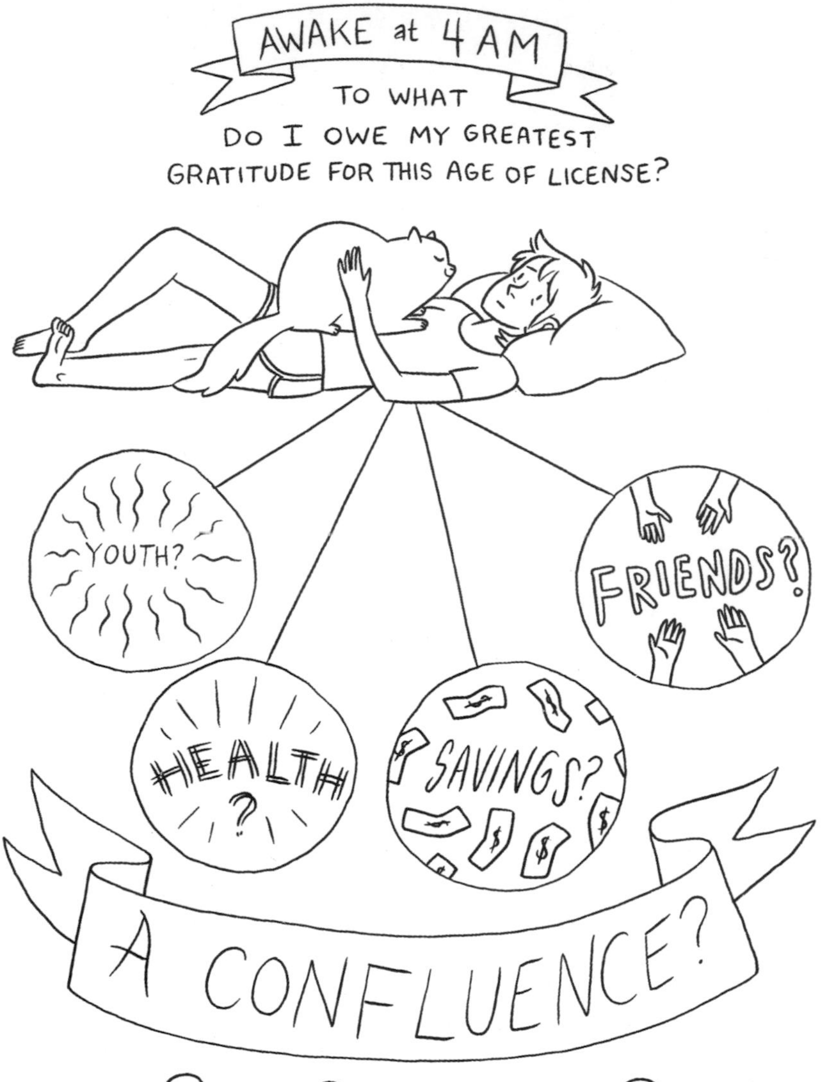
AWAKE at 4 AM
TO WHAT DO I OWE MY GREATEST GRATITUDE FOR THIS AGE OF LICENSE?
YOUTH?
FRIENDS?
HEALTH ?
SAVINGS?
A CONFLUENCE?
GOOD LUCK?

Seeking a place for my gratitude,

I turn to that great comforter:

THE INTERNET

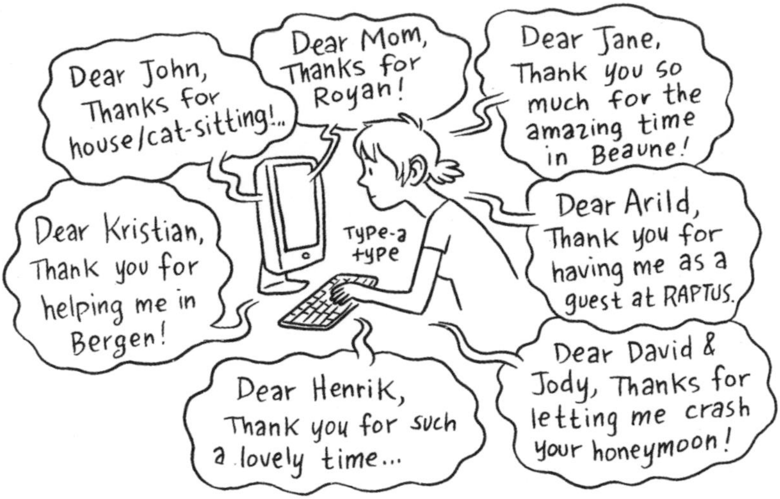
Dear John, Thanks for house/cat-sitting!..
Dear Mom, Thanks for Royan!
Dear Jane, Thank you so much for the amazing time in Beaune!
Dear Kristian, Thank you for helping me in Bergen!
Type-a type
Dear Arild, Thank you for having me as a guest at RAPTUS.
Dear Henrik, Thank you for such a lovely time...
Dear David & Jody, Thanks for letting me crash your honeymoon!

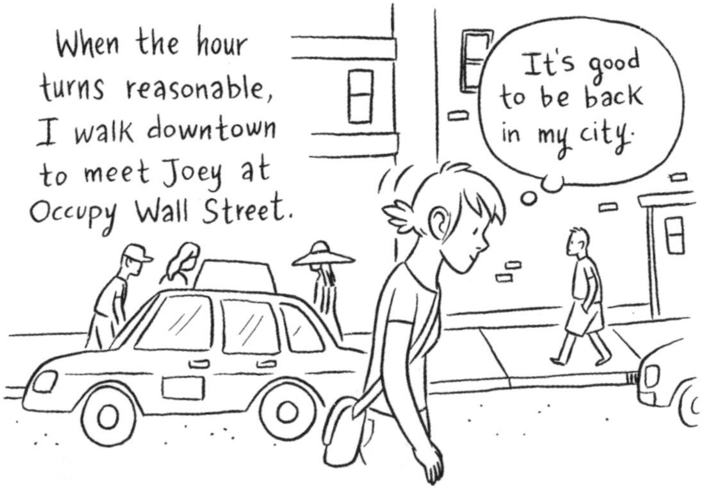
When the hour turns reasonable, I walk downtown to meet Joey at Occupy Wall Street.
It's good to be back in my city.

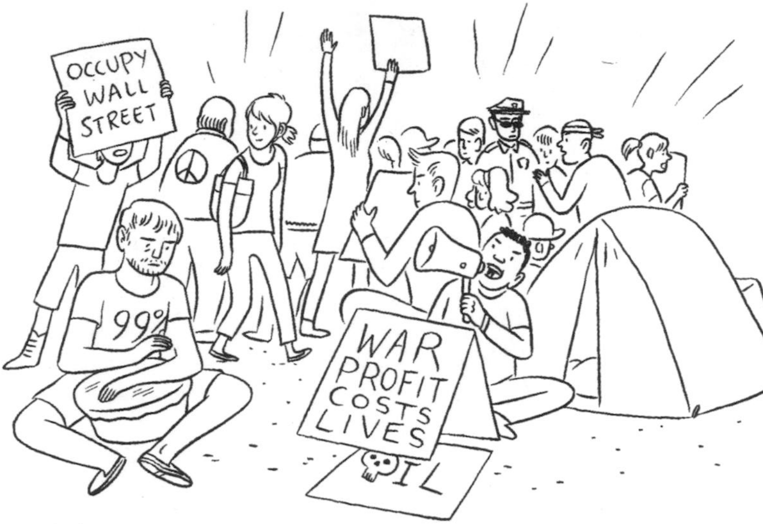
OCCUPY WALL STREET
99%
WAR PROFIT COSTS LIVES
IL

It's interesting to be here— the air feels charged with emotion, full of righteous and outspoken American fervor. It's only just begun to coalesce into a movement, so there's a certain lack of focus, but everyone seems to be standing against those in power who feel that they can do whatever they'd like without repercussion— That they have free license to do anything for profit.

Somehow, I find Joey in the midst.

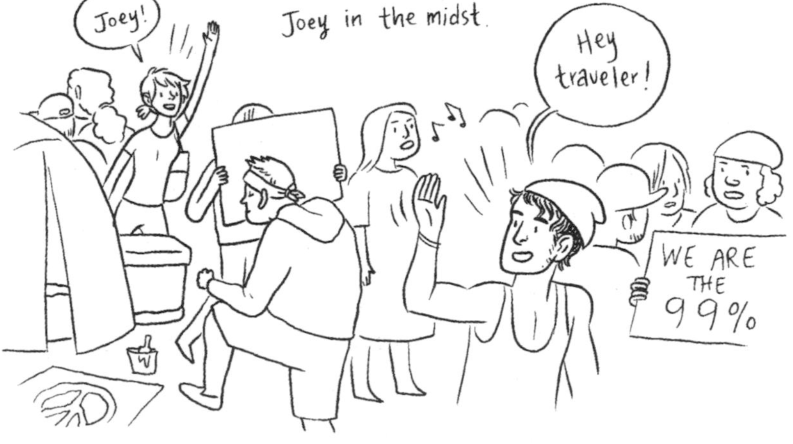
Joey!
Hey traveler!
WE ARE THE 99%

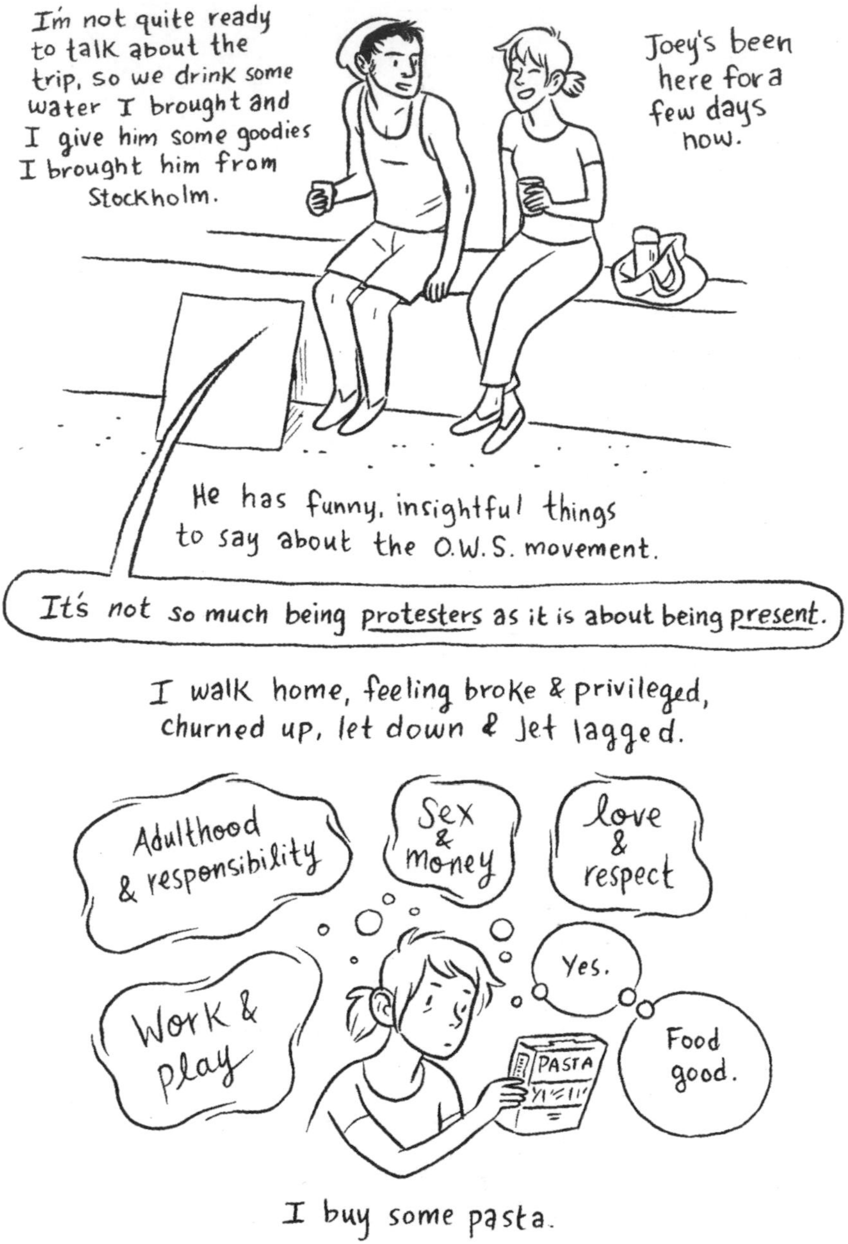
I'm not quite ready to talk about the trip, so we drink some water I brought and I give him some goodies I brought him from Stockholm.
Joey's been here for a few days now.
He has funny, insightful things to say about the O.W.S. movement.
It's not so much being protesters as it is about being present.
I walk home, feeling broke & privileged, churned up, let down & jet lagged.
Adulthood & responsibility
Sex & money
love & respect
Work & play
Yes.
Food good.
PASTA
I buy some pasta.

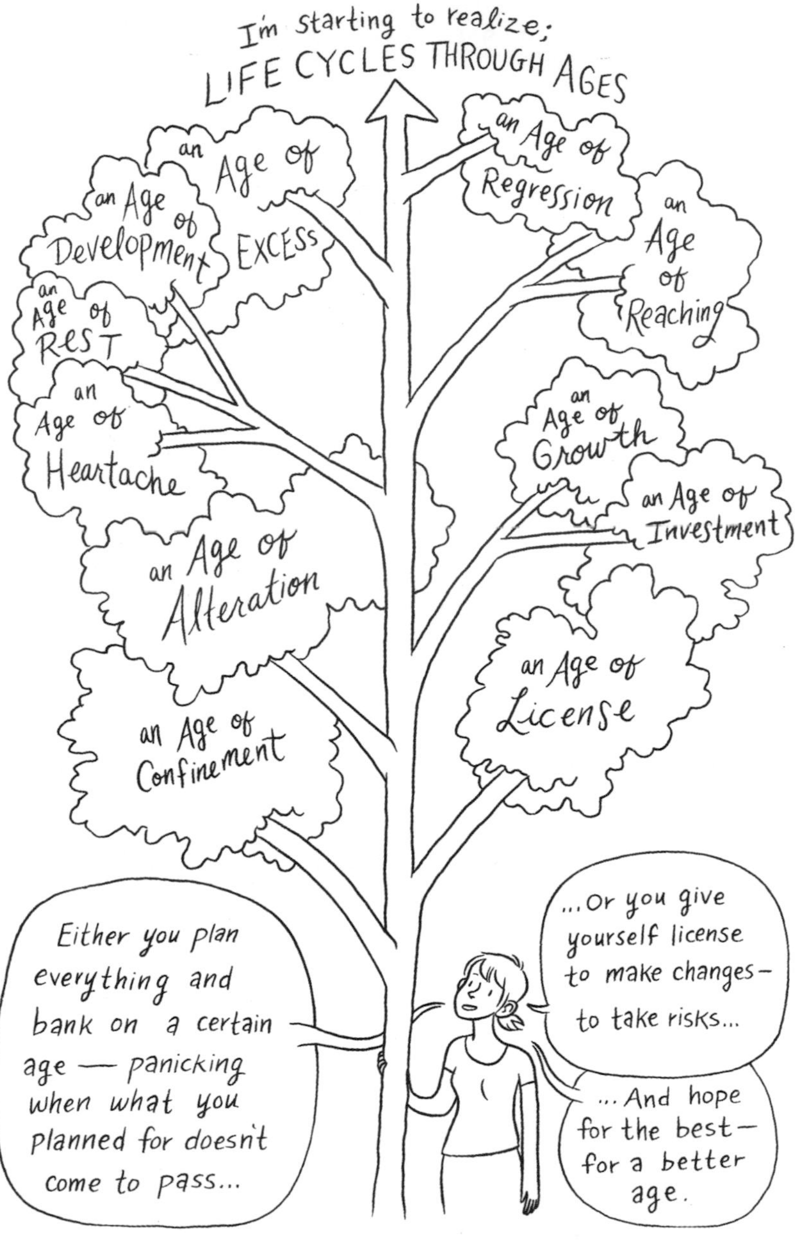
I'm starting to realize;
LIFE CYCLES THROUGH AGES
an Age of EXCESS
an Age of Regression
an Age of Development
an Age of Reaching
an Age of REST
an Age of Heartache
an Age of Growth
an Age of Investment
an Age of Alteration
an Age of License
an Age of Confinement
Either you plan everything and bank on a certain age — panicking when what you planned for doesn't come to pass...
...Or you give yourself license to make changes— to take risks...
...And hope for the best— for a better age.

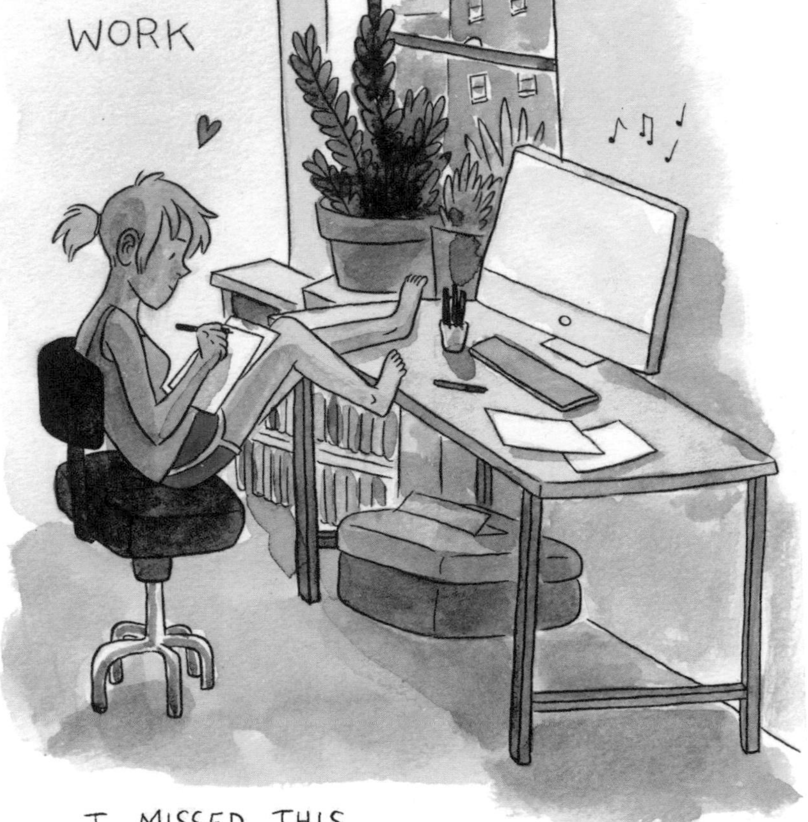
BACK
TO
WORK
I MISSED THIS.

What *is* my
"regular life?"

— From Henrik

Amazing, lucky, beautiful,
sad, boring, wonderful...

...Surprising.

(This book)

THE END OF AN AGE

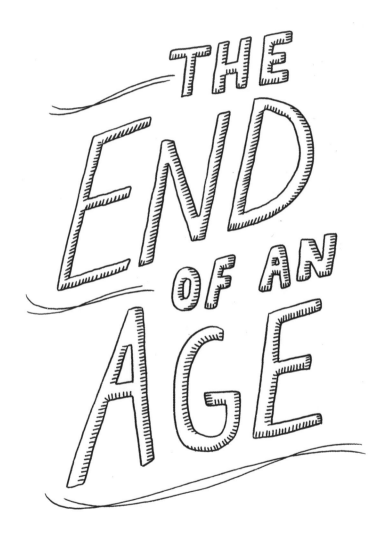

MY THANKS
(and apologies)

To Jane,
for showing me the incredible world of French wine and fabulous old friends.

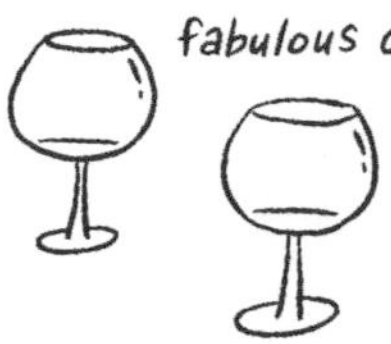

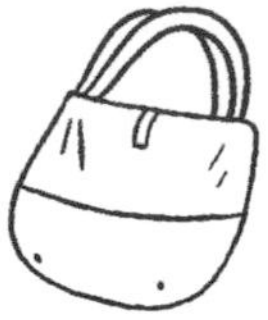

To RAPTUS comics fest and its organizers, for bringing me to Bergen and introducing me to Norway's comics scene through a great show.

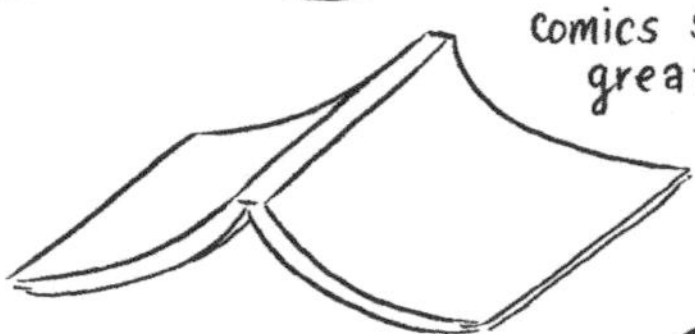

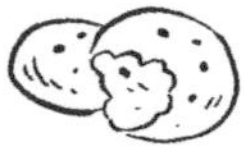

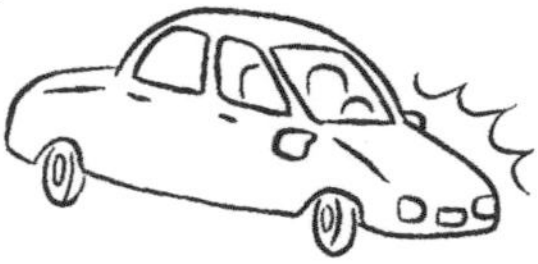

To Mom, Hilary & "Jen", for sharing our hilarious and surreal experience in Royan.

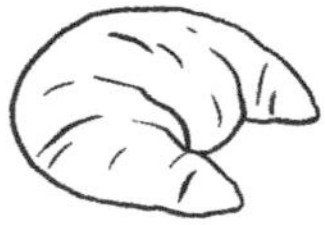

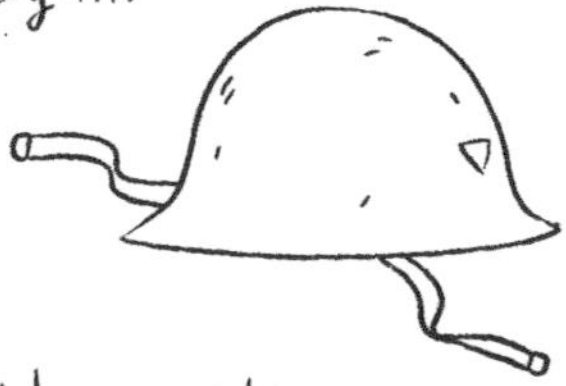

To David & Jody, for letting me tag along on part of your honey-moon, and forgiving me for missing the wedding.

To Henrik,

Thank you for a beautiful love affair. I'm sorry there wasn't more of it – that it couldn't last. But part of me is glad that it can exist, whole and lovely and complicated, in my mind. I think of you fondly, with a little wistfulness.

I hope you understand why I wanted to write it down – to share it, to remember.

With affection,

Lucy

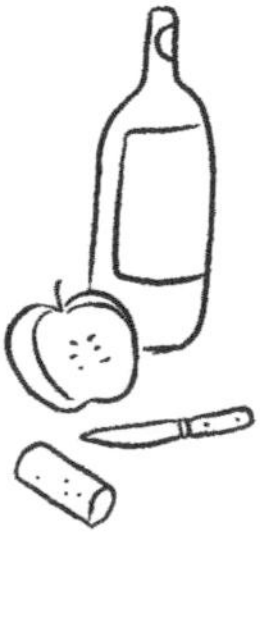

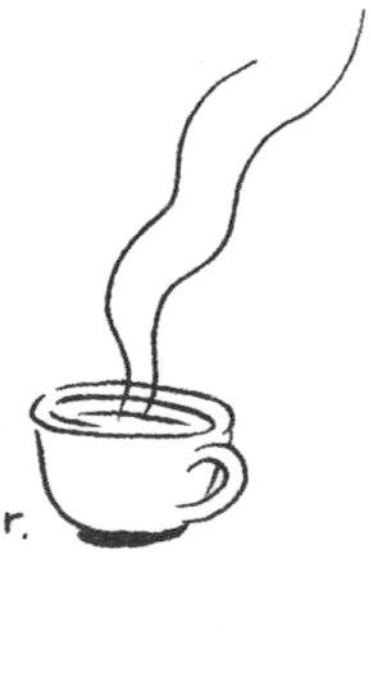

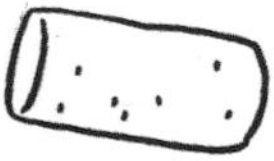

a cork from Beaune

a chestnut from a tree
outside the commune

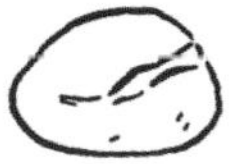

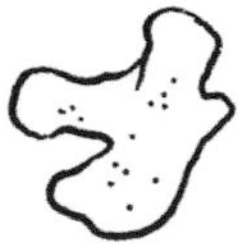

a piece of coral from the beach at Royan

A Short Afterword:

Over the last two years since the events of this book,
I've asked a number of French pals
if they've ever heard the phrase
"An age of license"
or anything similar.

————————— NONE OF THEM HAD. —————————

I don't know if Denis made it up,
or if it's super obscure or WHAT.

It's still a nice term for something
that, otherwise, doesn't really have a name.

And putting something in words —
naming it — allows us to recognize it
a little better when we come upon it.

It's sorta the point of all this.